HOME ALONE IN AMERICA

Letters Exchanged by a
Young German in the U.S. and
His Family in Berlin from
1946 to 1955

Elizabeth A. Dost

Edited by
Elizabeth Arnswald Dost

EAGLE EDITIONS
2004

EAGLE EDITIONS
AN IMPRINT OF HERITAGE BOOKS, INC.

Books, CDs, and more—Worldwide

For our listing of thousands of titles see our website
at
www.HeritageBooks.com

Published 2004 by
HERITAGE BOOKS, INC.
Publishing Division
65 East Main Street
Westminster, Maryland 21157-5026

International Standard Book Number: 0-7884-3149-8

Dedicated to the memory of

Paul, *who had the dream*

Helmut, *who made it come true*

Maria, *who never lost hope*

Martin, *who made this book possible*

CONTENTS

PREFACE

The remarkable collection of original letters that comprise this book were exchanged by young Helmut Dost, in the United States, and his mother and brother in Berlin during a nine-year period of separation from 1946 to 1955. They tell the story of a German teenager who, as the only American-born member of his family, was sent alone to this country to claim his birthright a year after the end of World War II.

As Helmut's second wife, I first became aware of these letters in 1993, when his younger brother Martin, who had saved and organized the correspondence, decided to turn the collection over to us. The previous year, at the age of 61, Helmut had suffered a debilitating stroke. Ironically, two years later Martin was diagnosed with a severe brain tumor. The brothers, whose close bond is reflected throughout the letters, both passed away just four months apart in 1994.

At that point I had not yet read the letters, about two-thirds of which were written in German. Eager to learn more about those early years of my husband's life, I first had to translate the German letters into English. After reading the whole compilation, I was amazed at the coherent, suspenseful, and often riveting story told through the medium of this correspondence. I realized that I had become the custodian of a very rare collective memoir that begged to be shared with a more extensive body of readers.

Drawing on my own journalistic background to edit the letters, and supplementing them with occasional narrative, I incorporated with them a number of excerpts from the translated diary of Paul Dost. These diary entries by the brothers' father were written in Germany between 1946 and his own untimely death in 1949.

Launching the story are four critical letters exchanged after the end of the war by the Dost parents and American college professor Carroll Dodge. These were not a part of the original collection but were found much later among the papers of his wife, Bertha Dodge, whose daughter graciously consented to their use in this book. It was the delayed receipt of one of these letters that changed the course of Helmut's life, and thereby that of the whole Dost family.

Many other people have contributed, directly and indirectly, to the book's creation. Among them I owe particular thanks to Mary King Critchell, of Franklin, North Carolina. After staying up half the night to read the suspenseful collection in one sitting, Mary consistently urged me to make the letters available to a wider readership. But I probably would not have completed the project without the additional support and encouragement of many unnamed friends whose keen interest in Helmut's story kept me going.

Among those who contributed their skills to this endeavor I am grateful to Gilbert Ward, translator of a number of Helmut's early letters, and to Ursula Kraul Manuel and Irene Faber McGregor, who made themselves available as consultants in my own translations. Finally, this book could not have come into being without the technical expertise of my friend Margie Rose, who succeeded in transferring the manuscript intact from my ancient Macintosh computer to a current generation PC!

INTRODUCTION

An Overview of the Dost Family Saga

It was September 1946—just a year after the war's end—when a young American-born German stepped off the ship alone in New York City to begin a new life in the homeland he had never known. In the dark days after the end of World War II the boy's parents had made an agonizing decision: to send their 16-year-old son to the United States, destination uncertain, to claim the privileges of his prized American citizenship—and hopefully pave the way for their own immigration. Little did they dream what lay ahead!

The letters in this collection, exchanged over a nine-year period of separation by Helmut Dost in California (and later Korea) and his family in Berlin, were written against the backdrop of the escalating Cold War between the Soviet Union and the West. They tell the dramatic story of a young man whose place of birth seems to have thrust upon him a mission far beyond his years, and his single-minded and sacrificial pursuit of that goal—to bring his family to America.

The political situation in Germany after World War II has a direct bearing on the story told by these letters. After the war Germany was divided into two political entities, communist East Germany (the German Democratic Republic), dominated by the Soviet Union, and West Germany (Federal Republic of Germany), a new democracy occupied and supported by the Western allies.

The capital city of Berlin, located in the middle of East Germany, was itself divided between East and West. East Berlin was essentially an extension of East Germany while West Berlin, a virtual island in the middle of the eastern state, remained a political unit of West Germany. Although the Russians were the first of the Allied forces to enter the city, they eventually withdrew from the western part of Berlin, which was subsequently divided into French, British, and American administrative sectors. The Dosts lived in Reinickendorf, a section of the city located in the French sector.

As the Russian noose was drawn ever tighter around West Berlin, uncertainty about the fate of the beleaguered city was a constant source of anxiety for the city's residents. Meanwhile, on the other side of the world, the division of communist North and democratic South Korea led to America's involvement in the Korean War of the 1950's.

The overriding theme of these letters is young Helmut's long-drawn-out struggle to bring his family to the United States—largely at the sacrifice of his own opportunities. In them we follow the development of an impressionable German school boy into a man—American no longer in name only, but in reality. From Berlin, through nine years of separation, the letters of his mother, Maria, and brother, Martin, describe vividly the impact of the city's isolation during the early years of the Cold War.

But these letters are actually part of a larger saga, which began with the abortive attempt of Helmut's parents to immigrate to the United States in 1930—a shadowed saga of separations, disruptions, and plans gone awry extending over a 25-year period.

Helmut's father, Paul Dost, was a restless electrical engineer who worked most of his life for a large German electrical company, AEG. An irresistible wanderlust seems to have drawn him into the overseas division, which assigned him to projects in various foreign countries. A few days after his marriage to Maria Starkowski in 1928 Paul had to leave his new bride to begin a new job in Central America. She joined him several months later.

Helmut later recalled that his dad always seemed driven to get out of Germany. As Paul's ultimate dream was to settle in the United States, the couple applied to immigrate directly from Guatemala. Having lost their first son there at birth, which they attributed to inadequate medical conditions, getting to the United States took on a new urgency when Maria became pregnant with her second child. But there was a serious snag. Helmut's arrival was due in July of 1930 while their immigration quota numbers made them ineligible to immigrate legally until October of that year.

Advised by the American consul (erroneously as it turned out) that they could come to the United States on a visitor's visa and pick up their immigration papers in Montreal, Canada, the prospective parents set sail for New York that spring. On this voyage Paul and Maria met an American couple, Carroll and Bertha Dodge, both professors of botany at Washington University in St. Louis, who would later play a significant role in their lives and that of their future son.

Life in New York City during the Great Depression was very difficult. Unable to work legally in the United States, Paul obtained lodgings in exchange for tending the furnace in an apartment building, picked up various menial odd jobs, and even accepted some limited help from the Salvation Army.

On July 18 Maria gave birth to a healthy son at Bronx Maternity Hospital. Come October, the couple made their way to Canada to obtain their immigration papers, only to be turned back at the border by Canadian authorities. On a second attempt at another border crossing, they were again refused admission into Canada. Later, in a letter from the State Department, they were told that it was not possible to immigrate to the United States in the manner prescribed by the consul. Unable to solve their dilemma, the little family was deported to Germany when Helmut was nine months old.

In Berlin jobs were also scarce in those days. Thus Paul worked as a mail carrier until a job opened up for him with his old company, AEG. During this time, in 1933, Helmut's brother, Martin, was born. The next year Paul was rehired by the AEG and assigned to a job with a sugar beet factory being constructed in Ireland. For reasons that are unknown, the family never did join him there.

Happier times came when Paul was assigned to electrical projects related to dam construction in Egypt in 1935. There the family lived in a modern apartment in Cairo, hired a house boy, bought a car, and enrolled the boys in a German school. Helmut remembered those days in Egypt as some of the happiest of his life.

Paul and Maria were active in the German community in Cairo, and it was there that Paul, apparently under considerable pressure from his boss, became a dues-paying member of the overseas division of the NSDAP (German Nazi Party). Paul, who actually voted for the Communists in 1932, was an improbable Nazi. Always the pragmatist, his brief interest in the party years before seems to have been its early emphasis on opportunities for German workers during the Depression.

Life was good until 1939, when war broke out between England and Germany. At this point German nationals were no longer welcome in Egypt, a British protectorate, and within a week were rounded up for incarceration by the British. But Paul, ever resourceful, managed to elude British authorities and get himself and his family onto a Bulgarian ship and back to Germany, even though it meant leaving all their possessions behind.

The family spent the early war years together in their Berlin apartment until the allied bombings became intense. At that point, in 1943, the boys' entire school was evacuated from the city, first to East Prussia and later to two successive locations in Czechoslovakia, as Russian troops closed in. Because Helmut's mother was employed as the school's secretary, she was fortunate in being able to accompany her sons in these relocations.

At the end of the war the family was eventually reunited intact, but by this time life in Germany was extremely grim. Malnourishment was rampant and TB a major threat. Paul and Maria could only think how much better off their "Ami" [American] could be in the country of his birth, and apparently assumed that having a child in the United States would soon open the American door to all of them. So once again, Helmut's New York birth certificate in hand, they consulted the American consulate—this time to find out what rights their eldest son might have as a United States citizen.

They were unprepared for the response. Helmut's birth in the United States, they were told, qualified him as a war refugee eligible for *immediate* repatriation. To this end the consulate advised that he leave the country as soon as possible after his upcoming sixteenth birthday—preferably on the next refugee ship! But without family members or close friends in America, Paul and Maria had no one to whom they could send their son.

Thus it was that they contacted the Dodges, with whom they had corresponded until the beginning of the war. Grasping at straws, they had also written a letter to Augusta de Boer, an elderly shirt-tail relative in San Diego, California. On receiving the Dosts' letter, the Dodges made arrangements for Helmut to attend an excellent boarding school in their home state of Vermont. Since the family spent their summers there, the plan was for Helmut to live with them during school vacation.

But by an inexplicable glitch in the postal service, the Dodges' airmail response, which would normally have taken a week to reach Berlin, did not arrive until four weeks later—several days after Helmut's ship had left Bremen for New York. Meanwhile, Mrs. de Boer, known to the family as "Tante [*aunt*] Guschen," was finally prevailed upon, as the only other alternative, to take Helmut in, although her ambivalence was painfully obvious. This collection begins with the Dosts' letters to Carroll and Bertha Dodge in the summer of 1946 and the Dodges' replies.

It was an irony of fate that the well-raised, intelligent young man who might have had a superior high school education, interested mentors, and in all likelihood opportunities to make a smooth transition to college, instead ended up sharing a small trailer house in California with an eccentric old German woman who would never get over the feeling of being taken advantage of. Why this plan was not reversed once the Dodges' letter was received remains something of a mystery, since Helmut spent some weeks in New York after his arrival in the United States and presumably could somehow have been contacted.

Insisting on more income than Helmut's meager refugee assistance was bringing in, Tante Guschen expected Helmut to go to work. Therefore, instead of attending a regular public high school in San Diego, he finished his education in a continuation school (attended mainly by drop-outs) while working during the day for a German shoemaker. When life with Guschen became almost unbearably strained, Helmut left—at his parents' insistence—and went to live in the home of his employer's sister until he graduated.

Without money or consistent guidance, Helmut's confident hopes of going to college did not materialize. Instead, he found himself working as a poorly paid hired hand for a German chicken farmer near Palo Alto, California, constantly waiting for the promised sponsorship of his family which always seemed right around the corner. While there he received news of his father's successful denazification hearing—to be followed, less than a year later, by the shattering report of his death in an industrial accident.

Three years after what was to have been six months on the farm, the Korean War broke out and Helmut was drafted for military service. Ultimately he served nearly five years in the Marine Corps, including a year in Korea, before his mother and brother finally joined him in California in October 1955. By this time Martin, in Berlin, had acquired the virtual equivalent of an American bachelor's degree. In June of 1956 Helmut, nearly 26 years old, started out as a freshman at the University of California on the G. I. Bill of Rights. He remained a student there until he had earned a Ph. D. in physics in 1965, and later went on to a career in defense-related research.

This chronicle of nine years in a young man's life begs many questions. It spans a period when the chaotic circumstances of war and its aftermath often prompted desperate decisions. Like that of many victims of war, Helmut's youth was largely propelled by a succession of circumstances almost totally beyond his control.

The family's sudden expulsion from Egypt, repeated childhood relocations in Europe, an involuntary "repatriation" to the United States, educational plans shattered by the accident of a tardy letter, the unexpected death of his father in Germany, and finally the outbreak of war in far-off Korea—these were among the formative events to which life demanded a response.

Finding himself with the man-sized responsibility of arranging his family's future, even while lacking the direction so greatly needed for his own young life, the boy rose to the challenge. He coped. Coped unquestioningly, with all the pluck, imagination, and dogged commitment a young man could muster, until the mission was accomplished. But, one might fairly ask, at what price?

How might the life of this family have played out had it not been for a son seemingly born to be an American? At the end of the day, one wonders, might they have fared as well in Germany? For Helmut, was his birthright more blessing or burden? Who can say? You, the reader, may judge.

EDITOR'S NOTE

Most of the letters in the original collection put together by Martin Dost have been included in this book. A number of letters that are exceptionally technical, repetitive, or unrelated to the main thrust of the story have been omitted. Other letters have been abbreviated for the same reasons. Brackets have been used within the text of the letters to set off editorial explanations and comments.

To differentiate letters translated from the German from those which were written originally in English, the translated German letters have been rendered in regular type and the English letters in italics. Segments of the translated letters—paragraphs, sentences, and even individual words—that were in English to begin with are also italicized. No modifications have been made to the spelling and punctuation of the letters written originally in English.

As a boy, Helmut devised a system of assigning sequential numbers to the letters as a means of keeping track of them. These same numbers have been retained at the head of each letter.

In the letters, frequent mention is made of persons who are called "aunt" or "uncle." In reality Helmut and Martin had no uncles, and only two aunts, both of whom had passed away by the time the letters were written. These people were thus not actual aunts and uncles, but family friends, aunts or uncles of their parents, or in some cases more distant relatives. The German word for aunt, "Tante," has been left untranslated when referring to Augusta de Boer, who was known to the family as "Tante Guschen." Also, the signature of their mother, Maria Dost, has usually been left untranslated as simply "Mutti."

1

A Letter Lost: *How It All Began*

Chapter 1 consists of four letters exchanged in 1946 by Helmut's parents and American botany professor Carroll Dodge, whom the Dosts had met many years before in their early attempt to immigrate to the United States. A letter from the Dosts, written a year after the end of the war, asks the Dodges if they can do anything to help their son get settled in the country of his birth. The Dodges' reply describes their plan to enroll Helmut in a private boarding school in New England and to have him spend vacations with them in their own summer home in Vermont.

Ironically, Professor Dodge's first letter was inexplicably delayed by four weeks—an incident which would radically change the direction of Helmut's future life. In response to the delayed letter, the Dosts explain that they have already sent Helmut on his way, having now arranged for him to live with a distant relative in California. They tell the Dodges that they want very much to join their son in the United States but intimate that they cannot do so without help from an American citizen who would be willing to undertake their sponsorship. Helmut will not be able to do this himself until he turns 21.

The search for a sponsor is the theme that dominates all of the letters exchanged by Helmut and his family. Because a prospective sponsor was required to sign an affidavit guaranteeing the immigrant's support during the initial period of residence, a sponsorship was not so easily come by even for one person, much less for a family of three.

These four letters between the Dosts and the Dodges were not a part of the original collection saved and numbered by Helmut and Martin Dost. They were discovered many years later by a member of

the Dodge family among the papers of author and botany professor
Bertha Dodge.

⌘

Berlin Reinickendorf, June 23, 1946

Dear Family Dodge!

*A few weeks ago we wrote to you our first letter after the war,
which we—thanks to God—survived all right. Of course in the short
meantime we could not yet have any answer from you, even if the
address still would be the same as we suppose.*

*We hope now that very soon we will get a sign of life and health
from you all. Now we are in a real hurry to write already again, for, in
the last days, we decided that our eldest son, Helmut, being born at
New York, NY 1930, shall become an American. So we went to the
American Consulate, and there they made no difficulties at all—the
contrary, he may have his Pass-Port right away, only he has firstly to
stay at least two years in the USA to be a full American citizen.*

*Now in August he is ready to leave Germany and to go over to
USA, your dear and from us beloved country.*

*But where to shall he go? We have no member of family or other
friends except you in USA...We are really not afraid that our boy with
his character and abilities is not able to make out of himself a man
without others help—But you know, we as parents should like very
much if he would have the opportunity to stay in a decent family,
possibly where he can finish his school and other studies, instead of
living in a strange house, learning any insecure trade or working in a
dirty factory. This would be a real pity insofar as the boy is physically
not so very strong (for food is too scarce over here) and mentally
extremely capable. He got, as the terrible war circumstances allowed, a
very good education. He likes sciences and music (plays piano and
violin) and his hobby is chemistry.*

*Now dear family Dodge we ask you—what advice would you give
us about this case? Do you know what we can do for this boy? You
must know that we lost all our fortune by the war and for the first we
cannot do much in financial respect for our Helmut—but this question
must be [solved] now, for this boy is too slender and he needs some
strong food, for his health. He is still going to secondary school and*

there one of the best pupils. He understands English pretty well and promises to be a very good company.

In regard that the time from now till August is too short to expect your kind answer by letter, we would ask you to decide as soon as possible, and then to telegraf us shortly your opinion about this matter. For we think that your answer by telegraf will reach us before August. Now please excuse our freedom to ask you such great questions and try to understand us in our actual position. We parents may follow Helmut as soon as he has majority and then we hope will come the time to recompensate your kind help in this case if not earlier. Naturally we will try to solve this question as soon as possible.

Be sure that we never would like to trouble you, but knowing your hearty, friendly feelings for our sort, we took the freedom to ask you for this familiar service. In case of the contrary you may be sure, we would do the same.

Hearty greetings as ever

Your true friends,
The Dost Family

Pawlet, Vermont, Aug. 7, 1946

Dear Mr. Dost:
Your letters of May 10 and June 23 have been received, forwarded to me here, where I am spending my long vacation from the University. We were glad to learn that you had survived the war without serious loss. I had not gotten sufficient data to answer your first when the second arrived on August 5.

Under present conditions, we do not think it wise for Helmut to try to live in a large city. The housing situation in them is very difficult, almost impossible to find a room, and very difficult to find work where he could earn his living, certainly not and continue his education. We do not have room for him in our home in St. Louis and adjustment to strange conditions in very large city high schools would be very difficult. [The Dodges later explained that they were also concerned about the prejudice Helmut might have encountered as a German in their heavily Jewish neighborhood].

Consequently I have arranged with the headmaster of the Burr and Burton Academy in Manchester, Vermont for Helmut to go to school and live in the boys' dormitory, or if that should be crowded, in the *headmaster's own home. Helmut can stay here in Pawlet during the long summer vacation. The school is being very generous in contributing his room and part of his tuition and board, which will amount to about $600.00.*

The amount he can earn will depend upon his ability. In spring and autumn some of the boys earn $4–$5 per day on Friday afternoons after school and on Saturdays on the golf courses.

Perhaps you will be able to contribute a little and I can arrange for Helmut to borrow the rest without interest until he has finished school and is self-supporting. He might even find a suitable position for the summer and earn the rest then. We can settle details better when we see how things develop the first year. The headmaster is very sympathetic as also two of the teachers with whom I talked, one of whom has done some graduate work in Heidelberg. My sister, brother, and I were all trained in this excellent school.

We expect to be in Vermont until Sept. 20, so he can come directly to us by train to Manchester, Vermont, where we will meet him and bring him to Pawlet until school opens in early September. If I know in time, perhaps I can arrange for my sister to meet Helmut in New York and see him on the train at the Grand Central Station for Manchester, Vermont. She works for the American Red Cross. He should allow at least $10 for expenses in New York and train fare to Manchester.

Since we feel you should know all of these arrangements, which are obviously too long to cable, we are sending this by air mail, which should arrive in about a week, giving Helmut time to arrive here before we leave for St. Louis. The school opens in early September. I do not have the exact date at the moment. Trusting that you will approve these arrangements, which are the best I can do, and looking forward to meeting Helmut, we are

Sincerely yours,
Carroll W. Dodge

Reinikendorf Ost, September 10, 1946

Dear Mr. Dodge!
Many thanks for your very kind letter of Aug. 7 from Pawlet, Vermont, which we received now, after our Helmut had already left Berlin since 28th of August in order to start from Bremen to New York. We suppose that his ship in the meantime will have started to his new home in U. S. A.

You were so kind to give us your advise in consideration of all possibilities to live and to learn, and even to earn a little for contributing himself for his education. By your fine arrangements you made us very quiet, although in the moment Helmut (knowing nothing about your good advise) will continue his voyage to our old good aunt Mrs. Auguste de Boer in San Diego (California). But who knows—the aunt of my husband is already 73 years old—maybe it is better for him to stay soon among younger, well educated people, in your neighborship.

We expect Helmut will have interrupted his long trip to San Diego in order to take occasion for a visit to you and your dear family. So, you will have seen and spoken to him, overthinking his situation after your personal impression in this matter.

Even the meeting for Helmut with your dear sister in New York at the Grand Central Station was a very nice plan. Please for all your help our hearty thanks and remember us to your dear family, Mrs. Bertha Dodge and the children.

It is a pity that the entering to U. S. A. in the moment is not possible for us. If you hear or see any possibility for us or at first for my husband (or me and the son Martin, who is now 13 years old) to settle over there, you would oblige us very much...Naturally you never must be afraid that we will make you any trouble in your personal life by our coming over there. My husband has...more than 20 years of practice in working as an erecting-engineer for electrical power stations and so on. Besides, he has practice in speaking several languages, as Spanish, English, some Arabic, etc. in order to understand foreign people, as much as it is necessary for his work at least.

I hope we will have once occasion to show you also from our side how glad we are to count you among our dearest friends in this new time. God may help you and all the other worthful people in the world to make forget the cruel enemyship from one people to the other. Wishing you all the best for the future, I remain with many hearty greetings from house to house,

Maria Dost

Oct. 25, 1946

Dear Mr. & Mrs. Dost:

Your letters of September 10 arrived Tuesday and Helmut Wednesday afternoon. I think it wise for Helmut to live with his aunt in San Diego, where he can attend High School and probably the first two years of the University. I have asked him to write me from time to time and if anything should happen to his elderly aunt, I will try to help him in any way I can.

Helmut seemed very happy. He told us he had gained 11 kg in weight and 5 cm in height since leaving Germany. I tried to meet him at the station, but missed him. He found our house address and arrived by taxi before I returned. He spent the night with us and Mrs. Dodge went with him to the train the next afternoon. Unfortunately I had classes and other appointments at the University so that could not spend as much time with him as I would have liked.

I am sure that Helmut will succeed in San Diego. He can probably find work there after school to contribute his share of living expenses. In high school there are no tuition charges and textbooks are usually furnished free of charge. He will profit by your aunt's loving care and his responsibility as the man of the household will be very good for him.

Mrs. Dodge joins me in sending our best wishes,

Sincerely yours,
Carroll W. Dodge

2

Hello, New York: *But Where Do I Go from Here?*

The first two letters sent by Helmut to his family were written in the Emigrant Assembly Area in Bremen, where he went through processing for 9–10 days while waiting for his ship to sail. After living for so long in near-starvation conditions, his descriptions of food served there are noticeably enthusiastic and detailed! Helmut's family never received his third and fourth letters, in which he described the voyage to the United States.

Knowing nothing of the plans made by Professor Dodge, the War Refugee Division of the New York City welfare department spent several weeks trying to settle the case of this young man who seemed to have no clear destination. When he presented a mailing address for Augusta de Boer, a distant relative in San Diego, it turned out to be simply General Delivery, and the caseworkers actually ended up enlisting the help of the FBI to track her down!

Meanwhile Helmut spent time in New York and Baltimore visiting with a number of German families who were apparently relatives of friends in Germany or acquaintances of his parents from their early days in New York. It seems that Paul and Maria had asked Helmut to look them up but did not know any of these people well enough to have asked them to house and care for their son.

Technically classified as a war refugee, Helmut was eligible for funds from public assistance. Even with this limited income, he immediately began sending packages of food and clothing from New York to Berlin. Because of restrictions on the number and weight of parcels that could be sent from the United States to any one family in a given period of time, Helmut quickly adopted a rather complex system whereby packages were sent to friends and relatives who then sent them on to his family.

On October 25, after receiving a less than whole-hearted invitation from "Tante Guschen" de Boer in California, Helmut boarded a train for the West Coast.

⌘

Letter 1   Bremen, Emigrant Assembly Area, August 29, 1946

Dear Parents, Dear Martin!

The trip here went well without any long delays. Only we arrived at 9:00 a.m. instead of 10:30 p.m. We had barely left and sat down in our compartment (Sybille and Herta Tiedtke, their friend Gerd—an 11 year old boy—and two nursemaids) when several Americans hurried down the aisle with mugs, crackers, tins of cheese and liver paste, and water.

The Americans, who accompanied the train, soon took a fancy to the young nursemaid, who was travelling to her husband in New York. So the whole night long there were at least two of them in the compartment.

When it got dark we discovered that we had no light—after all , we were travelling second class—while the cars ahead of us, filled with French people, all had light, and we also discovered that the seats folded out and fastened so that four wide sleeping places were available. I laid down on one side... and looked out of the window; it pulled out so that the window was open. Gradually it got dark. We were all expecting the second course of supper, but it never came. Herta and Gerd played with the Amis [*Americans*], until they were worn out and fell asleep. Then I fell asleep too after Potsdam, Brandenburg, and Magdeburg were behind us.

Then, after Salzgitter, the last two cars and our baggage car were unhitched and connected to a train heading north. Before this we had come to the foothills of the Hartz Mountains. Then there was a bustling trip to the north via Hannover to Bremen. Shortly before the station the train stopped and went through a few switches in the direction of Bremerhafen. After a while we were loaded onto trucks and driven back through Bremen.

Here in the camp they took out the big suitcases first. Then we came through registration and a short medical exam and delousing, with a pile of blankets and bed linen, to our assigned room. The whole building looked as if it had been a school. In our room there were eight bunk beds. Everything here is wonderfully clean. I made my bed right away and went to dinner. There was a small bowl of oat soup, two crackers, three cutlets with a dab of marmalade and grease [*a common substitute for scarce butter*]. With it there was a cup of milk-coffee. After the meal I washed up and brushed myself out. Then I tried to reach Otti [*Otti Schneider, a family friend who lived in Bremen*], but with no luck. It was uncertain when we would receive our exit passes.

I was just at lunch. The adults got two or three cigarettes. Otherwise there were three slices of bread, a small helping of potatoes, some gravy, and a dish full of beans. Also a cup of tea. Everything tasted first-rate. You couldn't believe how full I got. I heard somewhere here that the ship is supposed to sail on Friday, September 6, but it isn't official. I'm anxious to go on. I'm still hearing that we aren't supposed to take any unchecked mail with us. Instead, we have to send it by civil mail. I've received a piece of soap and will receive a new one in three days. I can even get my things ironed here, but I haven't tried that yet.

At Schneiders, August 30, 1946

Yesterday evening there were three slices of bread (white), one helping of red fish, similar to what I used to get in packets, a small bowl of pea and sausage soup, and a cup of tea. It tasted delicious. Before I went to bed I played a funny American game with a little American boy (civilian). This morning there was a small bowl of oatmeal, three slices of bread, two crackers, one small portion of grease, and a helping of scrambled eggs. Great!!

At 9:00 a census officer was with us. We only needed to show the letters to the censor. Paper, stamps, books, pictures, etc. weren't necessary. I also had to show my foreign money. He didn't even look at anything less than 20 or 30 dollars. Thank goodness! We will get the letters back before the ship leaves, and in a sealed envelope.

Then I took a shower. For lunch there was a small bowl of a strange sweet soup, three slices of bread, boiled potatoes, and excellent meat gravy, beans and peas, and tea. Scrumptious! At 2:00 p.m. there was a discussion. The trip is likely to last 10 days. We will probably receive our tickets on September 5. Otherwise nothing new is expected. At the end of the meeting I left right away to walk to the Schneiders, since the street car had just left and it wasn't far to walk.

Mrs. Schneider didn't seem terribly surprised. Likewise Otti, who was busy in their new home. We went to the post office, and then he showed me the cathedral, the city hall, the "Roland" [*a statue*], and a few more notable sights. In the evening...I picked up the pants I had taken to be ironed for one mark. In the evening there was another symphony concert.

August 31, 1946. This morning we had the same [*breakfast*] as usual. From 11:00 to 12:00 we had a voluntary English lesson for advanced students, which, since the teachers are among the passengers, can be continued on the ship. In the afternoon I went with Otti to the Weser [*River*] and finally to the barber. In the evening we had three slices of bread, three bowls of soup, half a can of sardines in oil, and tea. At 5:00 we always have supper; if you stay downstairs till 6:00, you can usually get something more, and that's good because otherwise you don't get anything else to eat for 14.5 hours.

In the evening we had a dance at 8:00. The music was really very good. A four-man band: one piano, one accordion, one fiddle, and one percussion instrument. In the beginning no one trusted himself (to dance). Then when the American from the supply house started, things began to warm up. I haven't told you anything about our room. Originally we were three fellows, 16, 18, and 19. Two days later nine foreigners came in. At first we were worried, but we needn't have been because the Hungarians, or Croats, or Serbs, or Bulgarians, or whatever they are, are very sociable and friendly and funny. One of them became the center of attention; he was really an outstanding dancer. Three bunks are still empty. There are sixteen beds (eight double bunks). In the future I am not going to write so much.

Greetings and kisses, Helmut

Letter 2   Bremen, September 6, 1946 [*Sailing Date*]

They woke us up at 4:30 a.m.; now it is 5:00. In half an hour we have to give up our supply of blankets, sheets, and pillows. Then at 6:00 there is breakfast and between 6:30 and 8:30 the individual trucks leave one after the other. More later!

On Monday and Tuesday nothing special happened. I looked around the city with Otti. On Sunday evening we had a movie. Funny. Monday evening there was a dance; Tuesday evening a movie, but in the afternoon there had already been a fairy tale movie with nice commentary. On Wednesday morning I received a visit from Herr Miksch [*another family friend living in Bremen*] and was able to show him the camp; he was very surprised (in a happy way). In the afternoon we went together to the Fischerbrude [*an art gallery*]. Without exception they were horrible pictures by Meyboden. At coffee time we chatted over sausage and gelled meat pastries. I ate a lot of fruit. In the evening I went back again between "Show and Dance."

Yesterday there was a lot to do here. Early in the morning I washed out two pairs of stockings; then I took a shower. After breakfast the consul came and distributed the passports and ship tickets. I'm berthed with the majority of men on Deck B (1st between deck) in room II, berth 36. The American ladies are berthed on Deck A. The American men are on Deck B. The female emigrants are on Deck C and male emigrants on Deck D to E. The ship is the *Marine Marlin*, a converted freighter. It's supposed to leave between 1500 and 2100 (between 3:00 and 9:00 p.m.).

Helmut

Paul Dost's Diary, September 12:

We received two letters from Helmut that he mailed in Bremen. The letter from Professor Dodge was delayed; it arrived on September 9 (four weeks instead of one).

Letter 5   Farmingdale [*N. Y.*], Oct. 3, 1946

Dear Ones at Home!

I just sat down on a shaky bench in the wonderful sunshine. Yesterday and the day before we had terrible weather—that is, ice cold. Last night we had...about 45 degrees F., that's about 1–2 degrees Celsius. Yesterday and the day before we had about 55–60 degrees F., that is 10 degrees Celsius. In some northern regions the paper says there have been violent snowstorms, which is unusual here at the beginning of October. I've already posted the collection of mail that I was given for Kallenbergs (who meanwhile have moved to 49 Fairview Ave., Park Ridge, New Jersey) and Heimanns; it's doubtful if they still live there. [*Helmut's parents had apparently given him letters to mail to acquaintances from their early days in New York*].

One day when I was in a nearby park with Gerhard Koch (Gerhard is pronounced Gerard, with the emphasis on the second syllable and a "G" as in journal), Mrs. Koch suddenly arrived with a man who looked like a boxer. He introduced himself as Herr Heinz Feuerherdt or something like that, commissioned by Mrs. Kovaleff to transport me to Farmingdale. In the evening he put me on a bus going in the direction—but only in the direction—of Farmingdale, because it didn't go there at all. He had written down when and where I should get off, and that Mrs. Kovaleff would pick me up there in an old brown car. When the driver dropped me off at my destination it was night. All around everything was field and woods and no brown car. Here I was, a lost soul staring into the night—there was only a store and another one on the other side. A ways away there was a house with light. The whole day it had been hot as an oven; now at 11:00 it was cold. And I (what a dummy!) only had a day shirt on and nothing more with me. "We learn through misfortune"—*nocendo discimus* [*Latin*]. After waiting a while I just ran to the house. These people and others, after many mistakes and vain telephone calls, finally succeeded in getting me to the Kovaleffs.

Mrs. Kovaleff works here in real estate, that is she buys and sells houses. In the meantime I told them a lot about Germany, the Pisareks [*mutual friends in Germany*], the mood of the people, the occupation of Germany, etc. She always wants me to eat more. I already have a regular pot belly. Next week on Tuesday, Mrs. Kovaleff will take me back to New York, since she has something else to do in the city. She is very nice and understands my jokes very well. Tomorrow we want to take pictures. Then I'll send you some. The Kovaleffs have a very nice house here on a big hill. Behind the house are the hen houses. They have in all about 6,000 hens. Mr. Kovaleff and an old hired hand have a lot of work to oversee them. Mr. Kovaleff speaks Russian and broken English. Mrs. Kovaleff speaks German and quite a good English, but with a Russian accent. They have a piano here. Also on Saturday I was at the Russian Club. [*The Kovaleffs were apparently Germans who were originally from Russia*].

On the first, second, and third of October we had a great article in the newspaper about Nuremberg [*where the Nazi war crimes trials were in progress*]. I've cut out a few things for you. A quick close, because the mailman is coming right away. Write me something about Nuremberg.

A big bag full of greetings and kisses.
Your Helmut

Paul Dost's Diary, October 7:

Still no mail from Helmut [*from the United States*].

Paul Dost's Diary, October 8:

Tante de Boer got scared of the "responsibility" and told the United States government, which had advanced the travel money, that she will not be able to host Helmut (and therefore will not pay for the travel expenses either). She wrote Helmut off out of fear, adding that the Navy or Army would be happy to take him (according to the letter from September 23, airmail). Now we are anxious to hear where Helmut is going to stay, and how everything will work out.

Letter 6   Yorkville, Oct. 17

Dear Ones!
        I am still well and not homesick. Sure, I've often thought of you poor Berliners, but not with homesickness. I was with the Lentzens four days in Baltimore. They are very nice people. Regina has kept herself well; she doesn't look twenty-two. They have a very nice four-room place... in the suburb of West Arlington. I went there on a Greyhound bus. As you know, I was with the Kovaleffs...in the neighborhood of Farmingdale.
        Mrs. Kovaleff has a little old jalopy from the year 1929. She gets mad at it. With this monster we bumpity-bumped here in the neighborhood and to the beach, which is about 13–15 miles away. On Tuesday, Oct. 8, I was picked up [*by Mrs. Kovaleff*] from the bus in the hubbub of New York City. First she went to get a package off to Russia. We slipped into a movie with a news show, where something about the Nazi trial was announced outside in black letters. But we only saw the same pictures as in Berlin.
        Then we were swallowed up in the crowds of the city and drove in the direction of Yorkville to the mother of Heinz Feuerherdt, who had put me on the bus to Farmingdale. I was very well received there, and in the evening we went to Brooklyn. In the meantime I was persuaded by Mrs. Kovaleff and Mrs. Feuerherdt that I should go to San Diego—that a nice woman [*i.e. Tante Guschen*] would certainly be there.
        Now I have decided to take off in about 14 days. In Brooklyn with

the Kochs I waited for a letter from Baltimore...The letter [*from the Lentzens*] said I should come over for a week end to arrange everything; besides, there was a check for $10.00 to pay for the estimated customs fee. So I took this opportunity to pick up the rest of my baggage during the next few days. Since I wanted to leave soon for California anyway, the next week end was ideal. As the week end drew near, everything turned out as if it had been planned. Something like that doesn't happen every day. The other morning I got myself a ticket right away for Saturday at 2:05 p.m. Then when I explained my wish to move I was informed by the welfare department that I needed Tante Augusta's firm consent. So I wrote to her. When I got back from Baltimore I had the answer. But more about that later.

In Baltimore I went to a movie, "Caeser and Cleopatra," an English color film wonderfully produced from the play of Dad's beloved Bernard Shaw. Then once I went bowling with Regina and some friends. One evening the Lentzens were invited by friends for a birthday; there was coffee and cake and ice cream and conversation in abundance. Earlier we'd wolfed down "thick noodles" and had sworn to fast for two days; then the call came and we cursed the birthday feast. But when the magnificent fragrance ascended to our nostrils, we forgot our joking and our full stomachs.

In New York the answer from San Diego had finally come. She [*Tante Guschen*] would be pleased to be able to mother me but "What are we going to do with you coming so suddenly to America?" etc. A letter like this went to the welfare department and a similar one came to me. Today I got a telegram—read it yourself: *"Welfare says will not support you in Calif. Sorry I cannot take you. May later when I have a own home. Aunt Augusta."* Too bad. I will arrange everything with Welfare tomorrow. Mrs. Feuerherdt thinks that Tante Guschen is quite shrewd and would like to have money from Welfare for my support. Maybe. It's 11:30 p.m. More tomorrow morning.

                                                                    Helmut

Letter 6-A   Yorkville, N. Y., Oct. 19, 1946

Dear Berliners!

Well, yesterday morning I went to the welfare office (250 W. 57th Street). After a long wait Miss Osten finally appeared, she's handling my case. She's really nice—you must think I call everyone "really nice," but I mean it seriously—she seems to be Jewish, and her father was a regular German. In any case she speaks good German, although veeerry sslooowly, with a hint of something foreign, in any case not an American accent.

This Miss Osten read the telegram through, disappeared, and returned right away with two letters, giving me one with the words, *"Write your aunt that she can't be always changing her mind from one day to the next, in the end she's got to be definite. Deliver this letter to this address in San Diego when you introduce yourself."* Later, around Tuesday or Wednesday, I will probably take off by train, get off in St. Louis and later change for Kansas City and Los Angeles. In the letter to the San Diego welfare department it explained:

> *"As Helmut is under 18, we are anxious to arrange for supervision of his environment in San Diego and perhaps help in planning his future with him. Helmut is anxious to return to school to continue his education. He speaks English very well, is bright and intelligent, and shows evidence of having had good schooling and careful upbringing. If you are not the agency handling the supervision of children, may we ask you to refer H. to the proper child-caring agency?"*

So you see the kind of impression your son's been making!

Well, here I am at Mrs. Feuerherdt's. I'll send along pictures next time. The Kochs want quite a lot of money to stay five days, so I can't stay there any longer. The Feuerherdt family is a great substitute for them. Twenty-one ties, three shirts, a pair of pyjamas, and a pair of ice hockey skates with shoes that fit me all right. They've given me all this already. Besides expensive care and support, so that I can save money for myself or for you. Send off a letter to them. Also, you absolutely must tell me if you can receive one-pound packages from the American sector. Then I could send Uncle Karl one-pound packages that he could send on as individual packages.

I don't really have much money, but something should turn up. The day before yesterday I bought two pairs of new shoes. Brown oxfords, black dress shoes, both comparatively cheap, $6.00 each. I don't know if I already told you that I've gotten bigger, taller and broader. The pants I had to wear suspenders with six months ago so they wouldn't be too long, and a belt so they'd fit close to my stomach, barely fit me

anymore. At the bottom they only reach to my ankle (without sus-
penders) and as for the width I have to wear a belt so people don't see
that the top button is open. Pretty soon I won't be able to wear the
jacket any more since Mrs. Fabian took it in for me back then. The
narrow waist makes my bottom stick out so that there's no way I can
button it. You can talk about this, but please, please don't read this out
loud.

The day before yesterday Mrs. Feuerherdt and I were in the Bronx
at the Department of Health. We ordered a copy of my birth certificate
which will arrive soon. Yesterday we were only at the welfare office in
"Radio City" on 50th St. at the corner of 6th Ave. There we saw a
movie, and a performance—ballet, orchestra, concert, etc. In the evening I was in the Planetarium on 81st at the corner of 8th Ave., which
around there is called West Central Park. The exhibition was very, very
interesting. A lot of meteorites were displayed in the entry room. In the
next couple of days I'll check out all the notable sights. Bronx Park, the
Museum of Natural History, Miss Liberty, etc.

I still haven't received any letters from you. How is the garden?
May you stay healthy until the packages get there. Today I'll send a
CARE Package. Now it only costs $10.00 to mail the same package
that cost $15.00 before. Eventually I'll also send one to the Herbergs. I
must tell you that the postage stamps are as good as worthless here—
10 cents a set if one is lucky; that would be two packets without profit.
[*Helmut is referring here to a stamp collection that his parents sent
along with him in the belief that it would have some monetary value.*]
I could send a package of coffee to the Scherbiuses, but I think that this
only goes to the American and British zones; so you also have to give
me an address [*of someone living in one of those zones*] if one-pound
packages are allowed from there. Best wishes to all our dear friends and
especially to you.

Big kisses,
Your Helmut

Letter 7   On the Train, October 25, 1946

Dear Germans!

Since I'm writing while traveling on the train, you may not like my
handwriting much—or do you?

Recently in New York I was in your old apartment house. Right
where you were in Number 353 the janitors changed very fast. At least

the fourth one [*since 1930*] is there now. I asked about Netherkotts, Kallers, etc. No one knew anyone. Then the present janitor said that maybe the janitor on the corner, who has lived and worked there for 30 years, would know. Her name is Mrs. Schramm. Of course I took off like crazy. She was naturally very flabbergasted, and since she still had a lot of work to get done, I made the rounds [*to places remembered by his parents*]: to Weissbecker's, which has already been gone a long time (there is now a City Food store there), and then to Lindberg Hall, which isn't there at all anymore.

Auntie Schramm—I'll call her that, although she isn't—had a lot to tell me. As far as I understood, both of her granddaughters are married. The thin one has two children. The Waldmans live in New Jersey, but without an ice cream shop. Mrs. Schramm is a lively old woman of 76. It's really hard to believe all she does as a janitor at that age. She has probably been in the country 54 years now. Hearty greetings from her!

In the last days in New York I went still other places. I don't know if I wrote you about the planetarium. It's much better equipped than the one in Berlin. The star apparatus is of course by Zeiss in Jena. Then I was at the Empire State Building once. It's over 102 stories high. A couple of months ago it was very foggy and a pilot couldn't get his plane up very high so it was blown against the building. The motor came right out on the other side and fell down into the houses. It cut the elevator cables off so that it raced down with injured people in it. Fortunately no one was in the offices up there. Then after that I was at the ice show. Wonderful! It was a regular theater. I had a box of books sent to San Diego. I put a suitcase on my ticket.

I'm going to write to you about the trip another time, because otherwise the letter will be too heavy and I'll have to stick on 60 cents worth of stamps. More another day. Happy birthday to Rudiger and Gunther.

Your Helmut

3

California, Here I Come: *Tante Guschen's Trailer*

Helmut's first letter from San Diego describes his train trip west, including an unexpected visit to the Dodges in St. Louis on the way. Just a day before Helmut's arrival, Professor Dodge had received a letter from Helmut's parents explaining the delayed receipt of his letter and their subsequent decision to send Helmut to California. Whether the Dodges discussed with Helmut the plans they had made for him in Vermont is unclear. In any case, now that he was on his way to an "aunt" in California, they probably felt that they should not interfere with this new plan.

When Helmut arrived in San Diego he found Tante Guschen living in a hotel while looking for a small house to buy. For a few weeks Helmut lived there also, supported by the Los Angeles welfare department, and actively joined in the search—which culminated in the purchase of a small trailer.

Many aspects of Helmut's personality reveal themselves in this chapter. In spite of his frustrations with the ambivalent and often verbally abusive Guschen, he exhibits an understanding and tolerance remarkable for a sixteen-year-old. One begins to sense his feelings of obligation to help solve the problems of the adults in his life, even at the expense of his own best interests. He tries to advise his parents on ways to expedite their immigration to the United States—sometimes more imaginative than feasible—and even writes a letter to President Truman to solicit his intervention!

In his suggestions for devising a system of recording letters and packages sent and received, the creation of diagrams and maps to describe his new environment, and graphically detailed descriptions of places and objects we also see the emergence of a keen technical and analytical mind.

In this chapter Helmut mentions three different types of packages sent to Europe: CARE, "John," and private parcels. CARE was a cooperative of non-profit organizations which enabled Americans to send a ten-day supply of Army surplus food to friends and relatives in Europe for the price of $10.00. The organization guaranteed delivery and the sender always received a receipt from the addressee. Just what a John package was remains unclear, but a private package was simply an unsubsidized parcel of goods prepared and mailed personally by the sender. It will be noted that Helmut frequently included cigarettes in his packages. These were commonly used in trading for scarce food and other items. It is obvious that he not only sent packages to his own family, often through friends, but to various other families as well.

Helmut's decision to quit school and go to work is the focal point of this chapter. At the same time conditions of life in this country are seen in sharp contrast to the situation in Germany, where his father's future depends on the outcome of his pending denazification hearing.

⌘

Letter 8   San Diego, October 29, 1946

You Dear Berliners:

I've finally received your first mail. It was letter number 3, but the first one I received. The trip was very nice between New York and St. Louis. When we went through the Alleghenies —those mountains in Pennsylvania—it was night. When I woke up you could only see high hills. They were covered with either forest or meadows. You could see a lot of cows. After a while the land was very flat; a lot of woods, not like in Germany—no, little trees with tremendous undergrowth. It's all half wild. In between you could see a few meadows and fields. How well a couple of industrious people could manage here with a little piece of land and earn a lot!

I think the United States could feed the whole world. You just can't imagine such enormous spaces. The fastest express takes 68 hours to cross the states. At the train station in St. Louis I unfortunately missed Mr. Dodge. They thought that I would be coming earlier and that I wouldn't be staying overnight with them. I didn't deliberate long; I said: "I only want to stay one night with you." After much hustle and bustle a bed was freed up for me. We discussed many things, and all in English. Mrs. Dodge felt that I should speak German if I wasn't able to express myself. But that hardly occurred to me, or rather didn't occur to me at all; otherwise I wouldn't have learned anything.

The next afternoon Mrs. Dodge took me to the train station. First I went to Kansas City. From there I travelled almost the whole length of Missouri, about five hours. Soon it was dark already, but I saw a whole lot. The Missouri River is about 100 to 150 meters wide. It looks kind of dirty. On its banks there are some small mountains, covered with American woods. In Kansas City the train to Los Angeles was already there. I only had to look for a seat and finally I sat between some Negroes. But that doesn't matter.

You can sleep very comfortably in these trains. In one carriage there is always a row of seats on the right and left, always two next to each other. Each of these seats has an adjustable back. In the middle of the car is an aisle. Each pair of seats can be turned on a shaft so that it becomes a compartment; then, when the train isn't full, you can stretch out your feet on the opposite pair of seats and sleep peacefully with full support. That's what I did after St. Louis. Even then it wasn't entirely pleasant. At all hours someone comes through offering food: milk, cheese sandwich, meat sandwich, candy, fruit juice, anything your heart desires. Besides that, you can also eat in the dining car.

When I woke up, it was early morning. We were on a flat table land. Everything was fields and pastures. No trees and not many villages. Every 5-10 kilometers or so, you'd see a little town, or, to say it better, one or two larger farms. There were, of course, little trees in these places. I could never have imagined something so vast.

Can you please save these letters, or, if you want, recopy them? You see, I've completely forgotten to keep up a journal.

Hopefully you are still hale and hearty. I have sent a Christmas package to Uncle Karl Koch He should then send the one-pound packages for you to Berlin. For Martin, two pairs of gloves, four pairs of socks, and a carton of cigarettes to trade. For mother, two pairs of stockings and a pair of gloves. For Dad, two neckties, a can of tobacco, and cigars. Besides this, for everyone three boxes of cocoa, five cartons of cigarettes, a can of coffee, a can of milk, and a can of shortening. Five cans of coffee are for the Scherbiuses. Uncle Karl himself will also get something. Today as ever, many heartfelt greetings from

Your Helmut

Letter 9   San Diego, Oct. 31, 46

Dear Berliners!
    After tomorrow airmail to Germany will only cost 15 cents per 1/2
ounce. You can send up to one ounce. I'm writing here in the post
office like my aunt next to me. Do you always call her Tante Guschen
when you write her? I just now realized that I need to have a copy of
the letter the Department of State sent you from Washington. [*This was
a letter written in 1930 explaining why his parents could not stay in the
United States*]. You know what I mean. Send me a copy, and please, it
would be best if you could have it certified by the consulate. It would
be good if I had something like that here. Dad, have you got a job with
the Americans yet? How is it going with your denazification? The next
thing I do will be to get some corn seed and send it to you. I just bought
myself a pair of pants. Very good material. Everything is terribly
expensive here. I paid approximately $8.00.
    Yesterday I went to an eye doctor. My eyes were examined so
thoroughly within 45 minutes that I was completely astonished. The
eyes were prepared with eye drops. I noticed that suddenly I couldn't
read anymore. I no longer recognized the dirt under my fingernails.
Strange, isn't it? Then I had to sit in a big chair, similar to a dentist's
chair. My eyes were examined two and three times with many
instrument-like devices. Finally, when I was finished I received still
more drops and a note and then I was able to leave. I conclude that my
eyes have gotten worse. Please don't read every single letter from me
out loud. The teacher doesn't need to know everything in so much
detail. In the train coming here my glasses broke again in the same
favorite place. Glasses here are very expensive: between 15 and 30
dollars. That's an awful lot. The welfare department will pay for them,
as it also paid for the eye exam. Now I've had my broken glasses
repaired. $1.00.
    Aunt Augusta and I continue to look for a house. From her
husband, who died 28 years ago, she inherited several houses, plus
money, all of which she lost through carelessness and ignorance. She
only had two houses left on a little piece of land. She sold these a year
and a half ago. The buyers thoroughly cheated her. She could have got
$10,000 for them but only got $4500. Since houses are very expensive
now we can't find anything so quickly. The Welfare is looking for
something else for me now. I think until I'm 18. I'll close for today.

                                              Love and kisses, Helmut

Letter 10   San Diego, Nov. 16, 1946

Dear Berliners!

Please, please forgive my laziness in writing, but I just didn't have the time. Well, we've now found a house. As you can easily see, our house is located in the rear, but we have a driveway to the street. [*Helmut is referring here to a diagram he has drawn of the house*]. Maybe you think it's something special to have a house here. But it isn't like that at all. Almost everyone here has their own home. They call them: frame, bungalow, cottage, tent-house, stucco...In all of San Diego there are maybe 100 apartment houses. In general people here are only familiar with rooming houses or hotels; the difference between them is that the rooming houses have community kitchens.

Well, we're in the third week of my being here. For two weeks we were looking for a little house. La Mesa probably has the best climate around here. That's where we finally found one. It's going for $4500 but it's only a nutshell. No bath, no water, no stove. Gas and electricity are included though. Tante talked them down to $3000. Even then it was way too high, but all the other houses were even more expensive in this neighborhood. It will still cost around another $1000 for: plumbing ($20); furnishings ($30); plaster and paint ($50); stove ($100); washing machine ($100); sinks; toilet, and bath tub ($100); fencing ($50); and miscellaneous expenses ($100).

You can learn a lot here at school. Besides the usual education you can also learn typing, shorthand, driving, citizenship requirements, etc. As long as you're not really lazy, you can always find work.

Dad, Dad, dear Dad, try to leave Germany as soon as possible, for Egypt or even better for Mexico. You could earn good money; you can speak Spanish and Arabic. Then when you're a citizen you can have mother and Martin come after you. Otherwise you have to wait until I am [*earning money*]. And then it's still questionable if you can come over as Germans and [*Nazi*] party members. In this way you could immigrate here quickly from Egypt or Mexico. Dad, if you were in Mexico or better still, right on the border here, we could see each other every Sunday.

Dad, are you denazified yet? What kind of work are you doing? Something with the Americans? What are all the relatives and friends doing? Greet all of them very affectionately for me. Especially Fitzens, Pisareks, Wenzels, and Pohls. Please give my greetings to all the classes through the 2nd and 4th. You, dear mother, greet the whole faculty. But you don't need to show my scribbling to those people.

Now Mother, how are your legs? Your heart? The job? And, Martin, what are you doing now in the garden? Excuse the question, but it seems to me that it may be winter there now. Here there are only two seasons: rainy time, in the winter, and summer time. Martin, how is your school work? Are you doing well with it? Ask me if you're ever unclear or confused about anything.

Today there was a wonderful parade of *Masons*. It's a convention of loud rich guys who marched by us in extravagant costumes, with very old cars and wonderful music by at least 10 choirs. I am getting along very well with Tante Guschen. We joke around together quite a bit. Your letters 3, 4, and 5 have arrived so far. It's good that you're allowed to use more gas now. Today I'm supposed to be introduced to the school.

Greetings and kisses 1000 times!

Your Helmut

Paul Dost's Diary, Nov. 28:

We got good mail from Helmut...concerning the trip from New York to California, also a nice letter from Mr. Dodge who plans to keep an eye on Helmut.

Letter 11   San Diego - Dec. 19, 1946

You Dear Berliners!

Received:

Letter 3	Oct. 24, '46 (before I was there)
Letter 4	Nov. 4, '46
Letter 5	Nov. 5, '46
Letter 8 or 9	Dec. 18, '46
Letter 11	Dec. 18, '46
Letter 7	Dec. 19, '46

I don't know anymore when I received Letter 2, forwarded from Baltimore, but approximately Nov. 10, 1946. Could you also make a table like this, so that I always know what kind of letters have arrived, and when or approximately when. I'm very interested in that. From your letters I see that you've received my letters 1–9, except for numbers 3 and 4. How many could still be missing?

I'm going to have the postage stamps appraised all together and then sell them off individually or as a set. They aren't worth as much as we thought, but maybe $100–$150 or $200. Due to some kind of moisture Rolf's stamps got stuck together at the bottom of a big trunk. I've tried to restore them as much as I could. I will compensate him for them.

Have you received one of my three packages? The first was approximately 10 pounds. The second was a 49 lb. gross = 29 lb. net package from CARE. The third package was one with Christmas things, which I packed myself and sent to Uncle Karl in Wiesbaden; in it there were: three pairs of new gloves, two pairs of ladies' stockings, three or four pairs of stockings for Martin, four cigars, one can of tobacco, about eight or ten packs of cigarettes, a few ties, six cans of coffee, of which five are for the Scherbius family, two containers of powdered eggs, one container of milk, one container of lard, three containers of cocoa, and something for Uncle Karl.

After New Year's I'll be starting high school in Point Loma. Soon I'll try out part time in a clock maker's shop, starting something just to learn a practical trade. When I'm done with school, there will be plenty of time to become a chemist, or banker, or realtor (as in the real estate business), or mathematician, or electrical engineer, or physicist.

I think, in Letter 10, I described our "former" house in La Mesa. "Former" inasmuch as it is now no longer our house. One day, while we were busy there cleaning up sawdust and scraps, an inspector from the city of La Mesa came and made us sell the house back. The real estate man who sold it to us had no right to sell it to us according to La Mesa city regulations, since we didn't have 60 feet of street frontage. Finally, after a long, fruitless search we decided to buy a *trailer*. It's roadworthy, can be hitched to one's personal car—wonderful, a perfect house for vacations. [*Helmut included here a detailed diagram of the trailer's interior*].

The *trailer* cost, with sales tax, license, insurance, awning, etc. around $2250. The *trailer* —I don't know what you'd call the thing in German— is now parked in the Skyline Trailer Park, 2310 Hancock St., San Diego 10, California. When you write, just write "H. E. Dost" above.

This *trailer* park is a pretty large place with 60 *trailers*, each one on a *"lot,"* a piece of ground about 25 x 25 feet = 7.5 x 7.5 meters. Our *traile*r is about 7 meters = 22 feet long. On this lot we have hook-ups for water, sewer, and electricity. Gas which carries the special name of *"butane"* comes in a metal tank, out in front on the trailer hitch assembly. These tanks, with normal usage, need to be refilled every three weeks. Recently we ordered some wood, and I built a platform in front of the door and nailed together a wooden frame for the awning. The next thing will be to construct a little porch ("*veranda*") light outside the trailer that can be snapped on from inside. Here we usually have 110 volts or 120. More next time.

Hearty greetings and kisses, and for Martin one more extra "brotherly kiss,"

from your Helmut

Letter 12   San Diego, 22 Dec. '46

Dear Ones at Home and Those With You!

The day before yesterday I wrote you a long letter. I had just received three letters at once. Just think! In over six weeks I hadn't heard anything more from you. Today I got yet another letter. What have you received as far as letters go? Do you have letters 3 and 4 yet? In them I described all sorts of things about New York and my first impressions. They were sent from Brooklyn.

Have I ever mentioned to you a few of the speech differences in English? Here they say *streetcar* instead of *tram* for Strassenbahn, or *elevator* instead of *lift* for Fahrstuhl, as on the elevated train. Instead of "*I say*" careless Americans say "*I sais*" and "*you sais*." Then they say as a greeting if they pass each other on the street, "*Hallo.*" If they go into a shop or if they would like to begin an on-going conversation or business transaction, they say "*Hadidduu*" = "*How do you do?*," or "*Hai*" = "*How are you?*" When they're finished they say "*You are bett*" = Ihnen sei versichert, or "*You're welcome*" (even when they don't mean that).

Generally Americans seldom really intend to be friends. One can't buy true friendship (only false!!) Here people can only have friends if they have money. Tante Guschen has also convinced me of that through many true stories.

Now I'm going to tell you that I enrolled yesterday in the Point Loma High School. On January 6 school begins again and then I will be tested. They have predicted already that I will be placed in the low 11th grade. By the way, I already speak good English. I will have school from 8:30 to 12:00 and 13:00 to 15:00 = 5 and 1/2 hours altogether. Saturdays and Sundays are always free here.

With love, Your faithful son, Helmut

Letter 12-A   *San Diego, Dec. 23, 1946*

Dear Ones:
    Hai? Are you still alife? I hope so at least. How is everything at
home? How are my friends, likely well. In this country, my country,
there are not only Germany haters but lovers and worshippers too, as
you can see from those advertisements I cut out off the paper. It was the
"California Staats Zeitung" [California State Newspaper]. *A very*
patriotic paper isn't it? I hope you'll enjoy all I sent you with all of
your heart. Kindly greetings to all who ask for me!

                                        Heartily, Your Sonny,
                                        Helmut

Letter 13   San Diego, Dec. 23, 1946

You Dear Berliners!
    Now I'm alone in our trailer. I took Tante Guschen to get a
permanent wave. Tomorrow or day after tomorrow we want to go to
Los Angeles. Tante's niece Gretel—Margarete Gruppe—also wants to
come here. She is probably about 48 years old and I gathered from her
letters that she has a very nice disposition. She wants to marry a nice
former German here, I mean in Los Angeles, and therefore wants us to
go and make the man's mouth water since the two know each other
only from correspondence. Tante had placed an ad in the local German
newspaper, to which she received a whole bunch of replies. One of
these was from this Mr. Viermiesel....Then we can celebrate Christmas
at the Los Angeles German Club. San Diego doesn't have one
anymore.
    Now I want to write you something about Tante. Since she has
been betrayed by so many people she has become much, much too
cautious. She refuses to give even a harmless signature, because she
always thinks there is a trick behind it. Then I've been amazed from the
first moment that she still can't speak proper English, since she has
lived in the country 34 years already. She speaks almost worse than
you, Mom and Dad. She doesn't want to learn anything about it either.
It's come to that because the Americans are so flattering and no one
tells her her mistakes. Tante thinks she speaks correctly and always
wants to teach me the wrong thing. But I can speak better than she can
already. Whether she believes it or not. Many people tell her they like

to listen to her because she talks so funny. For instance, *"I be only"* or *"I could no found a home"* and so on. Then she is very easily discouraged. She always makes me feel guilty so quickly. She speaks first and then she thinks. So she insults not only me but other people too.

When she is carried away with anger and rage about something, she always hurls the sharpest insults at me. Then when I try to explain everything, she doesn't want to hear. Please don't let this letter go any further, and just write to me that you received it. Now I feel much better. When people hold everything in, they finally explode. From now on I will forgive everything, since I know Tante is that way because of accidents of fate. As for money—the welfare department keeps saying they're looking out for me, but for all that Tante Guschen does most of it. With hearty greetings and kisses I remain,

Your Helmut

Letter 13-A   San Diego, 28 December 1946

Dear Berliners!

Our trip to San Bernardino has just become a reality. When angels travel the sun shines; so it follows that when we took off there was a tremendous rainstorm. In San Diego it only drizzles a little, and since I'd forgotten my raincoat, we missed the train. Then we were going to take the bus. Just as we were about to climb on, Tante Guschen realized that in our hurrying we'd forgotten the address of the man in San Bernardino. So I rushed home once again. Finding it, in this case, could only be a matter of luck. But people have to be lucky, and finally I found the envelope under a thousand others. And fortunately I got back to the bus station in time for us to make the next bus.

We whizzed along at a speed of 60 mph = 100 kph on the magnificent state highway in the magnificent pouring rain. Los Angeles is about 130 miles (= 220 kilometers) away from San Diego. With a few stops along the way we made the trip in 2 and 3/4 hours, which in Germany might have lasted 12 hours. It got dark just as we got to Los Angeles, and it was still farther to San Bernardino, another two hours of riding, during which we mostly slept.

Because Mr. Viermiesel has an orange farm in San Bernardino and thus lives somewhere out in the country…we took a room in a hotel and drove out the next morning in a taxi. We noticed right away that

Mr. V. had the first "*farm*" on the edge of the city, really still inside the city limits. He is still thoroughly German, a mechanical engineer and a very capable man. He hadn't had much luck in marriage, and in his work had not yet figured out the right way to make money. He had two houses in Chicago. In San Bernardino, through a favorable opportunity, he'd been able to buy a large piece of orange and grape land very cheaply from the government. Of that he sold the two worst parts for as much as the whole piece had cost him. He still had the largest middle piece with oranges and grape vines.

It's magnificent up there. The high mountains are right in back. The only time it rains much there is in the winter. It's not as moist as San Diego. Over there he took us around in his fancy car. We went right into the mountains—from a terrace we had a really beautiful view. San Bernardino is located in a large valley. I have to clarify the idea "valley." San Bernardino Valley is a wide plain from about 25 to 30 km in diameter. On three sides there are medium sized mountains. On the fourth lie the San Bernardino mountains, a gigantic range; snow covers most of the tops. Most of San Bernardino Valley is covered with orange trees standing in rows and ranks in large layouts (groves). On the way back [*to Los Angeles*], which we traveled yesterday, it rained again throughout the entire trip. We drove through endless vineyards. When we happened to drive through part of an orange grove, every 200 meters we could see a high wall of eucalyptus trees standing as wind breakers.

Sometimes I irritate Tante, since I haven't been with elderly ladies much. I'll just have to get used to it. She is doing everything for me. The welfare department in New York provided for me much better [*than the one in California*]. Because Tante has had severe trials in her life, she is also rather nervous. When you see her you don't realize her age. You know that I always like to correct mistakes, but sometimes it isn't right of me to do it with her.

Thank you for your good upbringing, in which you have made me so independent; I still haven't been homesick for a moment, but I have had a longing (for you).

Most heartfelt greetings from your distant Helmut

Letter 14   San Diego, January 4, 1947

Dear Parents, dear Martin!

This morning is Sunday so you're going to hear from me again. The newspaper article [*enclosed*] should show you a little about how people here think of Russia and Germany. Unfortunately I forgot to cut out one article that I found very interesting, and now I can't find it anymore. It said that the American government has asked Russia for the third time to pay off the eleven million dollar debt (*lend-lease*) without any answer from Russia! In general there are a lot of people here who hate Germany and at least as many who have a good heart for Germany. Many think that world peace will only come when England steps down from its position of tyranny. Then the poor, oppressed people would finally have it better; that would be a blessing. What are people in Germany thinking about that now?

Well, Dad, do you have a position yet with the Americans or English? Recently, on the third of January, I received letter 12, from the 20th of November. Your letters take five to seven weeks for the most part.

Isn't it funny—a letter from you which contained newspaper clippings, although it was opened, came through well. No further letters are missing. Recently a letter from Tante's cousin came out of Hamburg, which arrived opened without the enclosed clipping. Uncle Hassan [*Hassan Shawkat, a close family friend from their Egypt days*] still hasn't written to me. The first airmail letter [*to Egypt*] cost me 70 cents; an enormous amount isn't it? Now the same item only costs 25 cents. Good! Maybe the answer will be lying in the mailbox tomorrow. Only patience! The bond is still too strong to break. I still have too much trust in Uncle Hassan.

Full of hope, I always think of the packages that I sent you:

Sept. 24, 1946   1 "John" Package

    2 lbs. Bacon
    1 lb. Salami
    1 one-lb. Ovomaltine (cocoa, milk, eggs)
    2 lbs. roasted coffee (beans)
    1 lb. sweet cocoa
    1/4 lb. tea
    1 lb. oatmeal
    2 cakes of soap   Price: $9.90

Oct. 20, 1946   1 Private Package to Uncle Karl

Oct. 31, 1946   1 CARE Package: $10.00

- 9. 8 lb. meat
- 6. 5 lb. cereals
- 3. 9 lb. sugar & candy
- 3. 6 lb. fruit jam & pudding
- 2. 3 lb. vegetables
- 1. 1 lb cocoa, coffee, and beverage powder
- 0. 8 lb. powdered milk
- 0. 5 lb. preserved butter
- 0. 4 lb. cheese

I sent off two small packages before Christmas via Uncle Karl. Both were filled with clothing articles that I couldn't wear anymore; I wonder if you'll have to pay duty on them. Or for the official packages? Pay everything back to Uncle Karl. It made a lot of work for him.

The welfare department here in California is very stingy. I only get $39.00 a month. That's $7.50 for rent, $21.00 for food, $5.00 for clothing, and the rest for incidentals and transportation. In New York I got approximately double the amount for food. Tante spends her whole little bit for food. She only has a small pension of $40.00 a month. With today's prices that's even less than Grandma gets, which isn't much to begin with. But still she sends out so many packages.

Tante Auguste next wants to take out life and health insurance for me. Nice of her, isn't it? Now, make sure you're all sitting down in case one of you should be standing up. I don't want anyone to get hurt as a result of the following:

Here in this country everyone thinks of how he can earn the most money. I heard recently that here people are only learning in college the trigonometry that they learn in Germany in the 5th class of high school, or are beginning to learn. What they're learning here I already know. For that reason I think I'll quit school. I'd like to find a little job somewhere. You can always start small here. Then you do whatever makes a little more money until you've found the place you're most comfortable with. That's what you hang on to.

You're required to go to school until you're 18 years old. Whoever quits before then must, with very few exceptions, go to "*evening school*." You can only work 44 hours (a week) as long as you're under

18, and then only if you have a work permit. I'll take the school leaving certificate as a certificate of completion. That's enough for me.

In *"Continuation School"* then I can choose, just like I'd be able to later in *"evening school,"* whatever subjects I'd like. I'll be able to continue my education on my own through my books, first of all in English but also in German. In the public school of course I can learn a lot being with other kids. You can't really do menial work eight hours a day. Once I give Tante my share (of room and board) from the money I earn, I can always put aside the rest to pay [*i.e. reimburse the government*] for my trip here. Afterwards I can save up for your coming. If anything more should occur to you regarding all this, share it with me in your next letter.

Tante Auguste understands, or rather recognizes, what's wrong with what you write. First of all, she doesn't take advantage of me. She's a nice person; I don't want you to think badly of her. Just think what a sacrifice it is for her to take me on here.

Affectionate hugs and kisses,
Your Helmut

Letter 15   San Diego, January 12, 1947

Dear Parents, Dear Martin!

Today is now Martin's birthday. What do you plan to do? It's 2:00 in the afternoon now. With you it's 8:00 in the evening and maybe you'll be at the movies, or having a good time over coffee with Mrs. Fritz, Aunt Greta , and Mieze, and maybe also Aunt Marta and Aunt Lori. Meanwhile, have you received the private package yet via Uncle Karl? There was also something in it for Martin's birthday When will Martin actually be confirmed—1947 or 1948? Could you tell me when you get a chance?

Now, something else. I'm working. As what? As a janitor and stock man in a dirty little old drugstore. Or rather I should say, I did work, and began on Jan. 8 at 1:00 p. m. Five hours. On the 9th, 10th, and 11th of January eight hours, from 10:00 to 6:00, for 25 cents an hour. It was like this: I was looking for work and in the process asked a druggist that Tante knows whether he could provide any work for me. He said that, since I had no work, I could start working for him. He is an employee of this drugstore, so he had to speak to the *boss*, as they call the owner here, and he hired me. So at 1:00 I started: tearing open cartons, clearing wood and sawdust out of a back room, unpacking bottles from boxes and arranging them on shelves, planing 100 drawers which were hard to move, ripping open a whole room full of cartons (I mean the cartons, not the room), clearing out aisles, etc.

At home I wasn't able to make Tante Guschen as angry [*as usual*] because I was tired. We had figured out what I could earn per hour. If she, as an old woman, could still earn 75 cents per hour, I should be able to earn at least that much. A man whom we asked said 65 cents would be the least. So I figured at 50–75 cents, I would earn at least $15.00 for 29 hours of work.

Then on Saturday, which was pay day, I asked the boss how much I would receive and he said that he and Mr. Mayer had thought 10 cents an hour! My heart stood still! I tried not to show it, but I was at least as red as a turkey cock from anger. He asked me if it would be too much; I didn't say anything at all, and continued sweeping. Then he asked what I had thought, and I said (informed, as always): "At least 25 cents an hour;" and then he actually gave me that. So, $7.25 for 29 hours of drudgery

Well, I'm not going back there tomorrow. He ought to see where he can get anyone for 25 cents an hour. I'm going to look for something, maybe in a large aircraft factory, where I can be trained as a mechanic. Auto mechanics are also in demand. I'm going to find out something in the morning. What do you think about it? Don't read this letter to anyone else and don't show the letter to anyone. It's very scrawled and I would have to be ashamed the rest of my life.

Has Martin received any [*sheet*] music yet? If not, he can get it with a few cigarettes. They were: Colorful Music No. 1; Collected Works of Munsonius (1+)2; Number 2 with "Free Butterflies," "Little Moor," and "Window Peeker." Then he can look around again for the single sheet music for "*My Name's Not Clark Gable Either.*" Maybe packages go out from the American and British zones to the USA the same way. If that's so, then I'd like to ask you to pack me up a darner, something you can't find around here yet. Maybe I can get a patent on it. I've already seen such a thing by AWAG at Alex's [*a store in Berlin*]. Stockings here are always getting so many runs. Mom, can you write me the exact length of your feet in centimeters? Otherwise I could send you a pair of good shoes of any size that you could trade. Soon a package [*addressed*] to any one of you will go off once more.

Don't write, "das alte Tantchen" [*the old auntie*] and so on. Tante isn't as old as she looks, so she just gets the wrong idea about you. Also, Dad wrote in letter 12 that Tante should be reasonable enough to

give me a break; that was wrong. Everything that she ought to understand, she doesn't get. And everything that she doesn't need to
understand, she understands, but not correctly. Tante Guschen was
immediately offended and then she gets the wrong idea. I am working
of my own free will.

Now once again, affectionate greetings and kisses from your
Sohnemann,

Helmut

Paul Dost's Diary, Jan. 12:

Sunday.
In the kitchen it is barely above freezing. Ice crystals are
glistening on the walls. Today is Martin's birthday...The schools are
closed until further notice due to the shortage of coals.

I have been summoned to the Denazification Office in Berlin-
Wilmersdorf for Wednesday, January 29. Helmut wrote that he
decided on work instead of school, and Tante Guschen writes that
she is not keeping him from attending school, although she is
always complaining about expenses caused by Helmut.

Letter 16   San Diego, Jan. 17, 1947

Dear, Good Berliners!
Since yesterday it's free to send private packages to all the zones in
Germany—but unfortunately uninsured. The day before yesterday I had
just inquired at the post office, but without any news. So I packed
something weighing three pounds, and unpacked it again yesterday
when I learned that all of a sudden packages were also going to the
Russian zone and to Berlin. Let's do with packages what we do with
the letters. Let's call the package that I sent out today Package 7.

The box (3 lb.) contains three small packages. To the Wenzels: 1/2
lb. coffee, two packages chewing gum, two rolls of yarn, three wallet
calendar cards; to the Scherbiuses: 1/2 lb. coffee, two rolls of yarn, one
wallet calendar card; to the Dosts: three wallet calendar cards, two
packages chewing gum, 21 packs of cigarette paper, four rolls of
sewing cotton, four meters of elastic, one overshirt, five cigars, four
boxes of cigarettes (don't smoke them all, Dad). Next time I think I'm
going to put in a few maize seeds (which they call corn here) so that
you can plant at least a little plot with it; it tastes so good.

Since the idea of numbering only came to me today, the others haven't been numbered. How long will it take for them to reach you? Which one will be the first? Please make yourself a register of individual packages in a little notebook like I have here. How long do my airmail letters take anyway?

On Monday, Guschen's birthday, I'll start working. Mechanic's apprentice at an airplane factory won't work out since I've got to be 18 years old at that place in order to join the workers' union. Because of this, Snyder Continuation High School arranged to get me into a laundry, the Balboa Laundry. There I'd be working from 7:00 to 3:30, with about an hour break. Since the laundry is located at the other end of town, I have to get up at 5:00 a.m. and leave the trailer at 6:00. I like this kind of work because it won't make you into a night owl. In the afternoon, after work, I have school from 4:00–5:00 (trigonometry) Monday through Thursday. One percent of my wages goes to the government for Social Insurance (old age pension). For 65 cents an hour I have to shake out the sheets and fold them.

It must be very cold where you are; we had frost last night. Just think, a polar bear in the zoo, while under water, was frozen in, and after being frozen in for an hour was hacked out dead. I could never have dreamed that it would go down to freezing here.

If I get a chance I might write a letter to [*President*] Truman about your immigration. But don't say anything. Warm greetings and kisses to you, and greet all our friends,

Helmut

Letter 17   San Diego, Jan. 25, 1947

Dear Parents, Dear Martin!

Today, Saturday, the 25th of January, I don't have to work; the same with tomorrow. Last week I worked 8 hours a day in the Balboa Laundry. There I usually have to sort out big carts full of washed sheets, which have become tangled up with each other individually. Because the sheets are sometimes so tangled up and you have to use so much strength to get them loose, I had back and arm muscle pain for four days. Now, yesterday, things went well again.

Next week, on Wednesday or Thursday, I'll get my first pay, and it's always that way for the previous week; 65 cents an hour. I get up at 5:15 in the morning and leave at 6:10 on the bus from here to Broadway, and from there I take the street car almost to my work place.

There I start work at 7:00 a.m. From 11:30 to 12:00 is noon break and from 12:30 to 3:30 I work again. Then there is a 10 minute break in the morning and afternoon. School is completely different here from in Germany. First, I haven't seen one old teacher here. Second, the children here are all wayward [*in continuation high school!*]. So the teachers here are completely different. In school you don't hear a bad word (from the teachers). It can happen that teachers get beaten up. In the continuation high school there are noisy young people all of whom work and go to school four hours a week. There are also men and women, 30–40–50 years old, who still want to learn.

The first day a nice teacher gave me a book that I was supposed to study. On Tuesday, the second day, a well-known teacher was there who said he wanted to test me. If I did well it would enable me to get my "diploma" and then maybe I would go to college (a small university) and study to be an engineer. Usually you have to pay $500 a semester (1/2 year) for that. But gifted students of moderate means can go to college free. Maybe I would be one of the lucky ones. I have almost finished my first algebra test. The second will be harder and with graphic descriptions of first degree equations.

I got through the geometry test well, how well I don't know yet because the teacher only looked it over hastily. Another thing about this school: the teacher only cares about the students who ask him questions. Everyone has a book in front of him and learns from it; if he doesn't understand something, he asks the teacher and the teacher explains everything very well. It depends on the student whether or not he wants to learn. From time to time a test is given and whoever does badly will get set back a class. Things go by grades here. The first five or six grades are called elementary school; from the 6th or 7th grade to 9th grade is called junior high school; and from 10th to 12th grade is senior high school. The students in the 12th class are called seniors. Now you've heard enough about that.

Yesterday at the laundry while I was working I made a remarkable acquaintance. The day before yesterday one of the young women in our group made a mistake. So an older woman of perhaps 45 or 50 jumped up. She spoke English with a southern accent; and because she said that she knew someone from France who knew perfect German, and I had heard her speak to someone in an animated language, I asked her, when I had an opportunity, "Comment ca va." [*French: "How is it going?"*] To that she asked if that was French, and if I also knew Spanish. Well, that was a broad hint. I asked if she was from Mexico (because she

didn't look like it at all), and she said she was from El Salvador. You
were also there for a while. After talking to her for a while I asked her
for the names of a few Germans down there. I asked about the names
Dost, Gottschalk, and Kron. The first two she didn't know at all. About
the third she knew of two daughters who were once introduced to her at
a night club as daughters of Herr Kron. Her own name is Marie
Rosales. Mrs. Rosales will soon go back to El Salvador for half a year.
Write her a letter in Spanish sometime.

The weather here is very beautiful now. Tante Auguste is also
doing well.

Warm greetings to one and all,
from your Helmut

Letter 18   San Diego, Feb. 1, 1947

Dear Parents, Dear Martin!

It's another week and since the beginning of January I still haven't
had any more mail from you from Berlin. The last, #12, was post-
marked from Berlin on the 21st of November. At that time you hadn't
received any packages yet. I have news though that you already have
both packages, John and CARE. Regarding the John package, I
received mother's signed receipt, and regarding the CARE package I
know that it arrived because I just received what Grandma and Dad
wrote from Wittenberg [*in East Germany where Helmut's Grand-
mother Dost lived*] on Christmas Eve. It only took four and a half
weeks. It's very nice that the CARE package arrived right on Christmas
Eve; nice that Dad acknowledged it right away.

Well, in one week I've earned $22, with about $4.00 deductions =
$26.00. One percent for Social Security, 1% for other taxes, and over
10% income tax. With the last alone I could at least send a CARE
package. Sometime I'm going to find out if I can have less drawn out
so that I can have something to take care of you. Then, I think, I would
have to pay less income tax. At the end of the week I try to lay aside
about $10.00. It's sure hard to live on $12.00 a week, but I have to save
money because I would like to pay back $10.00 to Tante Auguste for
all she did for me during the first 12 weeks, and then, after that, I want
to save for [*the reimbursement of*] my sea voyage.

So, about 14 days ago I had sent a small package via Frau Margaret
Wenzel with some coffee and sewing wool to Wenzels and Scherbiuses
and something for you. When is it likely to arrive? The CARE package

took seven and a half weeks and the other 11 weeks. Your thank you letter for Tante Auguste still hasn't come. How about that for a mix up? One letter arrives so fast, and you don't hear or see anything of the other after two and a half weeks. Odd!

Because of a mistake, Tante Auguste has received a bad impression of me. If I try to explain the mistake she prevents me and says she knows enough already. And she always says, when you put a nice word in a letter, that you only want to flatter her. She always sets wonderful food on the table. If I tell her that, she is sure not to take it as good; she says I won't be able to complain that I had it bad with her. When I tell her, since she often says she went a whole year without butter or meat, that we also got by many times without butter and meat...she thinks I'm not being fair. It's almost comical. When she sets something on the table, or buys something, and I take it (I can't really say, "Take it back to the store" or something) then she says she knew I'd enjoy it.

It's obvious that I enjoy it, but it isn't so necessary. "Too much of a good thing isn't healthy." I explain to her that she enjoys eating it too, but she thinks... she can get along without it; and I tell her it's the same for me. For her that doesn't make any sense... Enough of that. She is still a good soul and gives everything to her German relatives. She has a good heart. Tante Auguste has had to take a lot of money out of the bank. Everything costs a lot.

For this week warm kisses and greetings to all of you from your San Diegoan.

[*The following letter was written, in English, by Helmut to President Truman in the hope that the President would somehow intervene to help his parents immigrate to the United States. He did not receive a reply.*]

Letter from Helmut to President Truman

To: President Truman   *San Diego, February 2, 1947*
     Washington. D. C

My Very Respected President,
     I, the undersigning 16-year-old, Helmut E. Dost, born 7-18-1930 in New York City, were repatriated in August 1946 by the American Consulate General in Berlin—Germany.
     My parents, Max C. Paul Dost, born 3-15-1898, and Frederika W. Maria Dost (maiden name: Starkowski), born 12-18-1893, and my

brother, Hans-Ulrich Martin Dost, born 1-12-1933 are German citizens and in Berlin-Reinickendorf Ost, Genferstrasse 115, Germany right now.

My father is an electric engineer of the German firm AEG and was abroad almost always. My mother is a sekretary of a boys' and girls' school in Berlin. Both mother and father know English pretty well. My father was in Spain and the Canary Islands, with contracts of his firm, about 20 years ago; he was in Central America under the same conditions about 17 years ago (that time my parents were already married) and, as his American quota numbers were available soon, he went to New York City with his wife, as visitors, where I was born soon after. But, as my father had lost his quota numbers, he was to go back to Germany. In Spring 1931 he left the United States with his family on board of the "Bremen," Germany-bound.

Having had a bad luck like that and no money for the back voyage to the U. S. he was discouraged and didn't wait for his turn in case of a new quota number. He got new abroad-contracts with his firm and went to Ireland 1934 erecting a sugar manufactory; and finally got to Egypt in 1935. In winter '35-'36, we (my mother, brother, and I) followed my father. He erected several power stations over there. In 1939 we were to leave Egypt for Germany. Being in Egypt, my father joined the AO (Auslands-Organization) [an overseas affiliate of the National Socialist Party]. *During the war, my father didn't fight for Germany; he was not drafted.*

As my father could be useful for this country in account of his knowledge and leading ability, I'ld like you to help him get over from the Germany misery. If you want to know further details about my father I'ld be glad to inform you.

Thank you for having read my letter; I look forward to your being interested in this case.

> *Very truely yours,*
> *Helmut E. Dost*

Paul Dost's Diary, Feb. 16:

Martin is still not back to school on account of the cold weather. Our fuel supply is almost gone in spite of our extremely careful use. We were able to fire the additional iron stove with our trusty cooking machine (rubber fuel). The food situation is catastrophic. We are fortunate to have our acorn pancakes as a substitute for bread. (I had gathered about 100 pounds of acorns).

Letter 20   San Diego, 2/16/47

Dear good Germans!

Once again I owe you a weekly letter. Nothing very interesting has happened since last time. In the middle of the week I received a letter from you: Number 20, a very delightful, long letter. It did some real good, worked just like castor-oil, so that all of my anguish over your not receiving my letters went through the emergency trap door and took to the wide open spaces. I've become at least 20 lb. lighter, since the heavy stone in my heart dropped away.

To answer Martin's question: Our trailer sits on two good ordinary car wheels and tires. In front on the hitch assembly is another little up and down-screwable metal wheel. Since we're now going to be stationary for a little while, we've planted it on a wooden block, which must be raised up a little, since the wheels still touch the ground. I'm glad, little brother, that you gained eight pounds in December. Maybe since then it's become a little more. So now you're playing billiards in the evenings. Change is always really good. Our kitchen and living room are not divided from each other.

Mother's Question: The wheels do have a mechanism (electrical) for brakes, but it only functions if it is connected to a car latched in front of the trailer. There is something like that which would have to be built in; in the trailer this is already built in. So, when we stop, the apparatus is not working. Also, the trailer can't roll away in the wind (think of a car) and we haven't seen any of the American storms here; it's hardly blown at all. None of the trailers have a phone. The trailer park has a public one under the archway of the gate, and when it rings, the nearest person answers it and goes to fetch the person asked for.

We're having beautiful temperatures here, in the daytime about 80 degrees F (26–27 C) and at night about 16 degrees C (50 degrees F). We've noticed little wind here. Rain sometimes, but much too little, because our water reservoirs for San Diego County (nine in number) aren't half full. In the summer or fall San Diego may suffer a drought. Well, with you it will really be cold, brrr.

[unsigned]

Letter 21   San Diego, Feb. 23, 1947

Dear Parents, Dear Martin!

Hi? (How are you?) Well, another week is up, and at the beginning of the week, Monday or Tuesday, I received Letter 21 from you. I'm still missing 1, 6, 13–18, 22...! Well, what isn't yet can still be.

We two fine people are doing tolerably. If the prices weren't so sky-high we would do better; but just imagine: a pound of butter costs 65 cents here (at least). When I came here it was 96 cents. When you figure that if the mark were fixed at 10 cents, then a pound of butter in Germany would have to cost 6 marks 50 pfennigs now. What a difference! It probably sounds like a lot of money, but in reality it isn't at all. (I mean, what I earn).

Then I want to advise Martin to become an architect or carpenter, after finishing school. These occupations are the best here because in California building is done year-round. I say carpenter because here almost all houses are made of wood. For building, a person has to hire a carpenter. So if Martin can learn to be an architect with his high school education in Germany, or even here (better), but at least begin to take a step in Germany, then he can earn a pile of money here. Well, enough of that.

Letter 22 is going at the same time as the usual letter with trailer illustrations. Also there is in it a newspaper clipping about the cold weather in New York, and one about the East Zone. On the one general view that I've enclosed with this letter [*Helmut is referring to one of two post cards with views of San Diego*], I pricked a hole through each noteworthy complex; on the opposite side I have written numbers on the holes. This way I can explain everything well that's behind them.

[*Helmut wrote a lengthy and detailed description, omitted here, of the locations and buildings pinpointed on the two post cards*].

So Dad, are you actually in the middle of removing your guilt (dangerous war criminal)! Let's hope so. [*This is a reference to Paul Dost's projected denazification hearing*]. Well, it's terribly cold here and also in east and middle North America. But around here you don't notice much of it since it's often foggy in the mornings. I have a skin outbreak (tiny blisters in groups) on the right half of my chest, from the front middle around to the back middle below my arms, and as long as my arm. When anyone rubs it gently it's soothing; otherwise it hurts some all the time (like raw flesh). I have a doctor who I hope will cure it. Here people call this "*shingles*;" the same word is used for roof shingles.

> Warmest greetings and kisses from
> Your Helmut.

Letter 23   San Diego, 3/1/47–March 1/47

Como estan ustedes? [*Spanish: "How are you?"*]

Dear Ones!

Another week is here without any special events. But three letters came from you Monday and Friday (22, finally; and 23, 24). So you say that we could write off No. 1 and 6, but where are letters 13-18? Hopefully they aren't drowned. Otherwise I could only wish that they may have found a blessed end. *Let's wait; they might come pretty soon.* Well, with us nothing else special *gehappened. Except* that I *work* again *in the* group in which I first worked, because the sick ones showed up again in the Distributing Group. Now I'm working, for the moment, at the mangel; I "feed" it, together with another woman. Read through the newspaper clipping. The former president of the USA, Herbert Hoover, sometimes is here and many people call him a Nazi because he is so protective of the Germans.

Say, Dad, can't you try and find out how you could come to Mexico? I'm also going to inquire. That would really be very nice. You're surely going to try everything *anyway* to come into the world again. [*Here Helmut gave a detailed explanation of furnishings, etc. shown in the hand-drawn sketch of the trailer's interior which he had enclosed*].

You ask if I've eaten any oranges yet. And if I ate any on the ship. One day I ate 14. Here I eat three or four a day and bananas and apples and grapefruits (big yellow orange-like citrus fruits with a thicker skin). So I'm now five foot seven inches tall and I weigh about 140 pounds—35 German pounds more than when I arrived here. There is saccharine here too but tremendously expensive, $2.00 for 100 tablets; better to buy it there. I've never seen dried eggs and milk here in San Diego, only in New York City.

That Martin has become such a zealous stamp collector delights my old heart. No, Martin, it isn't so warm here that a person can bathe in the rainy season; it's a subtropical or mild climate; in the summer not too hot (especially at night), not like in Florida (and also not such hurricanes). I'm sorry that I thought your confirmation was next year. Otherwise I would surely have sent at least a pair of long pants.

Your Helmut

4

Heels, Heels, Heels! *Shoemaking in San Diego*

The next step in Helmut's American life began with his layoff at the laundry and subsequent employment by a local German shoemaker in San Diego's Point Loma neighborhood. Soon afterward he left Augusta de Boer and her trailer to rent a room in the home of his employer's sister not far from the shoe repair shop.

These moves led to the development of several new relationships with other German-Americans, including a Mr. Muehlke of the German Aid Society as well as a number of young people in his own age group. Preparing packages of food and clothing for family and friends in Germany continued to be a major preoccupation as Helmut learned the shoe repair trade and expanded his experiences in the new country. While repairing shoes one day he caught the attention of a local newspaper reporter who came in as a customer, with the result that he became the subject of an article in the "Point Loma Light."

Meanwhile, back in Berlin, Paul Dost's successful denazification hearing freed him to go back to work for his old company, the AEG, following the many social and economic disruptions after the end of the war.

There is a situation that should perhaps be noted here, although it is not mentioned in Helmut's letters. Helmut occasionally alluded to it later in his life, and it seems to be supported by a number of Paul's diary entries. This was the apprehension and interrogation of Helmut's father and several other men by the Russians soon after they entered Berlin at the war's end. Apparently Helmut's father was the only man of the group to be released. It was Helmut's belief that, in exchange for his freedom, his father had agreed to collaborate with the Russians in some way. According to Helmut, however, his father was never really comfortable with this connection and sought employment away from Berlin partly to put as much distance as possible between himself and the Russians.

⌘

Letters 24/25   San Diego, March 30, '47

Dear Parents, Dear Martin!

Now another week is up, and all kinds of things have happened; it's true that I had written you last Sunday, but I didn't mention any of this because I first wanted to present you with the complete facts. Actually the whole story isn't as bad as the preceding introduction could lead you to think, but even so you should rightly be curious. Mother has probably already asked, "What is the youngster really doing!"

What he has been doing is this: On March 14, Friday, which as you know is the last day of my work week, I received my pay check for the week and—was let go. Oh, no, Helmut let go? That's right; only not because of laziness—but because the owner of the operation had sold a part of it. Because he obviously couldn't discharge the long-standing employees, he discharged the latest employees in the whole establishment and put the most experienced workers in their places. So I was naturally one of the first. With it I received the following recommendation:

> *March 14, 1947*
> *To Whom it May Concern:*
>
> *Helmut Dost has worked for us for 3 months. He is a good, conscientious worker and I would recommend him as a good employee. He was laid out of here because of reduction in work and one of the last to be hired.*
>
> > *Esther Martens–Personnel,*
> > *Balboa Laundry*

The next week I looked for another job. Laundry work was not to be found. I didn't think about something different until a nice lady from the "*Junior Employment Department*" found a job for me. I had told her I would take anything at all, even if it were in a shoemaker's shop. Last Tuesday, March 25, she suddenly had me called into the school office (she is also of German descent and her name is Mrs. Bauer) and then and there I received a good job with a German master shoemaker, who owns the Point Loma Shoe Shop. So now I've been working for this Mr. Ernest Roll since Wednesday. Another former German works with me, who also began learning the shoemaker's craft four years ago in this very shop.

Mondays I go to my school from 8:00 to 12:00 (history and math) and I work from 1:00 to 5:00. Otherwise I work from 8 to 5 with an hour's break at noon, and Saturdays from 8 to1:00.Sundays I don't work at all. This shoe repair shop has already won the annual prize for shoe repair.

I was told that there I could learn shoe repairing from the best in all of San Diego, which is a good way to start out. To begin with I'm earning 60 cents an hour. First I learned to *"hack"* the shoes (*"hack"* = to mount heels) which is what I do now. Cobbling is easier here than in Germany: 1) The shoes are not as worn out as in Germany (also because of the wetness over there); 2) The tools here are better than over there (better and more highly developed machines)...This way at least I'm learning a real trade. I can then consider the laundry work as a secondary stop-gap if I'm ever out of work and can't find anything as a shoe repairman.

In the last week I received two of your letters: No. 28 and a second No. 27, a 150-gram letter, which contained all kinds of news, and was written February 16th; we'll name it No. 27a. You'll have to change that in your records. It went by way of the Los Angeles customs office as "free." In any case it came here really torn up, tied together with packing string. Thanks for the music; the newspaper clippings also really brought back memories. The needles (darning) in letter 28 require a little effort and dexterity. The stamp catalog was also quite nice. Send me the Beethoven sonatas first, if you can send them as a complete set. I haven't had an opportunity to play the piano; maybe I'll get one through these Germans. I play the violin almost every day and sometimes twice. Could you let me have the "Kaiser Etudes." Martin would know them.

Dad, you're wrong if you think that I was the one who came up with the idea for the Truman letter; the mother of the idea was Mrs. Feuerherdt, who told me that you had asked her advice regarding immigration. But the style and content were my creation and mine alone.

Affectionately,
Helmut

Letter 26   San Diego, 3/22/47

Loved Ones at Home!

Tell me, how are you getting along anyway? Do you read the San Diego letters in the evenings usually, when you're all sitting together, or do you start right in as soon as you get them? I usually let dinner get cold when Tante Auguste gives me a letter from you in the evening.

Now, you'll have to forgive me that I haven't sent you anything more since March 6. Then I sent you numbers 22 and 23. In the meantime I've now received four letters from you, one from Uncle Karl, and one from George, Rolf, and Anneliese Linde. Rolf wrote me for the first time when I mailed him a package. Have the Wenzels got their packet yet? I'll write Grandma for her birthday, tomorrow or the next day.

Answers (and reproaches):

Martin: Yes, you're right, the sun comes up on you nine hours earlier and not six. I'd forgotten the three-hour time difference from New York to California. We're going to send Aunt Martha a few California flower seeds, of which you can also take some.

Dad: Could you inquire sometime about the Warters, and other missing people, with the Hamburg refugee search place (I think with the Red Cross)? Where did you discover the diagram of my room with the Warters in Gumbinnen? [*Helmut and Martin spent a year in the town of Gumbinnen in East Prussia when their school was evacuated there during the Berlin bombings*]. You wrote the word *"electrician"* wrong. You wrote "elektricean." If I went for a job as an electrician trainee (as you write) I could earn after a year's training not just 50–75 cents an hour, but $1.50 an hour. That's how the wages are here.

A plumber or carpenter earns $2.50 to $3.00 an hour. Dad, if you came here, both of us, or at least you, would earn good money. Of course, the cost of living is also terribly high here ($10.00 a week for food alone for one person if they're frugal), but people who earn $500 and $1000 a month notice that very little. Tante and I are of course managing with difficulty. When I've finished my trigonometry I will probably learn technical drawing.

Mother: When I read your English writing, I really felt superior. Besides a few sentence structure mistakes there were the following: *"Film"* means, in American at least, a "filmpack" or "roll" for cameras. A film (kino) is called, in New York American, a *"movie,"* derived from *"moving picture,"* and in San Diegan, a *"show."* They don't say, *"Have you the..."* but *"Do you have?"* To exercise means physical exercise; piano exercise, on the other hand, is called *"to practice."* Also, they don't say *"neighborship"* but *neighborhood.* You can say, *"letters till 11 o'clock,"* but not *"till one pound."* Instead it's *"up to one pound."* *"Till"* is time-related; and not *"Something what you like,"* but *"that you!"*

Since you're asking what we would like, always a tube of Syndetikon (sticking plaster), as large as possible, which is available at Weiss's. Then always a stocking run repair device; a couple of new sheets of violin music for the first level to add to the old. A good German-English, English-German dictionary, not too heavy; a good textbook on technical drawing; a wood scraper. First send something so that we can see whether we have to pay duty. A good (although second-hand) roll-on girdle is enclosed in one of the two clothing packages. Mother, Tante Auguste and I are getting along together very well. Recently your letter came in which you mentioned our disharmony or whatever; Tante was sick then and very discontented. Did you misunderstand me or we you? In any case, don't write in such a dreamily philosophical way anymore. Instead tell me what was taken out of the Fritzens' cellar by the French and whether you had noticed something regarding the attempted burglary at Beckers. What kind of American movies are showing now in Berlin? Maybe I've seen some of them? If the English movie *"Caesar and Cleopatra"* should arrive over there, go see it—technicolor and a wonderful cast. I saw it in Baltimore. That's all for today. I'm really done in. Keep the lock of hair. It's from the front, in the middle.

Good night, Helmut

Letter 27 San Diego, April 14, 1947

To you whom I love!

It's been two weeks again since I last wrote you. You must know that I'm working for a shoemaker now. The work there is real nice, in any case better than in the laundry, although it's actually pretty messy. You often cut your fingers. I loosen and fasten the heels to be repaired. Then comes the initial cutting (trimming) with a knife, and finally the boss trims everything with a machine. Then I have to sand, polish, and shine. Last of all I do the same things with the soles.

Dad, do you still remember how you asked whether it could be arranged for me to only sleep at Tante Guschen's and spend most of the time, at least meal times, outside? That really offended Tante Guschen. I tried to explain it to her, but everything that she gets backwards and turned around in her thoughts can only be straightened out with difficulty, or not at all. On the other hand, many things that are childishly simple I have to explain to her; sometimes it takes all day. Mother's idea about the boarding house, she (mis) understood in just that way.

She thinks mother is always speaking "under the rose" (with a secret meaning) and that you're criticizing her, and in fact suggesting that she toss me out and that I have no further obligation to pay her back for the money loaned in the first months. And then she actually did throw me out, but not on the street; she only said, "Look for another place. I want to be free now. People have been telling me all along I'd come into trouble with you..." Then and there I looked around a bit and finally found this little room. Right now I'm living with my boss's sister, who has a rooming house, sort of. It's a little room with an opportunity for cooking.

I have four "*blocks*" (crossroads) to walk to get to my work place, so I'm saving transportation costs. Besides, Point Loma has a wonderful view; from here you can see across the Bay, San Diego, North Island, and Coronado, and still farther inland as far as the mountains in La Mesa and towards Mexico. It should be one of the seven wonder-views of the world. $4.00 rent a week.

Shortly after I moved out, on Friday evening, Tante Guschen received Dad's letter. She was very pleased and moved by it all. Write her another letter like that in which you "knudel" her with a thousand signs of thanks, saying that she really has been a great help. Because in the first three months of my being here she really dug deep in her pockets. I only got $1.20 per day for eating in restaurants, and after that about 70 cents (a day) for the time I lived in the trailer. It probably cost double that. Please forgive the many smudges and mistakes, but I'm very tired right now and want to go to bed. In the morning I'll write more...

April 15, 1947

Now, let's go on. Tuesday evening, 8:00. I've just washed my dishes, which I do after every meal. I had a couple of slices of bread with peanut butter, lemonade, and vegetable soup with noodles.

Letter 30 contained all stamps, as mentioned. However, it was censored—funny, isn't it? Letter 31 also contained everything mentioned: music, newspaper clippings, and letters. Many thanks for everything. Where I'm living now I have an opportunity to play some piano. So the music really came in handy. I don't think it makes any difference whether you send letters from the American, English, French, or Russian sector.

My shingles went away after one week. I had received a salve which soon helped: carbolated vaseline. Martin, you made me happy with your English letter; I am returning it and writing in improved English on the next page. It sounds better this way: I think you understood everything well. [*A rewritten version of Martin's English letter followed here. Martin's original letter was not included in this letter collection*].

So you've already waited five weeks again for a letter. I think I wrote the last time a week before Easter. On Easter, which is celebrated only on Sunday here and without a vacation, we spent the week end in Balboa Park. There was a wonderful concert by 135 youngsters (11–13 years old), a San Diego club. The next Saturday, on April 12, I was drawn away by Tante Guschen. On that Saturday-Sunday-Monday it was terribly hot. I was very lazy about writing. On Sunday I laid in the sun and, having cleaned up and put everything in order beforehand, on Monday evening I finally got myself together and began the letter.

Then the next Sunday, when I wanted to finish the letter, I was invited to my co-worker's in National City (5 km south of San Diego). The people are also from Germany and their name is Krause. Mrs. Krause is 83 and her son is about 40. I stayed there all day. On the week days I have no motivation to write. I go to the boss's most of the time after dinner, up above on the hill where I live. I always have fun there. Either I play the piano or we sing or all talk together or we listen to the radio or whatever. Or I go to T. G.'s [*Tante Guschen's*], or upstairs to the people I live with. They and the people in National City also have a piano.

Last Sunday I went out early with a nice fellow on a boat. He put us out to sea and I tasted the sea air. From 12:00 to 2:00 I put together a package for you. After packing the box, I went with T. G. for a real German butcher-banquet—$1.25 entrance. The money was used for packages to Germany. Someone contributed the pork, someone else the potatoes, another the sauerkraut, another six kegs of beer, another the hall, etc. Today I've been invited to Rosales' for lunch. After that I'd like to go to the zoo.

Affectionately, Helmut

Paul Dost's Diary, April 19:

Today another letter from Helmut arrived, the first in four weeks. He had been let go at the laundry shop and was unemployed for ten days; now he is working in a shoemaker's shop...My denazification hearing has been set for May 9.

Letter 28   San Diego, May 11, 1947

All You Three Loved Ones:

A really great "Good evening;" today is Mother's Day—9:00 pm . I've just finished writing a letter to Uncle Hassan, which I began early this morning. This afternoon I was at Tante Guschen's. She was very pleased that I was there with her today. Besides Mother's Day there is also a Father's Day here in America, which comes in the fall.

Since I'm really tired, I want to keep this letter down to four pages. My job is always the same: heels, heels, nothing but heels. At school too, it goes on and on.

How are you doing with your chilblains, mother? If only I could pick up a good ointment for chilblains, but there's nothing like that here. If only I could get hold of something good for Dad's leg. Mother, I made a mistake with the sweets I got for $2.00. I mixed them up with vitamin tablets. Say, Martin mentioned in passing that you "buried Grandma Schelske a couple of days ago," and that "Mr. Plettich and many other people from the neighborhood have also died in recent days." I didn't know anything about it. Who all died?

Pablo sago malo, kennsto duo eino gewissi Hospitalto Rosales inio El Salvadore? [*German in Pig Latin, meaning: "Say, Paul, do you know of a certain Rosales Hospital in El Salvador?"*] Miss Maria [*Rosales*] asked me to ask you about it.

Little Marty, you got a lot more than I did at confirmation!! I can't believe it. Hopefully you've gotten a little bigger. In the pictures it looks as if you've forgotten how to laugh, which I can't believe at all. The union between Tante Guschen's niece Gretel and Mr. Viermiesel is moving forward very, very slowly, because Tante Guschen can't or won't vouch for her (I think she can't).

A quick close,
Helmut

[*The following excerpt from Paul Dost's diary describes his long-awaited denazification hearing. After the war all former members of the Nazi party were required to present their case before a panel of Allied judges. Paul Dost had become a member of the party while working with his German company in Egypt. One of the questions asked by the judges had to do with the "Volksturm." In October, 1944, when the war was already being lost, Hitler, in a desperate last stand, required all civilian males between 16 and 60 to join this military home guard led by members of the Hitler Youth.*]

Paul Dost's Diary, May 9:

Day of the denazification hearing. We gathered at about 10:30 to 11:00 at the Friedrich Ebert High School in Wilmersdorf. My turn started at 12:00. The witnesses were: W. Schmeer, M. Genz, Frau Stein, Frau Klauss. The visitors (audience) were: the Raabes, the Genzes, two Schillers, Schade, Loos, Niessingh who also volunteered as the main defense witness, Lore Haase, Mutti and Martin, and five gentlemen..

First question: "How can you justify the fact that you joined the NSDAP [*the Nazi Party*] in 1936 while abroad?" I was startled at first, of course, to hear this question that felt like the stroke of a whip, and it took me a moment to compose myself and answer it properly, roughly like this: " When I joined the party in 1935, Germany was not only respected abroad but also downright popular. The great exhibitions, the Olympic Games, etc. had elevated Germany's reputation even more, so I didn't see any crime in joining this party as a dues-paying member only, especially since my boss, engineer Kunze, had practically forced me to do so."

An agitated debate followed. Then I was accusingly asked why I joined the SA [*"Sturmabteilung," a paramilitary division of the Nazi Party*] as a candidate in the labor service in 1933. I answered that I wanted to take a look at these things and that I had made a fool of myself there (because of the Jewish question), and that I stayed away from the SA after only six weeks and sought refuge in the FAD [*probably the "Freiwilliger Arbeitsdienst," a voluntary labor service*], from which I returned to the AEG, which had a job for me.

The questions, answers and discussion which followed then were of a more pleasant and chatty nature until, towards the end, a hard and whipstroke-like question was asked again: "Why did you want to fight in the Volksturm? You had gotten ready to go and then a female resident in your building persuaded you not to go." "Yes, that is true," I answered. "I was to report to the meeting point at 8 a.m. At 8:30 a messenger came and demanded that I come at once. I answered 'All right, I'm coming, I just have to get myself ready.' I pretended to get ready and said my farewells to the people in the air-raid shelter for appearance's sake. Then I went and hid in the basement until everything was over." This was a dangerous moment and had to be handled very carefully.

After this, the witnesses...were heard, and the judges retired for deliberations. Fifteen minutes later, the verdict was read from a standing position: "Your application for denazification has been granted."

Paul Dost's Diary, May 17:

A letter from Tante Guschen arrived. She writes, "Your Helmut has moved. It is your own fault. You write too much, and he is disrespectful and lazy." We cannot share the good Tante's opinion, of course, since we know our Ami [*American*] better than that, and we are happy that he has his freedom.

Letter 29   San Diego, May 19, '47

Dear Ones at Home!

Now it's Monday evening again—8:00. In the last week nothing special happened. On Sunday I went to the Rolls' (my boss) up on the hill at 9:30 in the morning and helped them in the yard. They have a charming garden with a patio; that is, a platform—with comfortable garden chairs and tables—similar to an arbor, with a raftered roof, covered with grape vines. Nearby are various kinds of flowers, two orange trees, and a Japanese lemon tree.

At noon I had a wonderful meal with them: roast, mashed potatoes, gravy, peas. Because a man from the German Aid Society had come with his daughter Gisela, there was also coffee with cream puffs and whipped cream. Then, at perhaps 4:30, Mr. Muhlke asked me whether I wanted to go with them to the movies. I went. It was "The Yearling." A very nice animal film. Afterwards he brought me to his house and there we listened to German music records, talked, and had pastries and coca-cola until 10:00. Then he brought me home again, up to Point Loma. Since he had two two-pound cans of lard with him in the car, he gave them to me to send to Germany. You'll receive the second one the next time.

Say, could you write a friendly letter to the Rolls and the Shopps, with whom I'm living; they're very nice to me in every way. Of course, to Tante Guschen also. She's always the old dear.

Now again an affectionate squeeze from your *Stranger*

Paul Dost's Diary, June 8:

Helmut writes about his master shoemaker and his relatives with whom he is staying. Nothing but heels, heels, heels! That is really something for the poor boy; he is sacrificing much—for us! With all our hearts we wish him more schooling and a better side job.

Letter 33   San Diego, June 22, 1947

You Dear Berliners!

How are you doing tonight? Last week three letters came from you again and one from Dieter Scherbius with one set of stamps (dry). A few of Martin's were once stuck together; Dieter didn't press them together like that in a little pack but put them in a strong stamp bag.

It's now just a quarter to seven a.m. (ante-meridian). The sun is already shining into my room. A *"mockingbird"* is singing its melody (a bird the size of a water-wagtail, the tail is also similar). With symmetrical grey feathers, he has one white stripe on the wings; he is probably the only songbird. There are sparrows here too (Mexican); then also *"finches"* (a kind of robin) and *"hummingbirds"* (kolibris).

The last can sometimes fly out of one flight position and as quick as an arrow into another. They're supposed to fly over the Caribbean Gulf [*Gulf of Mexico*] (600 miles) in about two days.

Well, up till now the weather has been moderate. Except for a few clear days, like today and yesterday, and a whole week two months ago, in the mornings it's heavily overcast till 10:00—12:00. Then it suddenly clears up and stays that way, for the most part, until night. Once, about four weeks ago, we had a hailstorm, which is a rare form of precipitation here, and there has never been one before at this time of year. A few times a thunder storm can come up in August. The day before yesterday in the evening a few drops also fell from the sky that never came to anything.

I've taken a picture of the house where I'm living. Yesterday at 9:00 I went to National City to the Krauses, you know, with whom I work. We dug holes three and a half kilos deep and have already installed two door posts, because the Krauses want to build a fence in front. Then later we'll take a couple of pictures. We also had a good meal and at 10:00 p.m. I was back home. National City is located about 12-15 miles from here on the other side of San Diego on the Bay. Now to your letters—

Martin, you're right, when I go out the door [*of the trailer*], I don't hit my head; but if I stretch, I do hit the top, also with my heels on the floor. We don't need to pay any duty on gift packages, only for the goods and the postage. There is no premature age of majority (18) here. If Dad wants to come over here before 1951 [*when Helmut would be 21*] I can't help him; that would have to happen from over there...

San Diego, June 29, 1947

On Monday evening, when I really wanted to finish this letter, two young people (one is half German) took me with them to play golf. It was the first time and I like it very much. Well, last week two more letters arrived. Number 47 on Monday evening, and Number 45 on Tuesday. I want to answer all the questions quickly.

Dad, are you denazified yet? Well, you will have written everything in Number 43, which isn't here yet. Your envelopes have arrived in bad shape for the second time; in the future please use only the strongest kind. Only the young people have bicycles here, and mostly only the newspaper carriers and messenger boys. Otherwise adults don't ride bicycles. Here every second family has at least <u>one</u> car. With rich people everyone has one. I'll still get around to flying too, but not for the present. Dad, when you come over here, you'll also have to give up your walking stick, because it [*carrying one*] absolutely isn't the custom here.

I'll soon be completely finished with heels. I'm already perfect in men's heels, and Mr. Roll is now also showing me how ladies' heels are trimmed.

That I'll come back there in two years is highly unlikely because then I'll probably be in college.

And then I won't be finished before two–three years. I will send you as much as I can spare. I've now paid back a fourth to Tante Auguste. Every week I pay her about $5.00.

Yesterday I bought two $20.00 savings bonds, which will bring 2% interest this year—and I can withdraw them any time. So that makes about $100 altogether that I've saved in three months (of about $350 owed). Besides, in that time I've sent off to Germany four packages worth about $25. So you see how saving I am, as I net only $22 a week. Living costs me: Rent—$4.00, food—$3.00, transportation and pin money—$1.00, Auguste—$5.00. Then I try to lay aside at least $6.00. Also, the packages and clothes. I don't go to the movies or anywhere else.

Martin, Point Loma belongs to the city of San Diego, as do Ocean Beach and Oldtown; from here a bus goes to San Diego (plaza) in about 20 minutes, approximately every quarter hour.

Recently a customer of the Rolls came into the shop and donated two super pairs of ladies' shoes for Germany (about $15.00 in price). I received them. I only need to pay for the soles and heels that Mr. Roll put on them. One pair is similar to the brown shoes (pumps) that you, Mother, got at the beginning of the war as a "refugee" and one is a pair of summer shoes. Both are very fashionable and modern. If the summer shoes (dark blue patent leather) don't entirely suit you, then trade them for a good pair that does. The size (American) is 7; if they should be too big, then trade them both in. They're both practically new. Soon another package will go out to you: sugar, flour, lentils, pudding, shoes, rice, lard, etc., and maybe powdered eggs, raisins, soap, and soap powder.

You write just the right amount. I write a lot more but therefore somewhat more seldom. A letter like that takes me about six hours, so you have to understand that I can't write one after another.

Greetings and kisses, Helmuttichen [*Little Helmut*]

Letter 34   San Diego, July 14, 1947

Dear Parents, Dear Martinusch!
In the last 14 days three more letters came from you. Dad's letter
46 is sure enormously long; and above all, written so small and tight.
I don't usually see such a thing from my old Dad. A few answers to
questions:
About Fritzes' book, I didn't know that it dealt with technical
drawing. For this reason I would like to have it here very much. I don't
need a rasp anymore because Mr. Roll has a wonderful modern workshop up on his property for tinkering, with the most modern tools, like
a big electric fretsaw, circular saw for three-inch boards, a bench vise,
turning lathe, and every imaginable implement.
And we have wonderful adhesive material in our shoemaker's
shop. It's liquid celluloid, which only glues celluloid to celluloid. So if
you want to glue wood to wood, etc. (any material to any material), you
first have to vigorously rough up the surfaces to be glued, then smear
both with the fluid celluloid (allow it to be absorbed) and dry. Then
when coats of celluloid have built up on the places, you only have to
spread some more fluid celluloid and press together. This combination
will never come loose again and looks outstanding if you don't smear
it. [*Helmut included here a detailed diagram he had drawn of a shoe*].
With the men's soles it's a little different. Celluloid is only put on
the oblique cut (between arch and main sole). Rubber cement is put on
the slip-sole (main part of sole), as on rubber heels. Leather heels are
attached with a _nail_ machine. For a press we use an easy Spannpresse
that has a rubber mat as a base, which is electrically warmed. The
men's soles and a few women's soles are then stitched with a powerful
machine.
I will probably graduate next February. Then maybe I can visit the
polytechnical college in San Luis Obispo, half way between Los
Angeles and San Francisco. There, if the field isn't filled up, I will take
up illuminating engineer or power plant supervisor or maintenance. The
Rolls' only son (Milton) and another fellow (Hugo Klinkert, 20) will
probably go there now in September. Here the high schools and colleges are not only set up for theoretical but for every kind of practical
instruction. In the basement there is a machine shop or an auto repair
shop, etc. so they're much more goal-oriented.
Martin, a.m. means "before noon" (ante meridian) and p. m. means
after noon (post meridian); so if you write "11:00 a. m. and I'm so
tired" I don't believe you. And then people don't say "my eyes shut

them" or "shut themselves" but rather, "my eyes close" or "fall asleep."
You misunderstood me about the German Aid Society. It's a committee
that meets and organizes social events to raise money for needy
German people. Then packages are sent, and Mr. Muehlke has special
responsibility for this. There is no certificate of legal age here. I haven't
heard anything about a university here [*in San Diego*], only the state
teachers college.

This is how it was, and is, with Tante Auguste. In the beginning of
my stay here we were best of friends. We joked around and had fun and
everything. Then, you know how it is, an older person likes to give
some wisdom to the younger one. It was mostly right, but sometimes
not; and then I sometimes contradicted her, which I should not have
done. That was the first squabble.

Then Tante Guschen was sick with bronchial catarrh. I still made
fun and jokes. But because she was really sick and still didn't go to
bed, I thought it wasn't really so bad. In any case, I should not have
made so many jokes. Sometimes it was probably too much. And then
she could hardly put up with it. (She was just sick). And I wrote to you
about that.

You probably had not understood me too well, and then asked me
sometimes in letters, "How is she acting now? Is she nice to you?"
Naturally Tante Guschen didn't like that. That aroused her anger and
mistrust, and she began to doubt that we would reimburse her for anything. She felt betrayed. She made an elephant out of an ant, didn't
sleep at night, and so on. Then I left, because she began to think out
loud and insulted you in my presence [*talking to herself*]. If you,
especially mother, want to write her a letter of apology and say you
know that she really had only the best intentions, it would make me
happy.

Last week end we didn't work (on July 4, 5 , and 6); the 4th is a
national holiday here. Then I had a nice day with Hugo Klinkert and his
relatives. He had a birthday. We went swimming. On Saturday the 5th
the Rolls were with me at the *county fair*. It's a fair like the Leipzig
one—an exhibition of industry, agriculture, and amusements.

On Sunday Mr. Muehlke picked me up early for a church service
and afterwards I went with his children and a few people from the
Sunday school to a swimming pool (similar to Heliopolis). It's lovely
here all the time now. This afternoon I'll probably go to the Rolls and
in the evening to a movie: "*Fantasia.*"

Most lovingly,
Helmut

Letter 35   San Diego, August 7, 1947

Dear Ones at Home!

I spent my birthday [*July 18*] with the Rolls. Mrs. Roll had baked a cake and invited me in the evening for "cake and ice cream." I received from them three pairs of socks and the cake, half of which I took home with me. It was a *"sponge cake,"* with an egg white-sugar icing on it. From the Shopps I got three pairs of socks, a handkerchief, three bars of toilet soap, a bar of chocolate, and of course there were the nice things from both of you—the music and the book on technical drawing.

The next Sunday (July 20) I washed down Tante Guschen's trailer. I got up early at 6:30 in the morning. After that I wanted to wax the trailer, which one needs to do now and then, just like with a car. But by 7:30 it was already too hot for that. At noon there was a chicken dinner. The next Sunday also I kept Tante Guschen company in the trailer.

Last Sunday I was with the Klinkerts at Krauses' Ranch (which is a house in the mountains including a big piece of land). On the land they have a few cows and horses, a swimming pool, hunting area, etc. However, at this time of year the swimming pool is as good as empty; last winter there was too little rainfall. You have to picture the mountains as piles of rubble (big and small); in between is sand and earth where grass and shrubbery grow. In the long, rainless summers here everything dries out terribly. It goes without saying that there are awful fires then that sometimes burn 2000 morgens with all the houses in the area. [*A morgen is a measure of land varying locally from .6 to .9 of an acre*]. Our climate is changing as a result. When we have a west wind, there is pleasant, mild weather; with an east wind it's terribly hot, like in the last 14 days. Then the heat comes from the mountains, deserts, and fires above us here. Here in Point Loma it's still the coolest of all San Diego. Los Angeles has a terribly hot (and humid) climate. The same with the valleys, like the San Gabriel Valley, where San Bernardino is located, or San Jose near San Francisco. Enough of the weather!

This is how Tante Auguste was left in the dark: I had fixed the light and thereby of course undid the connection between the trailer and the electric main, which I had forgotten. Because I had finished and left in daylight, I didn't notice that I had forgotten it. Tante Guschen was naturally in quite a dilemma, because I had done it and not a specialist and she didn't want to tell anyone. But on the third day she called the manager and when I came back on Wednesday the light was of course in order again. However, she didn't scold too much.

Martin's school report is really a good one. However, he needs to concern himself more with English and math. If there were dehydrated potatoes here, I would gladly send them to you; but I have never seen them in the USA. *"Off Limits"* means trespassing is forbidden (out of bounds). Martin, in the next package there will be a new pair of canvas shoes for you. From the Rolls' workplace you'll also get something. For mother (or for trading) there are also four pair, two pair in excellent condition, and two pair "slightly used."

I spend between $3.00 and $4.00 [*per week*] for food. Now and then in the evenings I can sponge on other people (Rolls, Klinkerts, Roberts). I still haven't heard anything from El Salvador. Yes, for sure, Tante Guschen speaks badly of mother, without reason. She misunderstands the letters and absolutely cannot think herself into another person's point of view. [*Helmut next presented the two self-made charts shown below evaluating different models and prices of cars.*]

A car costs:

	Good Makes	Medium	Low Quality
New	$3000-$4000	$2000-$2500	$1500-$2000
Slightly Used	$1500	$1000-$1200	$800-$1000
Old	$500	$200-$400	$100-$300

In the cheaper classes there are also some good ones. I am going to classify them a little differently: (Getting better from bottom to top).

Heavy 8-12 cylind.	Medium 6-8 cylind.	Light 4-6 cylind
Lincoln*	Dodge*	Plymouth x
Cadillac *	Chevrolet #	Chevrolet #
Crysler *	Buick x	Studebaker #
Buick x	Pontiac x	Mercury #
	Studebaker #	Ford *
	Mercury #	Nash x
	Ford *	De Soto #
	Oldsmobile x	

* = good car   x = medium   # = less good
If I were to buy myself a car, it would be either a Chrysler,   Dodge, Plymouth, or Ford.

$1500-$2500 New
$1000-$1500 Used (1940-41)

It isn't advisable to rent a car, and a person doesn't have to bother with a garage. If you have a house, you have your own; otherwise you can leave the car standing in front of the door or pay a rent of $5.00 per month for one. A house suitable for us with all the paraphernalia would be: New, $25,000; Used, $10,00–$20,000. So, it won't take so long. Engineers make $500 per mo. (a few, $35,000 a year). Here you can buy everything in installments (House: $8000 down, $100 a month). Naturally, there are a lot of taxes. There is a state old age pension from age 65. The laws vary from state to state. In Calif. it's $65.00 a month. There are of course private insurance plans also, but only a couple.

Now comes Dad's long question letter:

I eat the following things: Mornings: open faced sandwiches with milk, or corn flakes with milk and sugar and fruit (raisins, applesauce, prunes). Noons I eat two-three sandwiches, which I fix in the morning. In the evening I eat mainly at the house, soup and/or stew, noodles, etc.)

Everyone, from businessman to worker, has a car here; thus the Shopps, Rolls, Klinkerts, Roberts (two), etc. I often go swimming now after work. Doctor, engineer, lawyer, but also politician are well paid professions here. I was recently at the movies: *"Red Stallion,"* a horse movie (in color) very nicely produced. Sometimes in the evening I also play golf. There is no ferry going from Point Loma to North Island or farther. Instead you take the bus, which is in the city in 20 minutes. In the next package will come three maps (San Diego city, San Diego County, and California), so that you can fully orient yourselves.

The horoscope is very interesting. But it's probably only a sun horoscope. Mrs. Klinkert can make accurate horoscopes. She also has books, and in one book, about people born in Cancer [*Helmut's astrological sign*], it states that '47–'48 is going to be a year with financial questions for them. *"Money-money-money"* is how it begins. It doesn't tell people to get into debt but says they will often be in financial predicaments. Towards the end of our astronomical year, however, everything will clear up again and people can expect to receive money from unexpected sources. It also said that on March 4 a far-reaching change will take place because some planet will shine on us. Strange to say, the college quarter begins right on that day, on which I will probably enroll.

Thank you for the jokes, puzzle, and newspaper clippings. I always pass them around. Yes, indeed, Dad, you're a "graduated engineer" and for sure: power plant supervisor,—maintenance, and —erector, installation and illuminating engineer. That I once called Tante Guschen an "old bag" was when we were laughing heartily and making jokes. Then I said that I never thought I would be able to do such a thing with such an old bag! At that time she took it in the right spirit.

Meanwhile I had seen and paid Tante Guschen on August 9 for the last time—$5.00 a week up to that time, altogether $85.00. I asked her if she could forego being paid off for now, and let me pay her off later (after college) or let Dad continue to pay her. She didn't want to hear anything about it. When I left her I said I had to think about paying her further.

When I didn't pay her by the 16th (didn't go to her at all), she came with a friend to our shop on Monday the 18th and raised cane. Fortunately I wasn't there. They both talked for an hour and a half and made me out, and also mother, to be terribly bad, and demanded that he [*Mr. Roll*] deduct $5.00 a week from my wages. When he said he had to ask me, they said Helmut wouldn't give permission. But Mr. Roll didn't make anything of it and calmly allowed her to babble on.

Meanwhile the local court has taken over my guardianship, which Tante Guschen doesn't know yet. So if she gives me any more trouble, I'll just refer her to my caseworker, and he will give her information—of course I've explained everything to him. In the worst case she will receive an official prohibition to visit me, call me up, correspond with me, and talk to other people about me. As a last resort, Dad has promised to pay her back for any money she spent on me, and not I; although I understand that this is my own concern and it goes without saying that I myself will pay it back.

Enclosed is a newspaper clipping about Helmut Dost [*from the "Point Loma Light"*]. I'm also sending one to Grandma.

> Big greetings and loving kisses,
> Your Helmut

Paul Dost's Diary, September 9:

Fat letter from Helmut, #34 and #35 [*together*]. Tante Guschen is angry because Helmut had announced that he would slow down his repayments (he only has $65 left to pay). She even went to Roll's shop with another woman and asked Mr. Roll to deduct the money from Helmut's wages!

5

Visions and Schemes: *Dreams of Life Together*

We see from the next several letters that Helmut fully expects to enter college after his graduation from high school. He does not seem to have understood very well the realities of funding a higher education in the United States. Why he was unable to procure the hoped-for scholarship or to receive more helpful direction from school counselors remains a mystery.

While envisioning a future at California Polytechnic Institute in San Luis Obispo, Helmut tells his family how they should prepare for life in America. He writes in great detail about domestic life in the United States and his visions for their future here together. Again, Helmut the boy is advising the adults, who may not always be entirely able to distinguish realistic plans from youthful dreams.

Interestingly, his parents' understanding of the American immigration system sometimes appears to be more limited than Helmut's, as they seemingly failed to grasp fully the functions and responsibilities of an immigration sponsor and Helmut's inability to assume this role himself before the age of 21.

This chapter includes a poignant letter by Helmut's mother to Augusta de Boer. In it she defends her son against Guschen's constant complaints, and explains why she and his father finally encouraged him to seek lodgings elsewhere. How is it that we have this letter? Did Tante Guschen actually give it to Helmut? No one knows.

Meanwhile, Helmut's father is preparing to move to Essen in West Germany to take a work assignment with the AEG, while Maria and Martin stay in Berlin.

Letter 37   San Diego 6, Sept. 21, 1947

Dear Ones at Home!

It's 14 days again since I last wrote. Four things have come from you, and there's also a little bit of news from around here. To sum it up:

Last Sunday I swam in the Bay for a while in the morning, and in the afternoon I was with the Klinkerts and Muehlkes. Mr. Muehlke and I put two 3 and 1/2 lb. containers of milk powder in tins, of which you will probably get two, and afterwards we were with a young woman from Berlin who is the first German war bride (about 30 years old) in San Diego—that is, she just flew here last June from Berlin-Marien-dorf. We all had a real nice conversation. After a light supper with Mrs. Klinkert I went back home and turned in early, because I had to be back in school early the next morning, after three months of summer vacation.

Here you have to re-register each semester. Since I had figured on going to college next semester (that is, in March, after the end of school in February, thus earlier than my classmates would graduate), you can well imagine how taken aback I was when Mrs. Kox, my former school counselor, told me I still needed 3 credits (American history and, I think, Civics)—and that this would take till next June at the earliest (with 4 hours a week the first semester, 8 hours the next).

Now I knew that, according to my horoscope, in March [*1948*], the official beginning of college, a big change would take place in my life. Consequently, Mrs. Kox's calculation could not be right at all. I remembered a conversation with the director of the San Diego welfare department in which he referred me to a good friend of his with reference to consultations about college. This was Mrs. McMullen, the new principal of our school, who came here from San Diego College, so I asked Mrs. Kox to introduce me to Mrs. McMullen, and then everything quickly went right. She decided on two remaining history credits, which I will take this coming semester on Monday and Tuesday mornings. So my college probably will begin in March. Mrs. McMul-len asked me to make an appointment with her in about a week for a conversation about college and scholarships; she probably also wants to know something about Germany.

Yesterday, Saturday morning, I noticed that my pocket watch (Dad's "Omega," a World War [*I*] souvenir) had given out; it could always be wound up easily before, but then it stopped. The mainspring was broken. It cost me $4.50 [*to repair*], but the watch is worth it. You write about a great drought throughout Germany, and especially

Europe. Guess how long we had no precipitation here. Recently we had a very light rain all day (just like this morning); people hardly got wet outside. In this damp weather my alarm clock stopped—last winter already—it's also old; it was that way when I bought it. So I put out $3.68 for a new clock. So it was one thing on top of the other yesterday.

Today I went into the mountains for a picnic with Mr. Muehlke and his daughters, via El Cahon, Alpine, and Descanso to Cuyamaca. (You can look these places up on the maps I'm going to send you or in the atlas). We stopped there for two hours, including lunch, and then went back via Julian, Ramona, and Lakeside: altogether over 100 miles (165 km—Berlin to Halle) in about 7 hours including the stop. This is probably the most beautiful region in San Diego County—it reminds me somewhat of Germany—the trees (mostly oaks and pines) here are wonderful; the mountains too, of course.

Did I tell you something about my trip to Idyllwild? At that time I was spending Sunday with the Rolls. In the evening they received a visit, and in order to get out of the way, at about 7:30 I called Hugo Klinkert in the gas station down below the Rolls' to find out if he had anything planned for the evening. He immediately asked me if I would like to go with him, Milton (Roll), and his friend Don to Idyllwild—if Mr. Roll would release me [*from work the next day*]. I naturally wanted to go because something like that wouldn't be offered every day. At about 9:00 p.m. the four of us drove off in the Klinkerts' car via Escondido, Temecula, and Hemet to Idyllwild, where we arrived around midnight. On and off we drove 85–90 miles an hour. The whole stretch is 130 miles long.

Then we "slept" uncomfortably all night half in the car, half outside. It's about 5500 feet high there, thus 1700 meters, so you can probably imagine how cold it was. At 6:00 in the morning we drove further. First all around that region, then, after a hearty breakfast, via Hemet-Riverside to Los Angeles and from there down along the Pacific to Point Loma. Naturally I enjoyed it very much. From San Diego to Idyllwild we didn't see anything of the landscape of course, but from Idyllwild to Los Angeles and San Diego it was just gorgeous. The whole trip was about 400 miles long. After 21 hours, at 6:00 p.m. Monday we were back again for Mrs. Roll's birthday. One can hardly describe California in words—the weather and landscape and characteristics of the people, so come over and experience it for yourselves!

Also, in August I had a molar pulled with full anesthesia for about 45 minutes, by gas, which is injected into the blood through a vein in the elbow. About $20.00, completely painless. The Welfare paid for it, just like the glasses I got last November (-2.5 r./-2.75 l.)—nice and clear, good-fitting horn. Yes, the doctors are terribly expensive in this country, so have all your ailments "cured" in Germany.

At the beginning of last week I went to the movies with Milton and Don, *"The Great Walts,"* [*Waltz?*] which we already saw in Cairo at the "Strand"—open air—just three crossroads from us, and *"Make Mine Music,"* a Walt Disney feature. Walt Disney is the company that produces pictures like Mickey Mouse or Popeye (and his spinach) or Donald Duck. So *"Make Mine Music"* was various musical pieces, modern and semi-classical, on film, or rather shown on the screen, with music present of course. Also on Monday evening I heard *"The Seventh Veil"* over the radio. That was a wonderful radio program.

Say, before I forget it, could you send right away the address of Fritz Starkowski's wife, the one with the many small children. [*Fritz Starkowski was a cousin of Helmut's mother*]. Since Uncle Fritz is dead, I of course want to persuade Mr. Muehlke to send her one or more packages, which I already obtained for Mrs. Scholz (Aroser Allee 171), about 18 lbs., around Sept. 10. Of course, he sends almost exclusively to unattached young mothers with many small children and to frail old people (mostly refugees); so the address quickly please!

Yes, it's just amazing how long the powdered eggs can keep. How are mother's formerly frozen fingers now? A lot of soap will come with the next package. I'm not buying a wrist watch because my pocket watch is in such fine condition. I still have my lovely signet ring also (not lost). Only now I wear it on the right ring finger and no longer on the left middle finger.

So good night then; tomorrow morning it's to school for the first time after vacation. It's now 10:00 p.m. Up again at 6:15 tomorrow morning.

Bye-Bye, Your Helmut

Letter 38 [*typewritten*]   S.D., Oct. 5, '47

Dear Berliners!

I'm right up here at the Klinkerts and fumbling around a little on their typewriter. Hugo came here from his college at 4 a. m. yesterday (after a ten-hour ride on the bus, which is cheaper than a train or airplane), to spend his Sunday, or rather, his week end, at his mother's.

He had already written about it, but not whether on Saturday or on Sunday morning. Yesterday evening I was busy moving furniture around in my room when he knocked on my door. I was naturally kind of surprised, but he sure came at just the right time. In order to move the bed, I would either have had to take it apart, or lift it over the small oven table nailed to the wall—which Hugo helped me with. So now I have a combination of bedroom and kitchen and the table and chair for eating and writing as a living room—very nice for such a small 3 by 2 meter room, don't you think? The chests are like those long ones, you know, that you have in the basement, with a dividing shelf in the middle.

Last Tuesday I had a talk with the principal of our school *[Mrs. McMullen]*. She asked me some questions, for example whether I wanted to continue my education back in Germany, or what college I was thinking of going to, what I wanted to be, etc....and when she heard that I was thinking of going to San Luis Obispo *[location of California Polytechnic Institute]*, she thought she knew one of the directors up there and with his help would be able to arrange something for me; — in an astrological newspaper for October it says under my birth date that last Wednesday something favorable for me was being developed behind the scenes—so there you have it!

So how is it going for you in Berlin? Are the four packages (for Wenzels, Genzes, Hintzes, and you) already there? Instead of fresh eggs I've also bought the canned ones now because they're cheaper (a dozen and a half fresh $1.35, a dozen and a half in one can, $1.09). But everything here is terribly expensive.

Last Saturday I bought myself two pairs of nice shoes. Shoes will keep increasing in price; when Mr. Roll ordered the shoes in Los Angeles they were 30 cents less than what he had to pay when they were bought; that was only 14 days later. The shoes are going to be for college; I'm not going to wear them yet, so they can be exchanged if necessary after Christmas in case my legs should still grow a little in the meantime.

After school tomorrow I will probably go and have my hair cut. I go there as seldom as possible, but once in two months it has to be cut (it costs at least 65 cents, which I would rather send to Germany). Imagine my thoughts more than the writing in this letter, and forget all the mistakes you find, because this is the first time I've written on a typewriter since Senochraby. *[Senochraby was one of the towns in*

Czechoslovakia to which Helmut's school was evacuated during the war. Actually Helmut's typing appears very good].
    I wish you well, and stay healthy...

See you later, Greetings, signed Helmut

Paul Dost's Diary, October 19:

A few days ago, Helmut wrote us a letter that was again very upbeat, using a typewriter. His friend Hugo Klinkert came from San Luis Obispo for the weekend, helped Helmut to rearrange his room, and told him all about the engineering school there. Helmut's principal knows the principal at San Luis Obispo, and she promised to put in a recommendation for him there.

LETTER FROM HELMUT'S MOTHER TO TANTE GUSCHEN

[The following letter was written on a typewriter by Helmut's mother. It is the only one from another family member to become a part of this collection before 1951, when Helmut began to save the letters he received. This impassioned letter, which bears Maria's signature, appears to be the original and not a carbon copy. How it was obtained is not known.]

Berlin-Reinickendorf, Oct. 26, 1947

Dear Tante Guschen,
    Although, after perusing your letter, we had decided not to go any further into its offensive, incomprehensible contents, I would like, for your peace of mind and ours, to give an explanation of our present decision.
    So, listen: When we suggested that Helmut should perhaps look around for lodgings elsewhere, it was only to free you from all the trouble and economic hardship on his account, because finally, of course, it became too much for us to bear your continual remarks about excessive costs, etc. for you, a poor widow, without trying to find a remedy.
    It was far from our intention to place upon you any kind of burden by your taking our oldest son, who in general would have found more sympathy anywhere else. In our Christian view of life we know neither

hatred nor ugliness, much less dishonesty. Such accusations [as Guschen has apparently made] are inappropriate at the least. Much less should they be associated with an elderly woman. For there is a God who punishes all injustice. All guilt is avenged on this earth.

But now, in order to close the painful subject of money, you will receive the remaining claim of about $65—as far as we know—as soon as this is possible for Helmut. How much we would prefer to do it for him! We have written him to this effect; as a result may you again find peace about it.

We obviously believe and trust in our well-brought up son and will continue to, and such hate-filled accusations could apply neither to him nor to us. Such things always come back to the one who utters them. Everyone reaps what he sows, sooner or later, in life.

You have so often misunderstood both Helmut and us that a separation was probably inevitable. But even this separation could have been peaceful and civil, without stupid insults, which were not on our part, because as sincere, idealistically-inclined people we had only good in view, and surely in your case a mutual support and help between old and young.

This could have succeeded with harmony and good nature from both sides. But everything turns out in the end the way it should. Therefore, in spite of everything, you again have our thanks and best wishes for your future.

It is still a puzzle to us that you have remained so lacking in understanding of this innocent young boy. You have completely misunderstood him and us. We will not accept any slander about our son. People are different from one another and this is good; and if two people don't really understand each other, it's best that they separate in peace. No one has the right to stifle the individual personality of his fellow man, but rather ought to respect it as much as possible.

Helmut has never complained about you; on the contrary he has had only good words about everything; but it has distressed him and us to have to continually hear that you, as a poor widow, are too heavily burdened. So we had to choose this solution, which could only be the right thing for you. It's good if he—responsible for himself—learns to budget his money. Everyone must adjust expenditures to income. Incidentally, Helmut also has school on Mondays, which you probably did not know. He is industrious and ambitious, but naturally he also needs relationships with other young people his age, which we wish him from our hearts.

Now I hope that this letter may finally bring clarification and peace into your thoughts and feelings concerning us all.

In this understanding be greeted by Maria

Letter 39   San Diego, November 9, 1947

Dear Ones at Home!

It's now 5 weeks again since I last wrote you. Meanwhile a lot has happened, which I want to review quickly. On Sunday, October 12, the women's lodge (a German lodge called Tusnelda, a branch of the German-American Hermannssohne Men's Lodge) installed a new president. Mrs. Roll was elected president. Everything was in German; about 125 people were there. Afterwards there was food, with which I had a lot to do (giving out beer). Mr. Roll paid for me (75 cents).

The next Sunday there was something similar. A German goulash dinner for the benefit of German aid, so that we could send packages overseas again. It cost $1.50, but I went free. Forty-four singers from Los Angeles (the German Men's Chorus) were guests and approximately 350–400 people were served.

The next Sunday I visited a Heuschele family in Encanto (look on the San Diego map)—a couple with three children: Werner, 18, who goes to San Diego College and is studying to be a doctor; Catherine, two; and Roland, five. They are certainly the nicest Germans that I've met here. Mr. Heuschele and his wife were in the dt. Verein (NSDAP) and, because they were still not American citizens, were incarcerated in an internment camp. [*The Deutscher Verein was a patriotic German organization, apparently affiliated in some way with the National Socialist Party.*]

They had a nursery here, but had to sell it very cheap ($2,000 instead of $10,000); Mr. H. also had to leave the Pacific Zone (California, Oregon, Washington, Utah and Arizona) as an enemy of the State; these people, who weren't in Germany at all during the Nazi period, and had never learned the real truth [*about the Nazi Party?*] had to suffer so much. When Mrs. H. came out of the camp they didn't have a penny left. They had to start all over again. Mr. H. is a taxi driver for the moment. He works from 5 p. m. to 3:30 a. m. So he works hard to earn money 10 hours a day, 6 days a week. The Heuscheles send an enormous number of packages to Germany. Recently they sent two that cost over $37.00 for postage alone. Werner is a nice, intelligent, well-brought up young man (like a German). He was two or three years old when the Heuscheles immigrated. The Heuscheles have now acquired a home of their own again.

Last Sunday Hugo was here in San Diego again. His mother had let him work on the family Cadillac and now he has received it for school use. Friday, October 31, I sent off a package for you (for Christmas). Today I've packed another two for you. One will probably go out tomorrow and one next week, because you are only allowed to send one package a week. Package 19 contains: rolled oats, one pair of used pants, one white shirt (from the Roberts), one pair of black shoes (soled) for Martin (as a present from the Rolls), cream of wheat, prunes, 2 lbs. raw coffee, one quart of oil, one Christmas sausage, two bars of soap, three cans of fish, chewing gum, yarn. Number 20: 5 lb. sugar, milk powder, one pair of pants, one white shirt (also from the Roberts), white beans, one pair of brown shoes for Dad from Rolls' shop, chewing gum, yarn, one can of fish, 3/4 lb. currants, two bars of soap, and again prunes.

More good news in that connection. I received the following letter from CARE (from New York):

> *"Dear Mr. Dost: You will be interested to know, I am sure, that the two people you mentioned in your letter of September 1, 1947, have received a General Relief CARE package. In each case the name of the person donating the General Relief package was mentioned and your name was not, so that you might not have heard of their good fortune. Yours very truly, Donald A. Ostrander, Director, CARE Mission, Berlin."*
> *Hurray, it worked.*

The beautiful days here in San Diego have now ended. Last week it was so cold at night that it almost froze. Today we had the first real rain since June. Martin, continue to study hard. Maybe, if you want to, you can finish the 6th class and afterwards study marine architecture. Look into it. However, maybe agriculture would be better for you—but for that it probably would have been better for you to have grown up on a farm.

Well then, good night and goodbye,
Your Helmut

Letter 40 San Diego, December 6, 1947

Dear Little Berliners!

It's several weeks again since a letter went out to you from my end. Meanwhile Christmas is coming and, most important, mother's birthday [*December 18*]. So my best wishes to all of you for the all the festivities at once. May we be close again in the coming year, or at least be getting closer.

I now have received all the letters up to 66-a (from the 6th of November). To go into all your questions (from about 10 letters) in detail wouldn't make sense, but I will share with you in general what lies on your hearts and mine.

1) My education after graduation (next February): If I should receive a scholarship, I will of course go to college, to SLO [*California Polytechnic at San Luis Obispo*]. I'll probably share a room in town with Hugo and eat together at school (altogether about $50.00 per month). The scholarship appears to be as follows: $1200 for 4 semesters = 1 and 1/2 years uninterrupted—or 2 years of school with 2 and 1/4 years summer vacation. If I'm lucky I could get another scholarship for the remaining 4 semesters. Otherwise I'll have to work and maybe Dad would be here by that time and could help me.

2) College in General:

You can receive a qualification in 2, 3, or 4 years (or without vacation in 1 and 1/2, 2 and 1/4, or 3 years); of course the longer you go to college the better employment you receive later in life.

3) During my studies I will probably move to SLO, but later will probably live in San Diego (with you).

4) Your pursuits, in case your coming here soon should be delayed: Martin: will work somewhere (as with me, it's best to learn to speak English, because he's already receiving the written instruction now in high school, perhaps somewhat more than I did). Mother:—about night school English. Because you know Spanish, it won't be hard for you to find something good early on; in San Diego there are so many Mexicans who hardly know any English. Dad: night school and engineer status (likewise Spanish).

For all of you it would be necessary to review your knowledge of the spoken language. You would probably do best to live here in San Diego in an apartment. Most of the friends and German people are down here and, above all, the opportunities for Spanish employment. I would then of course come here every 3–4 weeks and for the vacations.

Should I not receive a scholarship, which seems to be a pretty sure thing, I will in no case go to college soon, but will wait until we can afford it on our own. As soon as I'm 18 I would begin to work in the airplane plant where I could about double my income.

5) Regarding Tante Guschen: That I should pay off the debts soon is completely clear to me. Only how? The debt (as I figure it) is $212 (which she...demanded for food) less$ 85 (which I already paid her back) = $127–$130. For packages, which she sent to you and Grandma, about $100 = $230. For other things she did for me, about $100 = $300–$350 total. By other things I mean: a trip to San Bernardino ($30), movies ($5), some clothing ($10), violin bow and a few pieces of music ($10), transportation money to the city ($20), and little things = $100. Then, with the rest of the $350, everything would be paid. Of course, if we were to strike it rich, we could even pay back the money for the trailer ($2500). So Tante Guschen can't, or shouldn't, be able to make any extra claims beyond $200 plus $130.

[*Helmut included in this letter diagrams of four two-bedroom houses, each with a different design. Below he offers his ideas about what the family could earn in the United States, and how much it would cost to buy a house. He also describes the contents of an American kitchen and current prices of household appliances.*]

When we are happily together, everything may develop in the following way. As soon as one or more of us has a permanent job and we have earned the first few thousand dollars (which, if everyone is willing, industrious, and patient should take no more than a year) we will pay down about $3000 on a house, and then pay it off at about $100 a month. Mother would earn about $150–$200, Martin $50–$150, Dad $200–$500, Helmut $200–$500 (monthly, of course); so you see that here it isn't at all hard to become rich, if one can be organized and not afraid of work.

In general we could own our own house, two cars, etc. in five years, but maybe we could have a small house and car after just one year. The lots are on an average 50 x 125–150 ft. in size. For us the first [*house*] would be about $5,000–$7,000 (about 10 years old); later on a new one for about $10,000–$12,000. The prices are for two-bedroom houses (see diagrams); also the prices are very high at the moment. All of the figures that I've mentioned so far are as they would be now; but they could easily be reduced to lower prices and payments, because both would probably go down proportionately.

On the next page are a few diagrams with explanations next to them. One should really draft the designs according to the lots (considering the sun exposure, slope, light). [*Detailed interpretations of the four house plans followed.*]

I am going to send, maybe in a letter or package, one or two kitchen models (from the newspaper). To an American kitchen also belong an electric mixer, for dough, whipped cream, etc.; electric washing machine with wringer; and dishwasher. Of course there are a large and a couple of small radios. In rich homes you also see television sets!

PRICES NEW

Gas Stove $75–$300	Washing Machine $100–$400
Television $800–$1500	Sink $50–200
Wringer $300–$500	TV & Radio $1500–$3000
Refrigerator $200–$500	Dishwasher $300–$500
Small Radio $10-$50	

Well, I've just gone through a lot of newspapers and dug into the ads. In doing so I found a number of interesting things with regard to what I mentioned above, and autos. I'm sending along a picture of a kitchen arrangement. So, mother, if you come over here, you won't have it too hard. Also you can buy all vegetables in cans (of course the vegetables taste better fresh) and for dishes that take a long time to cook they have the "pressure cooker," a thick pot with a lockable cover, in which the food cooks in a quarter of the time under steam. For instance, a chicken is completely cooked in 20–25 minutes, and potatoes only take 5 minutes. So everything is very practical. Also, there is of course warm water in every household.

In the last week the weather has now turned completely to rain. Not lasting rain, of course, but on and off. Everything is still going very well with me. I'm enclosing a few pictures from the last Thursday in November (the 27th), which is always Thanksgiving here.

Greetings and kisses,
Helmut

Paul Dost's Diary:

December 14—Herr Fleck in Essen sent a telegram saying that I can start a job there in January [*with the AEG*]. I am in the process of getting interzone travel tickets.

February 28—Helmut has still not written. No word from him since December 6. What could be going on?

6

Chickens and Apricots: *Becoming a Farmer*

After graduation from high school in February 1948, Helmut tried to enroll at the California Polytechnic Institute in San Luis Obispo, only to be put off for lack of funds. To earn money, he was advised by the college to apply for a job with the Westinghouse Corporation in the San Francisco Bay area, but found he could not be employed there until he turned 18.

Subsequently Helmut went to work for Otto K. Kern, a German farmer and doctor of agriculture in Los Altos, for what was to have been a period of six months. Instead he became increasingly involved in the work of the farm while the Kerns held out the promise of sponsoring his family.

Meanwhile, after a short time in Essen, West Germany, Paul Dost was sent to work at a power plant in the nearby town of Lünen. Living conditions there were very poor after the war, housing being almost unavailable. In addition, Paul began to develop some worrisome health problems. Back in Berlin the historic Berlin Blockade was put into effect by the Russians, who were attempting to isolate West Berlin completely by cutting off all ground transportation to West Germany.

Then in January 1949, the unthinkable happened: Paul was tragically killed in an industrial accident at the power plant! The situation in Germany, coupled with the sudden death of his father, lent even greater urgency to Helmut's sense of responsibility for bringing the remainder of his family to the United States.

By the spring of 1949 the ability of the Kerns to sponsor Maria and Martin hinged on the settlement of certain financial matters in Germany, which first required a trip to Europe by Mr. Kern. This was a period of radical currency reform in West Germany, where the old, greatly devalued deutschmark was replaced by the new so-called westmark.

It is in this chapter that Helmut first mentions certain coupons which he sent periodically to his family. What organization or agency issued these coupons, and the types of items for which they could be redeemed, is not explained in any of the letters.

It will be noted that Helmut is beginning to write more of his letters in English [*an English that is remarkably good*]. As mentioned in the editorial note, all letters and segments of letters that were written in English have been italicized.

⌘

Letter 41   Los Altos, March 7, 1948

Dear Ones!

It's a long time again since I wrote to you. I was so busy and just had no time (or motivation) to write. Meanwhile no small change (or more than one) has occurred with me. I spent a nice Christmas with the Rolls and Klinkerts. Five pairs of socks, a thick green sport shirt, $5.00, chocolate drops, and imagine: from the Welfare a good, new tennis racquet. During Christmas vacation I was mainly with the Klinkerts. Hugo was home, and we tried tennis, and practiced math, etc. He went back to college on January 5. Then my school started again.

In school there was intense activity after vacation. The exam came sooner than I expected, so I had very little time to look up the presidents. However, it worked out well. Social Science B and History A, both of which in Germany would be combined in history class. So on February 6 I had my diploma in my hands (without the ceremony); that was a Friday. On Thursday, February 5, I stopped working for the Rolls, and, because Mr. Muehlke was going to Frisco on Saturday,…I went right with him to San Luis Obispo. I was in San Luis Obispo for three weeks. I stayed with Hugo. San Luis Obispo is a nice little town, numbering no more than maybe 5000 inhabitants; not so modern, mostly little single-family houses.

I had a letter of reference from the school, but there they [*the college*] considered my money problem to be acute and turned me over to the electrical engineering instructor, who immediately sent a letter to Sunnyvale, California, where there is a Westinghouse plant (Westinghouse = a small AEG). When there was no answer after two and a half weeks, I decided to go there myself—since my money was running low. And so I got another letter of reference from the school (Cal Poly) and put myself on the train on Saturday, February 28—at 2 a.m. yet! We were in San Jose at 8:00 and there I called Sunnyvale around 9:00, but no one was in the Westinghouse employment office on Saturday.

Through one of Hugo's friends in San Luis Obispo I had received an address of some German people in Los Altos with whom he had worked a few years in farming. If you look in the atlas, you will find that three places lie, with Palo Alto, on the route to Frisco, only that Los Altos lies somewhat off to the side.

So I took a chance and went to Los Altos [*near Sunnyvale*]. At about 11:00 I had arrived at the Kerns, which is the name of the people. After getting acquainted, they invited me to a meal, and then also to stay overnight and till Monday, when they wanted to take me to Sunnyvale. They have a small piece of property, on the border of a large plain around San Jose and San Francisco, well into the hills, but behind us are high, forested mountains (like in the Black Forest), behind which there are supposed to be some California Redwood forests, and in front of everything Santa Cruz and Monterey and Pacific Grove. Look it up sometime on the map.

So, as I said, the Kerns' land is located in a very hilly area. They have 1500 hens, 5 lambs, 8 cows and calves, one bull, about 5 cats, a sheep dog... and a lot of work, no children, both around 50, one house in which they (and I) live, and two where they have renters, a new '47 Ford, 2 Ford trucks, and a little caterpillar tractor.

On Monday I was driven by Mr. Kern to Sunnyvale, and after some searching and waiting they told me that they wanted very much to oblige me but that I would have to be 18 in order to enter a useful position. However, they would soon have a job for a messenger boy, which of course is at the best about $120 per month. But until then they said I should stay with the Kerns, so I can save money; of course I'm making myself useful as far as I can by cleaning the weeds out of the paths, which is not that easy.

Los Altos, Beginning of April 1948

With the Sievers, whom I mentioned in the last letter, I went one Sunday to Carmel Beach, probably the richest and most famous bathing place in California. The trip was just wonderful, via Saratoga, Los Gatos, Santa Cruz, Castroville, Seaside, Monterey, and Pacific Grove in a 1946 Buick, which drives so beautifully, just like all heavy cars. I brought back a star fish to dry (as a captured souvenir). On a rock I also saw sea lions, which wander around freely here—and driving along the other coast I saw the spray of a whale splashing up two times.

The week before Easter we were busy sanding, shellacking, varnishing, and waxing the floors (parkett). The rest of the time I helped to clean the house. Then I'm collecting most of the eggs now and I feed the chickens and pack the eggs that Mrs. Kern doesn't need for private use. Apart from 100 dozen a week which are sold wholesale, there are still more to prepare for private customers; either they are picked up by the latter or Mrs. Kern delivers them every two weeks (each time about 200 dozen) with which I help her. So I'm halfway busy here. We went to the movies twice: *"Golden Earrings"* with Marlene Dietrich (a Zigeuner film about Germany) and *"A Double Life."* And yesterday I was at the movies again: *"Gone with the Wind"* with Clark Gable, etc., while the Kerns were at a wedding.

Last week your mail finally reached me; the last was from January 1 and the next from January 27. I assume that there are still about two letters missing. In these two you probably wrote me about Martin's accident, which I still don't know anything about. I did know that my little brother spent a month in the hospital [due to a broken leg], from which I myself have mail from him, including puzzles, that he came out with a plaster cast, and that it was already going fairly well for him the middle of February. Martin, I'm really sorry; thank you very much for your effort with the puzzles. But there's no point in still feeling sorry for you now, because in the meantime you will have gone back to school.

I was also glad that Dad is [*working*] in Essen and is staying with Dr. Hoffman's mother. If only you two could also leave that inferno Berlin. A war will probably be almost unavoidable soon. Then they'll snap me up here too and put me in a uniform somewhere. For this reason I've played with the thought of joining up voluntarily. Then I can choose a branch of the service and a special field and have an occupation with good wages. Also, a veteran has a lot of standing here—especially in getting jobs and studying. I think this is definitely the best solution to my problem. Maybe I'll go to Europe. They told me that if I were 22 I could enter the *C. I. C.* [*Counter Intelligence Corps*] where I could use my German English. Well, we'll wait and see.

I'll ask you one thing: Don't tell anyone the least bit of this. If the Russians should find out that I'm an American soldier, they'll keep a much sharper eye on you than before; and should it come to a war they might use you as hostages. Above all, try to join Dad [*in safer West*

Germany], naturally by legal means. The only one who should be permitted to know, except for Dad (I mean about the talk of becoming a soldier), is Mr. Swope [*the American consular officer*]. So—absolute discretion!

> Well, stay well and in good spirits,
> Your Helmut

Paul Dost's Diary, March 28:

This week I got a telegram from Mutti saying, "Helmut probably Obispo, 844 Upham Street." So that must mean that the boy is going to college now.

Paul Dost's Diary, April 13:

A telegram and a letter came from Mutti and Martin. Helmut, who is now in the San Francisco area, wrote, and they went to Vice Consul Swope who gave them three applications and it sounded like it might be possible for us to immigrate even this year, if I can document my democratic views. I wrote to Hassan Shawkat right away and asked him to send a letter of recommendation...confirming my democratic views while in Egypt.

Letter 43   Los Altos, May 2, 1948

Dear Mother, Dear Martin!

Yesterday I received the first mail from you sent directly here. It made me very happy that you received such a nice answer from the consulate. Or, in any case, it's a ray of hope for the future. You will probably get the political permits together, but it will take some efforts to receive the affidavits [*for sponsorship*]. Look, this is how it is: we don't have any real rich relatives or friends here. Those we know belong to the middle class, that is they have a house, car, and business or a small bank account. If they have a business, like the Rolls for instance, they only have a small income, and if they have a small bank account, they are always thinking of increasing it; we'll be like that too. So we don't have any really rich people.

So you see what a risky undertaking it is for someone to be a sponsor. And not only that: people naturally figure on the worst; if you,

let's say, should have an accident of some kind on the ship or in your
first days here, and if the obligation could not be accepted by anyone
else, they would have to bear all of the expenses and take care of you
the rest of your life, or at least as long as you were unable to work. And
then it depends on their financial ability and on the initial costs—about
$1000–$2000, which they couldn't avoid unless I already had the
money. At the moment I'm still almost at the zero mark. And how is it
going with the work permit for Dad? Did the consulate ask about it, or
was that your own idea? Maybe I could get one for him.

I've calculated the expenses to California as follows: (3 persons)

Consulate and passage:	= $500
New York:	
lodging, food, recreation, and clothing	= $600
Cross-Country Trip:	
transportation and food; airplane, train, or bus to Calif.	= $375
	$1500
First Month in California:	$500
	(total) $2000

Future Months (self-sustaining), altogether 4 persons:
        Three persons working
        Income: $400–$500?
        Expenses: $250 (food and living)
        Remaining balance: $100–$150–$20

        Dad and Helmut—fully employed
        Martin—half time work and half time school
        Mother—household

Everything is going all right for me personally. How are things
going with you? Are there more groceries now, or vegetables, or just as
little? I have to finally write Dad now. My laziness is doing me in.
More tomorrow.

                        So good night, Your Helmut

May 9, 1948
Now to continue: I want to write more now about my new environment.
First, the day's routine:
   I get up about 7 a.m. Then I go briefly to feed the calves (two in
number, 4 and 5 months), and 4 sheep and 3 lambs, about 15 minutes.

Then I go through the hen houses, see that everything is in order, that they have enough laying-food, and that none of them are dead, change the water, take the sick and weak ones into a separate stall, and set the rest of the hens free (every hen house has an extra fenced-in area for this).

At 8:00 there's breakfast; before or after that, depending on the time available, I straighten up my room. Then I wash dishes and about 9:00 I'm free for other work. That would be: pull weeds, spade, help Mr. Kern tidy things up, clean the hen houses, fill the containers with chicken feed, etc. At noon there's lunch; if Mrs. Kern is home she prepares it; if she has to go somewhere in the morning, I prepare the food and set the table.

After lunch the hens are fed (by me) with wheat, barley, or oats, and the eggs are collected, about 350 to 400. Then I wash up and rest for a while. From about 2:00 till 5:00 we do general work, and at 5:00 we have supper. Then gather eggs again, but no feeding (about 125), wash up and then feed the calves and sheep again from about 6:00 to 6:30. That's about all. Don't think I'm overworked because it's all just light work. Some days there is heavy work but only for 1–3 hours. On Sundays I only take care of the animals and wash dishes.

Mrs. Kern takes care of the young hens and chicks; cleans, sorts, and packs the eggs; and feeds the geese. Besides, she takes care of the household, serves the egg customers (sometimes I do that too), and every two weeks, on Friday, we (Mrs. Kern and I) take the eggs out and deliver them to private customers. Mr. Kern looks after things, takes care of the vegetable garden, milks the cows, and works around the place.

Since I've been here, Mrs. Kern spent a week in Santa Barbara with relatives. During that time I took her place, that is, eggs and housekeeping. And now Mr. Kern is on a short five-day vacation in the Sierras. Till now the Kerns could hardly go on these little vacations, so I'm glad that I can help them.

So I'm working an average of eight hours a day, and since the work is easy, and above all I'm acquiring experience for later, I figure about 50 cents an hour, with deductions of about $2.50–$3.00 a day for lodging and the best possible board. That leaves me with about $6.00 a week and much valuable experience, which I would not have anywhere else since both Mr. and Mrs. Kern are doctors of agriculture. Mr. Kern could be a professor at Stanford University (about 8 miles from here in Palo Alto), but he declined it because he wanted to be alone and independent.

Now stay very well and in good spirits and bear all the strains as well as you can. Write me how everything stands with the consulate, and what I can do from here on out to make the earliest possible passage available to you. Employment for Dad and a place to live aren't the worst problems, but sponsorship will be hard to come by. Well, we'll see. By the way, I'm also smoking cigarettes now, about one pack in 3–4 days.

> With hearty greetings and kisses,
> from your Helmut

Paul Dost's Diary:

May 10: I worry about my left leg. Yesterday it was swollen badly and full of knots...am feeling depressed frequently.

May 12: A continuous, aching, internal tingling sensation (blood congestion)...never completely goes away. A tumor-looking, varicose vein-like growth is forming; the leg is somewhat jaundiced up to about mid-calf. What will come of this? Will I be healthy enough to work for a number of years yet—and support my family? Will Helmut find sponsors? And will we not end up having to disappoint them?

May 17: The tumor thing on my left leg does not seem to be caused by water retention after all, but by hardenings of the muscle—No mail from Helmut since the end of April.

Letter 44   Los Altos, May 29, 1948

Dear Mother, Dear Martin!

It's a little while since I reported to you about my life in this place, I think even with sketches. Meanwhile there is no further news. I've received three short notes from Dad. All of them, and also your last one, included inquiries about security [*for sponsorship*]. You don't need to be worried about that. The Kerns are willing, but since they don't have enough cash, having put everything into the farm, they and I are going to look for someone else who could make up the financial difference, I mean on the affidavit [*of support*].

I hope to be able to borrow the cash you will need from the Klinkerts and Dodges. So everything depends on that one thing. Tell us immediately *the minimum cash amount required for you 3 people*. The

Kerns would serve in the background; that is, we'll say they are the ones who will provide "room and board" even though it may actually be different. So don't say that you're going to work for the Kerns (which isn't true anyway), but rather that you will live and eat here, and the farm is certainly big enough for that.

My plans (concerning you) have now changed somewhat. If I had you three come from N. Y. to California on borrowed money, it would really not be as good as if I were to go East (N. Y. or Pennsylvania) on my own money, and we started out together there. And only then, after a couple of years, we would move here to California. Here in the West, you see, industry is just starting up…Also, there we would have Mr. Erich Heinz (a friend of Dr. Mueller) in Johnstown, Pa. or the Feuerherdts, who have connections with factories where people always will find work. We could live in an apartment, etc. Also, I know a certain Mr. Skiff (whose son gave me the Kerns' address in San Luis Obispo), who has some kind of connections to GE (in the East).Well, we'll work everything out.

> Many kisses, and here's to an early reunion,
> Your Tumleh [*Helmut spelled in reverse*]

Letter 45   Los Altos, June 11, 1948

Dear Mother, Dear Martin!

I've received some more mail from you. Mostly about affidavits. As I said, the Kerns are going to try to take care of all this. I think the Kerns, their friends, and Mrs. Klinkert are certainly prepared to do that. They can't find out that Dad has a job because the local unions have put a clause against it in the immigration law. Just say that you, or especially Dad, wanted very much to work, but that there is absolutely nothing to be found, and that at best you could help out on a farm.

Once you're here, it will be a different story. This is a trick question that the consulate may put to you sometime, so you would need to be prepared. I like your passport photos very much. Only mother needs to pay a little more attention to her beauty. Mother, you ought to buy a good fat cream [*skin cream rich in oil*], and I'm going to send you a good soap (Palmolive) so that all the little wrinkles will go away. The outfit from Mrs. Klinkert looks swell on you (as far as I can tell from the picture).

Of course, everything is going fine for me too. I'm working now during the haymaking season. Then come the apricots (in about 3 weeks) and after that comes vacation time; that is, then we'll all take turns going to the mountains. Right now I'm developing muscles. Regarding our residence in the United States, there's still nothing special to say—*that is, whether East or West, but it'll probably develop during the summer and fall. Now please quit worrying about everything. It'll all come out all right in the end. The question of affidavit of support will be settled here by the Kerns and Mrs. Klinkert and their friends, most probably during the next month or two.*

With best love, Yours, Helmut

Letter 46   Los Altos, July 3, 1948

My dear Dad!

I finally received your long letter with the temporary address in Lünen. I'm glad that you finally have a hide-out. [*Helmut no doubt meant a place farther away from the Russians*]. Mother has probably kept you up to date about my well being. The situation around Berlin has probably become critical recently. The newspapers here continue to be full of the Berlin situation.

About my dayly routine: I am not taking care of the pullets (baby chicks) in the brooder house. Mrs. Kern does that. I am simply looking after the chickens in houses 1, 2, and 3 and the sheep and calves, i. e. I am collecting the eggs and doing the feeding 7 days a week. Otherwise I am only washing the dishes as regular work; from 8 am to 12 am and about 2 pm to 4:30 pm I do some other things around the place, what-ever there is to do, sometimes with Mr. Kern and sometimes without.

There is for instance working in the hayfield (that Mr. Kern has leased from somebody), or tearing out weeds to make the place look pretty and partly to extinguish the fire danger (you know, it does not rain out here from April till October except once or twice and that dries out the weeds enormously. So in order to keep the dry weeds from burning from a single match or cigarette thrown away carelessly by some visitor, the Kerns have to clean up their place at least once every year).

Right now we're building a shed in the NW corner of the free area west of the barn and workshop, it is something I have never as yet done in my life and I'm sure glad I get an opportunity to help setting it up.

*We are still only working on the foundation, but since we have to finish
the shed before the cots (apricots) are getting ripe in a week or so, I
have to step on it (uns beeilen). But we'll make it all right.*

*Now, I might have made some mistakes in spelling but I think all in
all you'll understand what I mean.*

> *Good luck to you for your job and with a thousand kisses,*
> *Your beloving Helmut*

Paul Dost's Diary, July 12:

The Russian blockade around Berlin seems to get more and more
intense. For weeks, only airplanes have been going back and forth.
There is even some talk about evacuation.. Helmut's first letter
addressed to me arrived on the 12th of this month. He thinks that he
can arrange a sponsorship for us through the Kerns, etc

Letter 47   *Los Atos, August 29, '48*

Dear Ati-Dati! *[Daddy]*
    It's quite a while already since I last dropped you a line. *Although
laziness and no time should not be excuses used in such case, it seems
they are the only way out, right now. Anyway—the apricot harvest is
over for quite a while. August 13th Mrs. Kern left for her vacation for
the Sierra Nevada, which is located in California in Fresno County
about 200 miles SE from here. During that time I was the egg-boss,
that is I was the one who graded and packed the eggs, about 400 every
day. Of course I did other things too.*
    Last Tuesday Mrs. Kern and I went in his [Mr. Kern's] *truck to a
ranch close to Escadero; we went through Stanford LaHonda to San
Gregario which is a little N of Escadero. I have seen so many beautiful
things that it is impossible to relate them any different then by telling
about them personally. One of these days I'll mail a package of
apricots together with vitamins and cigarets to your address. I just
hope you'll get them there. Haven't heard from Mutti for quite a while.
I wonder how everything is going to work out at the Consulate General
in Berlin*

> *Best Wishes, Your Helmut*

Letter 49   San Francisco, Oct. 7, 1948

You Dear Berliners!

Mr. and Mrs. Kern had their vacation in August and September, and now I'm having mine. On the 5th Mr. Kern brought me here. I'm staying with a nice school friend of Mrs. Kern from Stuttgart, a Mrs. Arnstein. The Arnsteins came over here shortly before the outbreak of the war, that is the father, mother, and two children, George and Carole, who seems to be a nice young woman (about 19). Mr. Arnstein died soon afterward and Mrs. Arnstein works as a tailor. George goes to a university in Geneva (Switzerland) and Carole goes to college in Berkeley (near San Francisco). Mrs. Arnstein has a small house here, and I'm being put up in George's room.

I'm going around the city a lot here and looking at a lot of things. I eat breakfast with Mrs. Arnstein and the rest of the meals too, and when I'm somewhere else (in the city) I eat some place there. Enough about me.

Now to you. We're going to investigate further about the affidavit. The Kerns are willing to sponsor Dad. They can hardly do any more. For the two of you we will find someone else. Now to the passage money. If it would be possible to pay the money in westmarks, the Kerns could do it. Of course we would have to reimburse them later here in dollars. Then they would get the money for us somewhere else here. So ask the consulate right away whether it would be possible to pay in westmarks and reply to me immediately.

Mrs. Kern inherited over 100,000 marks which are somewhere in south Germany in the form of certificates. For a long time she received something paid out, maybe $50 a month, until Adolph Hitler stopped it. I think there are still between 250,000 and 150,000 marks in certificates over there. The withdrawal is in process. I don't think this money will be devalued against the westmark, but will be fully exchanged; because it isn't the Kerns' fault that the money is still over there. They should have the full value over there in dollars, about $50,000; in any case about 150,000 westmarks.

You always ask what shape my future will take. Well, I'm going to college—and also think of not going. I will probably stay with the Kerns a couple more months and after that look into a job with Pacific Gas and Electric Company, near Westinghouse, or with GE in San Jose. About three weeks ago I registered for the draft. However, I probably won't be called before '49–'50. Please send a copy of this letter to Dad, so that he also knows the information. I'm going to write him another short letter right away.

All the best and many kisses,
Your Helmut—*Bye-bye*

Letter 50 San Francisco, Oct. 8, 1948

My Dear Dad!

I've just written a letter to the two Berliners, in fact with coupons too, with instructions to send you a copy. We will have the passage money together for you within three months and (if necessary) also the affidavits, only in another way than expected. Enclosed are two sets of coupons. Please use them only if absolutely necessary, as before. Mother has received some too. Stay well and in good spirits, and here's to an early reunion.

Your son, Helmut

Paul Dost's Diary:

October 11: In Berlin Mutti has applied for quota numbers for the U. S. Helmut has not responded yet regarding the travel expenses, etc.

October 24: An airmail letter came from Helmut. He writes that he is planning to arrange for the travel money and the sponsorship.

Letter 52 Los Altos, Dec. 19, 1948

Dear Dad!

Yesterday was mother's birthday. I have certainly thought about that. She will probably have the letter that I got off to her last week. Well, here it is another Christmas already, doesn't the time go by fast. Last week I finally sent out two packages, one to Berlin and one to you. Another one is coming soon with vitamin pills, cigars, etc. Well, my best wishes for Christmas and everything good. Now for current news:

The Kerns are still looking around for sponsors. If they could at least find someone for Mother and Martin, then they themselves would be responsible for you, but that is absolutely the best that they could do. So that's the only thing still lacking. As a residence you could unquestionably give Los Altos, Route 1, Box 588, that's because the Kerns want to transform a stable building into a house and are going to do it soon (we already have the wood).

Fifteen years ago the Kerns had loaned out a concertina and had completely forgotten about it. They've gotten it back and I have it now. Those things are very hard to play, you know, because they aren't like accordion keys. Instead you have to play buttons, which produce various notes when you press them in and out; but I'm getting the hang of it slowly.

Tell me sometime about your money situation, whether you could use a dollar now and then, how much you would get for it, how one would send it over there, or what you could exchange it for.

> Well, all the best,
> Your Helmut

Letter 53   Los Altos, Dec. 20, 1948

My dear Berliners!

I want to try something now that I have never done before: to put together a letter on Monday evening after my work is done. First I wish you all a very happy Christmas (as far as possible) and an equally healthy New Year. Now it should finally be possible to get an entry visa for you.

On my vacation in San Francisco I went exploring around, joined a motorboat tour on the Bay, went swimming, shuffled through the aquarium and some museums, and even went once to Berkeley (behind Oakland), where I (superficially) looked at the famous University of California. Once, on a Sunday, I also visited the Lehners. They are extraordinarily nice people; I was invited to dinner (leg of mutton), and afterwards we all went to the German House, where we danced (I barely). There is a nice young Swiss woman (about 24) working here in Los Altos who came over here about the same time as I. She was at the Kerns' for a picnic once and played wonderful music for us on a concertina; her name is Heidi Soundso. I had danced with her once (about 6–8 weeks ago). Since then I haven't seen her.

Meanwhile the Kerns remembered a concertina that they received about 15 years ago as a gift from some rich people, but which after two years they "borrowed" back again. Now Mr. Kern wrote a sharp letter and the rich man came crawling back here the next day and begged for the Kerns' friendship. Well, now we have the concertina—or rather I do—and Mr. Kern wants to inquire about your sponsorship [*by these friends*] as the occasion presents itself.

The people have a big ranch in the mountains about six miles from here as the crow flies between us and the ocean. It's true that it's mostly still wild land but it also has big flat meadows for their horned cattle; maybe something will work out. Now I am trying frantically to get a few notes out of the concertina. I can play two country waltzes well. Now I'm trying "Ihr Kinderlein Kommet" [*Come Little Children*] and "Oh, Tannenbaum" [*Oh Christmas Tree*]. It's slow going.

Now—since yesterday—I want to finally try to catch up on my debt of letters. I've counted about 30, of which I've already written to the Shawkats, Wahbas, Dad, and you. The rest are coming by Christmas (maybe the next one—1949). Do write a nice letter sometime to Dr. and Mrs. Kern; tell them how quickly you could receive your immigration papers if only you had the affidavits there. Unfortunately I couldn't send the lady's stockings through the letter mail; they will come soon with the vitamin pills that I profitably exchanged for the German postage stamps with a German doctor. So stay healthy and all the best,

Your Helmut

Paul Dost's Diary:

December 28: Letter from Helmut. The Kerns would be willing to sponsor just me; they are still looking for someone to sponsor Mutti and Martin, which I hope will yield some positive results soon.

January 7, 1949:
Yesterday a much-bounced around letter arrived from C. H. Knierim who is looking for engineers to send abroad as train engine technicians and trolley bus installers, etc. Did not accept since emigration to the U. S. is pending.

[*On January 10, 1949 Paul Dost was tragically killed in an industrial accident at the power plant in Lünen where he was working. He suffered third degree burns over most of his body after falling into a high voltage cage when he slipped from a ladder. He died a few hours later. According to the accident report the ladder had a loose rung, but one cannot help but wonder whether the poor condition of his legs may have contributed to the accident. Paul was buried in Lünen, West Germany, near Essen.*]

Letter 54   Los Altos, Jan. 21, 1949

Dear Ones!

I just received your news from Lünen [*of his father's sudden and tragic death*]. Stay strong and be assured that I am with you with my whole heart. You will not have to stay over there much longer. Everything will be set in motion soon. Be well.

Your faithful Helmut

P. S. You will soon have a real letter from Los Altos.

Letter 55   Los Altos, January 23, 1949

My Dear Ones!

Two days ago I received your devastating news. Mrs. Kern and I had just come home from the egg route when we collected the mail; there was a letter in it in a familiar handwriting. Mrs. Kern had now become familiar with Martin's handwriting, but when she saw the "for Helmut E. Dost" she immediately gave me the letter personally and so I learned the sad news then and there. Actually Mrs. Kern regretted giving me the letter right away, but now it was done. Mr. and Mrs. Kern are both very shocked.

In the immediate future they are going to provide the affidavit for one of you themselves and will take care of the second one at the same time. They want to have you over here as soon as possible, so that we three will at least be together. So that you will receive the papers in your hands as soon as possible, tell us please by the fastest means either your final address or one at which you could be reached at any time and which is reliable. [*Maria and Martin stayed in Lünen, West Germany for a short time following Paul's burial*].

I wonder if the Steag [*the power plant*] will pay something. Surely Dad must have been insured. Otherwise it would be enough if they paid your living expenses for the present, as long as you're still over there. Once we're together we will soon be able to forget the terrible things and still remember our Dad.

Christmas and New Years were very quiet here, but after New Years Mrs. Kern was down for a week with the flu. And just at that time one of her cousins who had not been here in 17 years had to come for a visit (from Mexico City). He is a certain Mr. Berthold von Stetten whose family owns the Eichstetten Castle near Augsburg. Incidentally, Mrs. Kern is an acquaintance of the Countess von Wurttemberg who occupied the large estate in Nachod [*a town in Czechoslovakia to which Helmut's school had been evacuated after the Russians entered East Prussia*]. For Christmas I received two cartons of cigarettes, one nice tie, two pairs of work pants, two work shirts, a work jacket, a work rain jacket, and stockings. I have given the Kerns a nice bottle of good brandy in thanks for their kindness.

Have you received your packages? If you need money, you could get it from Mrs. Kern's German account. By the way, Mr. Kern will probably go to Germany in the latter part of next summer (1949) in order to settle various matters, mainly Mrs. Kern's inheritance. Then they would have all the necessary money themselves. They want to furnish a small house for us (as a start). I always have enough to do, so I never get to brooding. Don't worry about me; I'm satisfied with everything. Stay well and let me know your address right away. Mr. and Mrs. Kern will soon write personally.

1000 Kisses, Helmut, *Take it easy.*

Letter 56   Los Altos, Feb. 6, 1949

Dear Ones!

Yesterday I received your letter from Dortmund [*near Lünen*]. It only took five days. Actually I had hoped, in a senseless way, that you could stay in the West; but of course that didn't work out. And now at least you're back in your home neighborhood; that's probably better for you. Mother, if you ever need money, I can send some—in dollars from here, or in Westmarks (through the Kerns) from Schwabia. Just write. How much are you actually earning at the school? How much do the two of you need to live? What could you buy over there now—in groceries and clothes (with prices) and how much is the dollar worth in Berlin? I just want to compare.

Today, or rather soon, I want to send you another package; because about 10 days ago Mr. Kern and I were in the city (San Francisco) and went shopping. For Martin I have 6 pairs of khaki cotton wool socks, 2 pairs of white wool socks, 3 underpants, one warm undershirt, 3 other undershirts, and a warm sport jacket. For mother I have two pairs of warm stockings, and for both of you vitamin pills, and for Martin casein and other things for the liver—and soap, cigarettes, and probably two more jackets of mine.

What I need the most urgently are Martin's measurements, so that I can send him pants, and shirts, and shoes. Tell me exactly how the black shoes fit, which went out with the last package. Mother, you can surely use more. How are you for a corset and shoes? Could you use wool yarn or some gloves? How many? Just write everything, I want to send as much as possible.

Now something else. Dad must surely have been insured; shouldn't you receive a pension? If so, wouldn't it be better to have them give you a one-time settlement? Then you would have enough money for the present, and when you come over here you could leave it to [*friends*]. Because I don't think that you could exchange a hair of deutschmarks into dollars.

You ask how I'm spending my free time. From 6:00–10:00 [*p.m.*] I sit in the easy chair, smoke, listen to the radio (mostly chit-chat), read, study about chickens, think, plan (put in order), go to sleep.

On Sunday evenings I usually go with Mr. Kern to the movies in Palo Alto or Menlo Park. In Palo Alto there's a theater called the *"Stanford"* where we see films like *"The Bishop's Wife," "The Paleface," "Melody Time," "Ocean Liner,"* and so on, good honest American films; and in Menlo Park, which is located about 3 miles beyond Palo Alto, there's a theater called the *"Guild,"* in which mostly German, Italian, French, British, etc. movies are played, where we've seen "Die Fledermaus" (German), *"The Well Digger's Daughter"* (French), *"The Baker's Wife"* (French), *"The Upstairs Room"* (French), *"Carmen"* (Italian*), "A Yank in Rome"* (Italian), *"Fedora"* (Italian), *"Dear Octopus"* (British), *"Hamlet"* (British), and a Scottish one, the name of which I've forgotten. For the rest we have in all eight theaters in the neighborhood, but usually we just go to the two mentioned.

Sundays it's 8:00 eat; 8:30–10:00 hens, calves, and eggs; 12:00 eat and wash up; 5:00 supper; then collect eggs and feed the calves. Between 10:00 and 12:00 I usually read in illustrated magazines like *Life, Post, Look*, etc. and listen to the radio or instead (but seldom) we go to church; between 1 and 5 we sometimes have visitors or I write a letter, or listen to the radio. After 6:00 we sometimes go to the movies, or I read or listen to the radio. I think that's about all I would have to tell you.

Stay well and cheerful, as far as you can; don't worry about anyone or anything. Greet dear Grandma and all the relatives and friends.

1000 kisses, Your Helmut

Letter 57   *Los Altos, Feb. 13, '49*

Dear Mom and Mart,
A few days ago I had your letter dated Jan. 5 in my mail box.
Thanks a lot folks. Everything's still fine around here. I've been fixing
a couple of table and floor lamps for myself and the Kerns and thus
made everybody happy. Your package will get in the mail by Tuesday,
sorry but I couldn't do it any sooner. We are expecting about 700 baby
chicks in about 10 days, so we are busy preparing their accommo-
dations, i. e. the brooders and everything that goes with it. A brooder
is, I guess, what you would call a "Bruthaube," that is supposed to
keep the little chicks (about a day old) at about 100 degrees F.
Chickens still make a lot of work and we never fail to be busy.
We had a pair of newly born lambs last week, one of 'em died,
though; this coming week we are probably going to butcher a young
steer. I think I forgot to tell you about a Schlachtefest [slaughter day]
we had about three weeks ago. A friend of the Kerns butchered a great
big hog. At that Schlachtefest, *which was held at another mutual*
friend's place, I met three lovely girls, one is studying at San Jose State
College and is of Italian descent and both others are of Japanese
parents, sisters they are and one of them studies German at Stanford
University. Though I haven't seen anything of those two, Mariana and
her parents were here yesterday for supper and she said they were
going to get me one of the coming Sundays so that we could go hiking.
By the way, I had sent the Lehners a Christmas card and I think
they are lovely people. But if I were to keep up correspondence, I'ld
have to write to about 50 people every month, and I am not even doing
10% of that. Be good now, and chin up,

1000 kisses, Helmut

Letter 58   Los Altos, March 13, '49

My dear two Berliners!
Once again a Sunday is here, so you're hearing from me again. In
the last two weeks we had two storms; they didn't cause any damage
but we were thoroughly busy. Could you guess how much rain we had?
I think about 130 mm. or 6 inches. Of course all of us here are
especially happy about it. On the south side of the Kerns' farm a stream
bed runs by, which now for the first time in a number of years has

water running in it; and in fact so much that most of it is running over into side streams. Today was the first spring day; it was so nice and warm that we even ate outside. For the first time in several years some frogs are croaking again.

Thank you for your mail. Airmail usually takes 5 days; how long does mine take? I'm glad everything is working out with your pension. Say, see that you buy an accordion, possibly with either 36 or 48 basses, and then bring it over here with you; but maybe not until you get to the West [*West Germany*], because you would probably have to be flown out from there [*Berlin*].Unfortunately I can't send any more packages out [*directly*] from here to Berlin. I just heard on the radio that Stalin definitely has cancer and that his death is expected in 1949 (that's why Molotov rose up).

May things go well with you from here on. Hearty greetings to both of you.

Your Helmut

Letter 60   Los Altos, May 29, '49

Dear Mother!

Yesterday your nice letter arrived which you had mailed from West Germany; it was dated the 19th and stamped on the 24th in Karlsruhe (Baden), so it came to Los Altos in only 4 days—Very fast, wasn't it? Your letter contained much that was new to me. So I want to go through it systematically.

So Martin is earning 150 marks education allowance; great! You'll soon be millionaires, right? And if, as you write, he is 1.71 [*meters*] tall, I am only 1 cm taller; so the poor fellow will still have to wear my discarded things. It's good that he's going rowing; there's nothing wrong with a little physical exercise. Say, does he do gymnastic exercises sometimes on the horizontal bar or ring? I myself—in the evening when I'm tired—do 10 pull-ups from a hanging position. *It's nothing.* The dancing lesson [*Martin's*] is also all right. I came here not very good in dancing. In all the time I've been here I've only had an opportunity twice.

When Mr. Kern will leave isn't known yet; in any case not before September. Say, Mother, wouldn't it be better if you postponed your quotas till next year? Please don't misunderstand me—I mean, how would it be if you came later on to the West [*West Germany*] and waited, let's say, till next summer. Then gradually everything will be

worked out—because by then the Kerns matter will surely be settled
and you could come over here cheerfully and in peace. Till then it
would be better if Martin would take up something practical, let's say a
year of apprenticeship with a mechanic or watchmaker or something
like that, since he's certainly studied enough and will go to school here
anyhow, at least in a continuation high school. It will still take a while
to get travel money and an affidavit in his hands.

Another thing: now that you have some money, have all your little
physical problems (heart, kidneys, legs, teeth, and eyes) completely
taken care of. Have two pairs of glasses made, teeth pulled, bridges
prepared. Otherwise you would impoverish us here.

There's not much more news here. We've just begun to cut hay.
The haymaking will keep us quite busy for about a month.

So: many heartfelt greetings and kisses from your

Helmut

Letter 61   Los Altos, June 12, 1949

Dear Mother!
Haven't heard anything from you Berliners for a long time.
Probably you don't have much time either. Things probably aren't
going too badly for you. Now I have a request to make of you.—on
Friday, June 10, I took my written driving test; in order to learn how
to drive myself I have to have a learner's permit. This card is good
for three months and then I have to pass the driving test. After that
I'll receive the regular driver's license. At the written test I had to
fill out a form and answer some questions. However, because I'm
still under age, the answers must be attested to by my parents, in this
case just you.

Have you ever:
1. *Applied for a driver's license under another name?* <u>*No.*</u>
2. *Failed any exam for a driver's license or been denied a
   driver's license?* <u>*No.*</u>
3. *Had your driver's license revoked?* <u>*No.*</u>
<u>4.</u> *Suffered from paralysis, epilepsy, feeblemindedness, or
   other disabilities or "illnesses" which would restrict your
   ability to drive?* <u>*No.*</u>

5. *Suffered from fainting spells, dizzy spells, mental illnesses,
    or episodes of nervousness?* <u>No.</u>

You only have to confirm these *No* answers. And then of course
go to the consulate, prove your identification as Mrs. Maria Dost,
sign the white paper there in front of the official, and then he
will sign and press his stamp below it. Then put the white and red
papers back in the second envelope and send them back to me as
fast as possible. Do me this favor as soon as you can.

Hearty greetings and kisses from your Helmut

Helmut and mother enroute back to Germany in 1931

Maria, Martin, Helmut and Paul in Germany during the early war years.

*Helmut (front) and
Martin as young
children.*

*Helmut (left) and
Martin as boys in
Berlin*

The Dost family on Helmut's last day in Berlin before leaving for the United States in 1946.

Helmut at age 16. Photo taken during the time he was working in Mr. Roll's shoe repair shop in San Diego.

Helmut next to Tante Guschen's trailer, his first home in the United States

"Tante Guschen"

Helmut and his new friends Hugo Klinkert and Mrs. Klinkert

Helmut with chickens at the Kern farm

*O.K. and Mrs. Kern,
Helmut's employers on
the farm*

*Farmhand Helmut with
Mrs. Kern*

(clockwise, from top left) Lee, Norman, and Hilda Wade as they looked at the time Helmut first met them.

Helmut with some of the farm's animals

Maria and Martin at Paul Dost's grave in Lünen, West Germany, in January 1949

Martin at age 16

*PFC Helmut Dost (age 21) in full dress Marine Corps
uniform, wearing Rifle Expert Badge*

Helmut driving a jeep in Korea

Helmut in Korea

Helmut with Marine buddy

May 1954, Sergeant Helmut Dost, Pomona, California

Christmas 1954, Helmut at China Lake, California

7

Promises, Promises: *The Berliners Still Wait*

Due to a freak accident on the farm which disabled Mrs. Kern, Mr. Kern had to postpone his trip to Europe from the fall of 1949 to the spring of 1950. This situation greatly increased Helmut's responsibilities, as he now had to add most of Mrs. Kern's tasks to his own.

Meanwhile Helmut found a new friend in a teenager, Norman Wade, who came to help with the apricot harvest. He began to visit frequently at the Wades' home in nearby Menlo Park. A high point of Helmut's year was the boys' week-long backpacking trip in the Sierras—one of Helmut's few diversions from his grueling labor on the farm.

Spring of 1950 soon became spring of 1951 and, for reasons that are not entirely clear, Mr. Kern still had not made the required trip to Germany. Since Helmut had become eligible for the draft due to the escalation of the Korean conflict, Mr. Kern had now become even more hesitant to leave the farm.

Later, while preparing to leave for Germany, Mr. Kern suffered a physical breakdown seriously involving his heart. However, since he was not of much help with the strenuous farm work at this point, he went to Germany as planned in June of 1951, leaving Helmut in charge under Mrs. Kern's supervision.

Discouraged with the outlook for his own future, Helmut now began to focus on the fortunes of his brother, offering to fund Martin's education with back-pay owed him by the Kerns—especially if Mr. Kern could pay him in German currency after settling his wife's German inheritance. And surely, with these funds freed up, the Kerns' sponsorship of his family would have to follow soon!

Letter 62   Los Altos, August 31, 1949

Dear Ones!

If you have heard nothing from me in so long, it's mostly due to me. However, in large part it's also because of an accident that Mrs. Kern had, in which she smashed her right knee cap. So here's the story:

After we had finished with all the hay, the apricots began. At first Mr. Kern and I picked them all alone, insofar as we could. Then, when the neighbors offered us the job of picking their apricots, we hired two teams of pickers. So there was intense activity here. Altogether, besides our own, we have to pick the apricots from the trees of four neighbors; 65 acres in all. We've delivered 20 tons of apricots for processing and have dried about 8 tons ourselves. So we were amply busy.

My birthday fell in the second half of the harvest. We celebrated quietly (a bottle of champagne, a cake, a carton of cigarettes). Then two days later on July 20 it happened. Poor Mrs. Kern just wanted to feed the calves and had two feed buckets and a milk bucket under her arms. Actually I usually did that but at the height of the harvest Mrs. Kern had taken over most of my daily chores. Well, she slipped downhill, as if on roller skates, on a particular kind of seeds that had fallen from the trees. Mr. Kern took her to the hospital, where they operated on her immediately for three and a half hours. Then she had to stay in the hospital about three weeks with her leg in a cast.

Now she's been back home for almost four weeks. It's hard for her to get around (only on crutches, of course) and she's just beginning to cook again. Otherwise all the other work she had done before has fallen mostly on me. Meanwhile Mr. Kern and I now had to scrape the dried apricots from the trays and deliver them. Then we're still taking the hay out of the field now. The pullets (grown baby chicks) also began to lay already and quickly had to be transferred to a laying house, and at the same time be inoculated. Besides that, the prune harvest also came now, but that, thank Heaven, is already over. Approximately half a ton are lying on the trays to dry. Next week, on Wednesday, Mr. Kern and I are driving to Sacramento (the capital city of California) to the *"state fair."* Two years ago I was with the Rolls at the San Diego county fair. Every county has its own *"fair,"* and there is also a *state fair*, at which the counties of the state have exhibits all together. Mainly we want to look at horned cattle and farm machinery.

By the way, I completely forgot to tell you that, since 10 days ago, I am the lucky owner of a young dog. As chance would have it, he is an animal of the pointer breed about three months old. He is terrifically devoted and doesn't even mind having his paws stepped on all the time. His name is "Fritzie."

Because of his wife's accident Mr. Kern will not leave before October. About the accordion: if you can get hold of an old one, otherwise forget about it. Here they cost $500 (a good one), which is as much as a good used car. But if you could bring me a wrist watch, that would be wonderful. Regarding the vitamin pills, I had sent part of them to Dad at the beginning of January, and they never came back. Then a quarter went to you at the same time, but they did come back, because at that time package mailings to the Russian zone were stopped (and also to Berlin).

Well, warm greetings and kisses to you both,
from your Helmut

P.S. Last Saturday I was with Mr. Kern at a private reading of the famous poet Ernst Wichert. The old man was here for a couple of weeks at Stanford and has read from his works (which are very anti-Hitler). Mr. Kern talked with him personally.

Good Night

Letter 63   Los Altos, Nov. 6, 1949

Dear Patient Ones!

Finally another letter to you is coming about. Many thanks for your kind mail and, above all, I was happy with the really nice passport photos from August. I also have an enlargement of the picture of Dad's grave from Lünen with the enclosure from January. The Kerns were also immensely pleased about your letter. As I said, when the Kerns have your travel money, you'll be here in no time. Well, now about me.

On October 3, I went on vacation to San Diego. I rode down in a bus. It took 18 hours. Hugo was very nice and I slept in the Klinkerts' little house. I visited the Rolls, McComas, and Heuscheles, as well as Mrs. Kimbal and Mr. Andreen of the Welfare and Junior Ward, and the school. Then, of course, I also visited Tante Guschen in El Cajon. She's still living the same as before, was very nice, and lonely. She complained senselessly about how much the Germans were taking out of her pocket [*possibly people to whom she was sending packages?*] and doesn't know for sure if she should have her own little house built on her piece of land.

On Saturday, October 8 Hugo, his girl friend, her girl friend, and I
went to a first-rate dance and on the following Sunday the four of us
went out of San Diego into the mountains. (We wandered around for
three hours and then happily returned home). So then at 10:00 I went
back north. Since then Mr. Kern has also been on vacation. Also we've
worked hard on your little house, butchered another calf, I learned to
drive (I finally have the license now), cleared out the hen houses, and
got the eggs out.

Mr. Kern probably can't make it to Germany anymore this year.
Mrs. Kern is doing better. I also had some mail from Grandma; I want
to write to her too. The coupons are finally enclosed. I'll write more
another time.

Warm greetings and kisses and all the best,
Your Helmut

Letter 64   Los Altos, December 11, 1949

Dear Mother!

Your birthday has once again arrived, which you hopefully will
celebrate in good health and happy spirits in the circle of your good
friends and with dear Mart. My greetings must unfortunately come
from a distance, but surely now for the last time. Unfortunately I have
nothing more for you than these two tiny little pictures; but they give
you an idea of what I look like; I'm 1.74 (5' 8 and 1/2") tall (in socks);
hopefully Martin isn't any taller.

Unfortunately, Fritzie went to the animal shelter; he was a little too
wild, actually a hunting dog who never in his life would belong on a
chicken farm. I sure felt bad, but it had to be—*sooner or later.* Your
(our) little house has the roof on it now and the window frames are in.
Our carpenter is usually drunk and that's why the work is taking so
long.

Mr. Kern (O. K.) is going to Germany as soon as possible, which is
probably the Spring of 1950. Mother, this is the situation: If the
consulate has worked on your documents and lacks the sponsorship
document, it can't tell us anything. But as soon as we send the
sponsorship [*affidavit of support*], the processing of your papers will be
completed, and that means you will be told, "Here is your visa. It's
valid from (let's say) January 10, 1950 to April 10, 1950." Then we
could hustle here and maybe (also maybe not) scrape together the
passage money. But that isn't the worst thing; where would you live?

Why not have everything ready first (the house finished, passage money obtained, etc.)? Then if everything goes well, you could live in a house instead of living here, maybe three months, in tents being eaten up by snakes. This much is certain:

You'll come to the U. S. in 1950. The Kerns will give you the affidavit; but only when all the preparations have been made. It probably won't be later than March-May, because then we can use you here during the harvest. So don't worry.

I can already drive very well (Mrs. Kern says). During the last 14 days I've learned how to drive a tractor. That's a kind of caterpillar tractor (Raupenschepper) which they use here instead of horses for plowing, sowing, and harrowing; also a lot of scrubbing out the hen houses, packing eggs, etc. Mrs. Kern can bend her leg 90 degrees again; but it's still weak; she has to exercise and walk a lot, but without crutches, just with a cane. So, "Happy Birthday" and all the best from here on out, and many greetings and kisses to you and Mart.

from Your Helmut

Letter 66   Los Altos, Dec. 25, 1949

You Two Dear Ones!

I'm sitting here full of duck, red cabbage, potatoes, celery, olives, gravy, burgundy, water—coffee, chocolate cream, cookies, liquer, and cigarettes. It was a magnificent meal; and good Mrs. Kern played a trick on me with regard to washing up. She said after dinner, "Let's rest for half an hour first and then we'll wash dishes together;" but when I went over (to wash up) everything was already done, so you'll get a couple of lines from me right now.

To my greatest surprise and joy your lovely little package arrived, together with one to the Kerns from their sister, on exactly the 23rd; of course we kept them until Christmas Eve. There could hardly have been a nicer Christmas if you had put yourselves into the package and we had been happily united under the Christmas tree. But it was really one of the nicest that I have ever had. At 7:30 the presents were distributed. For Mr. Kern I had a bootjack (made by myself) and a bottle of liquer, and for Mrs. Kern a bottle of cologne and 100 clothes pins. I made them very happy since I had previously told them that I didn't have anything for them.

I myself received a belt from Dave MacKenzie (who lives with us in the little house down below), two pairs of British socks from the Sokol family (the Austrian professor of Southeast Asian culture, especially eastern India), $1.00 from the Stottman family (on the egg route; you know, just like you give Mrs. Heide, etc. 5 marks at Christmas), a wonderful little radio from the Kerns, also a lovely checkered flannel shirt, and a "cigarette case-lighter combination" from the Blinns (friends—German nursery). And of course your lovely package. Everything was in it as listed. Hearty thanks for everything. The marzipan was delicious, and the chocolate, well, I haven't tasted it yet, and these many pictures—I just showed them all to the Kerns—and the Mikado game, yes, and above all this nice little wristwatch; that was something extra special. This morning we went to communion at 8:30 a.m., and afterwards was the best time to take a few more snapshots. So you will soon get some more pictures.

So Gummbei (goodbye) now. Many affectionate greetings and a happy, healthy new year with a lot of traveling.

Your Helmut

Letter 68   *Los Altos, March 19, 1950*

Dear Folks,

Sorry about my long silence; I know, it is inexcusable and I can only ask for your forgiveness. I was fine all this time and very busy with a new hobby I acquired about four months ago. In November I started to knit a pair of stockings; after knitting about one hour every second or third night I finally got them done in January. [It was not unusual for German men to knit. Even Helmut's father knew how!] *They turned out nicely under Mrs. Kern's instruction and supervision and were finally completed in January or maybe February—and they fit too. Now in February I started on a sweater which is in its last stages now. I finished rear and front and one sleeve, and am working on the second one (I mean sleeve). All I have to do after I've finished that second sleeve is to sew all four parts together and add another two inches around the neck for a neckband. That's all for now. Wish me luck that the thing is going to fit. I have four pictures for you which shall follow as soon as I get a few 15-cent stamps; this was just to be a short note of good health. Now, bye-bye and good luck.*

Your Helmut

Letter 69 *Los Altos, March 23, 1950*

Hi Mom, Hi Mart,

How's everything out your way? Everything ok out here. Mr. Kern is just getting ready for his small spring vacation which is going to get under way on Monday. He will leave for Mt. Lassen in northeastern Calif. where there is supposed to be a lot of snow; you see, he likes to ski. We've had a very mild winter so far, but as it is we still don't have enough rain to see us through a normal summer. We can just keep hoping for some more of that precious moisture. Otherwise we will have to start sprinkling (irrigating) very soon. But then we will still have quite a little time ahead of us during which to expect rain.

As I might have written earlier, Mr. Kern and a very rich neighbor of ours have sort of gone together (into partnership) to raise beef cattle. So we were very busy, recently, building and repairing fences (aren't we always). Aside of that of course we did some work on the little cottage we are building for you "Germans." The electricity is in now and the waterline is up to the house and already we built a small bathroom including a toilet, washbasin, and shower. Although this is not quite finished we already have somebody living in the house. It is a friend of ours, who is very modest and of course very simple in his way of living. He usually does all the disking [light plowing] *for the Kerns and is not going to stay with us very long.*

On March 3, about three and a half weeks ago, O. K. and I went to Modesto in the San Joachim Valley (about 300 miles over and back) in order to get the 600 baby chicks; they are about 4 weeks old and just wonderfully developed. Well, you'll experience it all personally next year. O.K. still wants to go to Germany in August, and after that everything will surely be settled. There certainly won't be a war because all sides are too afraid of the notorious H (ydrogen) bomb. So don't worry.

My pullover is finished except for the collar and sewing it together. I'm going to take some more pictures. *Bye-bye now and be good.*

1000 kisses and all the good wishes, Your Helmut

[The following is a letter from Martin to Helmut, written in English. The underlining is Helmut's. The next letter, Number 71, is Helmut's rewritten and "corrected" version done for Martin's benefit.]

Letter 70   Berlin, March 27, '50

Dear Mr. Helmut!

*   At first have my best wishes for the Easter days. Our holidays begin on the day after tomorrow and end on the 13th of April; I'll be busy these days. F. i. [for instance?] I must read Schiller's tale "Don Carlos," "Kabal & Liebe" and besides I'll finish "Jury Jenatsch" (K. F. Meyer) and some English tales. In school-time there is no time to read. I've also made up my mind to build a little weekend-house with pasteboard, etc. Our teacher, Mr. Gollin, had ordered to make as an architect the plans for such a house (6 x 8). Dear Helmut, many thanks for your letter, you had written in English. Please, be not too hard with me, if you find the many big faults. Last week we have learned the poem "A Psalm of Life" by Henry Longfellow. It is a nice poem with serious contents. How we long for the announced letter with the four pictures.*

*   We were amused very much to hear that your last hobby-horse is knitting stockings and pullovers. In Egypt we had learnt it at first at school, isn't it? If we could do it we would send you some 15-cent stamps for our letters; but I think that you would not like it much to write us nevertheless. But the stars are due to it, for all "krebs" men—like Kurt Merboth and Uncle Hassan—don't like writing.* [Krebs, meaning crab, refers to the Zodiac sign of Cancer, which was Helmut's astrological sign]. *We have not yet heard if you know anything of the existence of our accordeon, and many other questions, we have put a long time ago. Or do you mean that we shall hear all these answers of you personally? That would be the best result.*

*   Yesterday the weather was very nice and for this reason we made a walk to the "Rehberge." After this walk we were in the "Mercedes-palast" near "Sustr." to see the colored film "Die Konigen vom Broadway"* [The Queen of Broadway] *with Rita Hayworth and Victor Mature. — We have not yet received the money, we must get from the Insurance Company in Aachen; everything is uncertain. Some days ago we received our 2 luggage pieces we had left in Bremen. Some of these clothes of Vati* [Dad] *are still very good, and we were anxious that they could perhaps go lost in the Magazine of the AEG. Among these things were f. i. 2 boxes of Circle, Vati's daily notebooks, many family documents and pictures, camel hair blankets, etc. Mr. Niessingh had arranged the transport...*

*   Now, have a good-night kiss of little Martin*

Letter 71 Berlin, 3, 27, '50

Dear Mr. Helmut,

First of all have my best wishes for the Easterdays. Our Easter vacations begin day after tomorrow and end on April 13; I'll be very busy (during that time); (f. i.) I am supposed to read.....During school days there is no time to read.....weekend cottage out of cardboard, etc...had ordered (had told) us to make plans (or a plan) for a little house like that, as an architect would.....for the letter you had written in English. Please don't be too hard on me for the many big mistakes I make. We learned the poem.....last week.....How we wish for.....We were very amused to hear about your latest (I hope not last) hobby to knit.....Didn't we first learn to knit (when we started) school in Egypt. If we were able to do so, we would buy you some 15-cent stamps for our letters; but I don't think that you would like to write much just the same (or nevertheless). But it is due to the stars; .....don't like to write....., whether you.....Accordion and the answers to many other questions we had put to you a long time ago.....?.....the best solution.....and so we took a walk....After that walk we went into the.....colored picture.....(We did not yet receive) the money we were supposed to get.....;.....A few days ago.....2 pieces of luggage.....of Vati's....., ...were afraid.....get lost in the warehouse of the AEG.....arranged for the .....kiss from

Martin

Letter 72 *Los Altos, April 4, '50*

Dear Martin,

I want to thank you so much for that really nice letter you sent me. I showed it to Mr. and Mrs. Kern and they both agreed that it was simply marvelous that a German boy, or should I say young man, can actually write such good English; they said—and I certainly had to agree—that no American who had never had an opportunity to speak the language in Germany could have ever written a letter in German with such natural fluct and still so completely understandable as you have proven you can. I am sending you back your letter, with my version of it and a complete explanation to every (im)possible mistake; I hope everything will be quite clear to you.

I am honestly sorry, if I never mentioned the Tonelly Accordion you bought. It certainly sounds like a good deal (Herr Kern returned

*from his short ski-vacation just yesterday; he was bubbling with joy
and good naturedness (he had been a little grouchy before he left) and
says he had generally a splendid time. He went due East (due east
means generally East) about 200 mi. to Yosemite National Park, then
due NNW to Lassen Volcanic Natl. Park and due SSW back home. He
went skiing and looked in on several friends; the whole trip was about
1200 mi. long. In about 2 weeks Mrs. Kern and I are going to take a
similar trip, but it is going to be quite a bit shorter because we will only
be able to get away for about 5 days but we'll have a good time.*

*My sweater is all finished; it fits fine and looks good! Good night
now. Many kisses and all the good wishes to you and Mutti from*

Your Helmut

Letter 73   *Los Altos, June 6, '50*

Dear Mom,

*Had your letter yesterday and thanks very much. The only darling
ever has been you; I hope you'll keep that in mind.* [Helmut's mother
has probably asked him if he has a girl friend who is occupying his
time]. *Do you know why I don't write so often? It's because I feel no
urge at all, I am with you constantly. When I am in the chickenhouse,
feeding my little dependants, I am talking to you, explaining to you and
Martin how to put the egg into the bucket; can you understand that?
I've never really been seperated from you.*

*We are only living over here, and nothing else; one has to work
hard, very hard for a living. One might have a few more comforts like
an automobile or so, but then one has to travel a distance of maybe 50
mi. whereas in Germany one would walk around the block. But just
because one happens to live in California does not mean that it is
paradise. So never once think that I am not your ever loving son.*

*Our vacation went off beautifully; we went up north to Live Oak
(between Yuba City and Chico), where we stayed with the Grunwalds;
one day we went up to Gridley and visited some other friends, then
another day we went to Chico and Richardson Springs, and back again
over Oroville. The whole trip took 5 days and Mrs. K. and I sure had a
jolly good time. I drove the car about half the time.*

*Right now I am awfully tired. I'll make the rest as short as
possible. I had my violin repaired (two little cracks from the voyage)
but decided to exchange it for a good repaired guitar, so now I am*

trying to study playing the guitar, which is certainly more popular than the violin. I like it better, too.

On May 20 I shaved for the first time.

That reminds me. You used the word darling where you should have used the word sweetheart. Darling is the term to use in case of closer relationship through blood or marriage (you are my darling); but if I had a girlfriend she would be my sweetheart. So goodnight everybody and an extra-special kiss to you dear Mom,

Helmut

Letter 74 *Los Altos, Sept. 1950*

Hi Folks,

I'm sorry, I must confess that I did not spoil you with any letter. The harvesting of the hay went comparatively easy, because we had a friend helping us. And, for the first time, this year we had all of our hay in the barn, before the apricots started. These in turn were pretty easy harvesting too. Although we worked long hours, it was half as bad as it could have been. Altogether we harvested approximately 65 tons of apricots, sending most of them to a cannery for juice, drying only a few.

Among other people cutting cots for us this year, we had a boy coming with whom I soon made friends. He is only 14 years old, but very advanced for his age. We are getting along very well. Well, since I was going to spend my vacation in the Sierra Nevada this year, and he was going there anyway, we decided to go together. First Mrs. Kern left for the mountains; then, when she couldn't get around the way she wanted, Mr. Kern joined her a week later, leaving the farm in my care.

Actually this was the first vacation the Kerns had together in 10 years, so I am really proud of the fact that I made it possible. During the time that the Kerns were away, Norm (that's my friend's name, Norman Wade) and I delivered the dryed apricots to the Association, and had a generally good time. Mr. and Mrs. Kern came back on Saturday, the 19th of Aug. and Norm and I left on Tuesday, Aug. 22, with another Los Altos boy, Wendell Lehr, 23 years, who owns a beautyful new Ford.

We left Los Altos at 5 o'clock, had supper in Los Banos, stopped shortly at Madera, and at Friant dam, and reached Huntington Lake at midnight, on the dot. We camped there for the night, had breakfast the other morning at the last restaurant, and drove the last twenty or so miles to Florence Lake, where we abandoned the car and started hiking. Florence Lake is about 7000 ft. above sea-level.

Well, we hiked about 65 miles in one week, making 10 or 15 miles a day, staying a day or so where ever we liked specially well. Second night we camped at 7600, then up at 10,000, next down to 9300, up to a lake (Lake Italy - 11,200). At Lake Italy we split up though; Wendell went on down Mono Creek to Mono Hot Springs, whereas Norm and I hiked to Florence Lake, picked up Wendell's car, and drove it around to Mono Hot Springs, where we picked up Wendell the next day. All in all we had a wonderful time, sunburn, blisters, and all. I am pretty tired now as you can probably see by the many mistakes I am making. Good night, now

With many greetings and kisses, your Helmut

Letter 75   *Los Altos, Nov. 12, '50*

Hello, Darlings,

How are you getting along? I was glad to hear that you are going to have a little more comfortable a winter ahead with glass in your windows and some heat. I was wondering whether there were still as strict controls over your consumption of electricity and gas as there were before I left Berlin. And I am sure happy to know that Mart is seeing an opera occasionally (or rather quite frequently), and has a chance to listen to some good music too. The only such entertainment you can have around here is the opera during winter in S. Francisco, but we have some very good concerts over the radio. Really the only outside entertainment we have is the movies (a television set we don't have); dancing is nothing special in this country. So I take to knitting in my spare time. We saw an amazingly good picture a week ago, it was "Hamlet" with Sir Laurence Olivier, Jean Simmons, etc. a wonderful word-for-word production of Shakespeare's masterpiece—better than it could have been done on any stage. We all enjoyed it tremendously. No wonder they gave it five Motion Picture Academy Awards (Film Akademie Auszeichungen).

About once a week I spend an evening with the Wades, watching Television, or Norm and I driving around a little. Last Sunday they came out here, where I joined them in a rifle shooting contest in a little neighboring gulch (small valley). I was right around the middle in my scores.

Mr. Kern is going to Oakland tomorrow, to arrange the last preparations for the Germany trip; so maybe he will be over there soon to arrange for your coming here. But today there is still nothing definite. He wants to go soon before I might possibly be called up, since I'm liable for military service.

Stay well and be heartily greeted and kissed by Your Helmut

P.S. *Don't write or say Mr. Dr. Kern. Only Mr. Kern or Dr. Kern.*

Letter 76 *Los Altos, Dec. 10. '50*

Dear Mom,

Birthday time is here again and yours is the first. I wish you many happy returns of the day and God bless you. You have been so very patient with me, not scolding me too much for writing so few letters; but then, you understand. Again, as in all other years, I have no special gift for you, except your constant memory and my gratitude for your patience. Things that I could send you could buy in much better quality over there, I know.

Like now, I am making about half a dozen coin purses; you know, the kind that you fold together. I have never seen one of this kind in the USA; but, because it is the best model I have ever seen, I am making one for every one of my special friends: Mrs. Klinkert, and Hugo, Mr. and Mrs. Kern, Norm Wade, Dave MacKenzie, and myself. The kind of purses you can buy over here is really very unpractical, so everybody is keeping his change in his pocket, and thereby ruining the lining. And yet, if I made one for you and Mart I know that they wouldn't even come close to the quality of coin purses you could buy over there. So please don't expect anything for birthdays and Xmas except my love.

Mr. Kern's sweater has progressed to a point of near completion, only neck and sewing together to be done. His Germany-trip only depends on one paper with certain signatures to arrive from Stuttgart. Mrs. Kern is busy baking cookies for Christmas, that being the gifts that are given away for Xmas.

How are you two kids getting along? Is Mart going to be able to finish high school? I just hope you will be coming over here soon now. We would have so much fun together. How are all my friends? Tell them that I send my best regards. Well, goodnight for today and a happy birthday,

Your loving Helmut

Letter 77   *Los Altos, Dec. 19, 50*

Dear Mom, dear Mart,
First of all let me wish you a very, very merry Christmas and a
quiet if not wonderfully happy New Year. Mr. Kern just came back from
S. F. [San Francisco] *and reported that his Germany voyage will take*
place in the very near future, early part of 1951. Since they are drafting
men my age left and right, he will naturally try to get away just as soon
as possible, so that I will at least be here while he is over in Germany.
In other words, you will very likely be here by next Christmas; we are
all looking foreward to it.
One certain package from Berlin came in today's mail, which I
gave to Mrs. Kern to place under the Christmas tree. My leatherwork is
coming along very well. I have finished 6 coinpurses, only 3 more to
go, then one wallet and one book cover. Mr. Kern's skisweater was
finished last Sunday. After Christmas I will make one Pudelmutze [a
fluffy cap] *and a pair of mittens from the same wool, so that he will be*
ready for the German snow.
The Korean situation looks pretty gloomy, but as a rule I like to
keep my mind on a lot nicer things. You know you can go crazy
thinking too much about the great mess we can get so easily into, but if
you don't think about it the world will not be any better or worse off
than if you do. How are you two holding out? Although the world
certainly is in a turmoil, there certainly is but little cause for alarm,
none at all for panic. I hear that Berlin is taking it stoically easy.
Well the best of luck to you both for 1951 and a merry Yule-tide,
10,000 kisses,

Your Helmut

Letter 78   Los Altos, January 4, 1951

Dear Mother, dear Martin!
Thank you for both of your nice little Christmas packages. The
contents were really delicious. I haven't touched the marzipan pig yet.
Otherwise everything tasted great. Say, are there by any chance more of
these chocolate cigarettes available to buy, so that a person could fill
this nice little box up again; everyone liked them so much. Dad's
lighter is standing on my little table and is used with each cigarette.
From Mrs. Kern I got two pairs of pyjamas, a flannel shirt, and a
bowl with marzipan strawberries, from OK chocolate and a one-year

subscription to a very good monthly magazine (illustrated): *"Popular Mechanics."* From Sokols a special sandwich-toaster, from Mrs. Sievers a pair of stockings, from Dave MacKenzie a $5.00 gift certificate, for which I can get $5.00 worth of goods at a certain store, and a few dollars from several egg route customers. With the money I bought myself a good white shirt, two *bowties* (I think they're called Fliegen in German), and one pair of cuff links and a tie pin to match. So the whole thing made me very happy. I spent New Years Eve and New Years Day with the Wades.

Now to you. Mr. Kern was in San Francisco today about his passport. Now the whole trip depends only upon the decision of the Oakland judge. Mr. Kern will explain everything to you over there. If all goes well, he will be there about February.

> With greetings and kisses,
> Your Helmut

Letter 79   Los Altos, Jan. 8, '51

Dear Marty,

First of all let me wish a very happy birthday among your mother and friends; say hello to everybody for me, won't you?

Thanks for those nice pictures in the Xmas package; I believe that I had forgotten to mention them before. It really looks as though Mom has put on quite a bit of weight lately. I was happy to see that you were both looking pretty good.

Now then let me get to this business about the president's right to veto any law-to-be. You probably know the Constitution of the USA. I hope I do not have to go into that. I would just like to explain the process of vetoing and let you puzzle it out yourself. First of all the president is elected by the citizens of the USA on a more than half majority; otherwise he is being elected in Congress.

This makes him usually the representative of more than 50% of the USA citizens. Congress is elected on a basis of about 1 representative to 300,000 people in the House of Representatives, and 2 senators from each state in the Senate. After Congress has passed a bill (law in proposition) through both House and Senate on a mere 50% maj., the bill goes to the White House, where, if the President agrees, it is made law by his signature; otherwise he vetoes it and sends it back to Congress with his reasons for having vetoed it. Then, after having taken all reasons into consideration, Congress votes once more on the passage of the bill, which this time requires 2/3 maj. to make it law and of course no signature of the President, which it would not get anyway.

Good night now and God bless you.
Helmut

Letter 80   *Los Altos, March 2, '51*

Hi Mom, Marty,
  Thanks for your really very nice letters. There was of course no reason at all for me not to write to you, so please forgive me. I didn't feel very good for quite a long time. You have probably heard about the flu-epidemic that we have been housing in and around San Francisco; that means that there is virtually no one around here who hasn't had at least a cold, or even pneumonia.
  On February 16 I received an order to report to the Armed Forces Physical Examination. This letter sure set some wheels magically into motion. The examination was to be in 10 days on February 28, '51 (exactly 3 years after my arrival at the Kerns' ranch). Well, usually it takes 4 to 8 weeks after the examination for one who has been accepted physically to be called into the Armed Forces.
  That would of course not have left enough time for Mr. Kern, whose Germany trip had to be postponed one month anyway (because of legal complications), to go to Germany while I was (under Mrs. Kern's guidance) taking care of the farm. So Mr. Kern asked for a deferment of my induction until at least October of 1951. No answer as yet as to that request.
  Well on Wednesday February 28, '51 I was herded into a Greyhound bus at San Jose, together with a lot of other young fellows my age. We were taken to San Francisco, where we had to fill out a lot of forms, answer a lot of questions, etc. Towards evening I got home again. Next week is supposed to bring us a lot of news now. First of all the official report of my physical examination and my consequent classification; secondly the report upon my deferment, whether yes or no; thirdly a Court's decision as to inheritances and their payability from here to Germany and visa versa.
  How would it be for you to study land surveying, Martin; that's a well paid field here in America. Mr. and Mrs. Kern, both of whom have also taken a course in water conservation, think that Germany is about

10 years behind in the development and application of teaching. Will write more soon.

Goodbye, your little Helmut

Letter 81 *Los Altos, May 11, '51*

Dear Mom, hia Marty,

I had your very nice letter with the pictures in the mail today. I am really sorry for not having written sooner; there is no excuse other than no initiative; although it is true that we had pretty rough going for a while. You know of course that there always had been a certain unclarity and uncertainty about my being drafted, which kept Mr. Kern from taking his trip to Germany. Well, as the draft rules have been considerably slackened in regard to farm employees, Mr. Kern had decided to go quickly and take a chance on my not being called into service. Now guess what happened.

Preparing for his absence, he speeded up his fence-building project to such an extent that he has suffered a sort of physical break-down. Now he cannot even walk for just a short distance without getting out of breath. Since his heart has been affected too he some-times gets attacks paired with severe pain in the chest, rising into his neck and arms. He can do some light physical work, but since there is very little of that on a farm, we all decided he was of little or no use to us over here in his present condition.

So Mr. Kern got himself a ticket on the German ship "Homeland" to sail from New York on the first of June. In other words, he will see you sometime in July probably. Let's hope his trip will come true this time. This constant waiting for him to go has affected all of us, as well as you two and all the other relatives of Kerns in Germany. Mabruk. [Arabic: Good luck, or May all go well.]

As to our general state of health...we are all in fine condition. I see Norm Wade quite often. Last Sunday we went to a church picnic in the Santa Cruz Mountains. Lots of fun. I played the first baseball in my life. Also Norm and I have been doing some target shooting. Your little Easter package had been received with great pleasure and I know what a great crime I committed by not letting you know sooner. My guitar had been in repair for a while, I am playing it again (not enough, though); whenever I have a chance I play the piano too (whenever we are invited to people who own one). I know a few verses of "Good Night Irene."

I am still on the farm and studying to be a chicken farmer (for the time being anyway). I like it fine. I'll stay here till I have my own place or Uncle Sam wants me in the Army.

Now to you, Marty, and your career. I have been thinking a lot about our future, because it must be referred to as ours together. I hope to be owning a chicken ranch of my own someday in the future, by no means because I want to be a chicken farmer, but because it is the only way I know of to make a living.

It would be good for you to study something good (Electricity, Gasolene-or Diesel engines) like especially Diesel Engineering or even Mining Engineering; study it as far as you get. Then when you can come over here, you can work on the farm for a while, if you want to, or, with enough training, get a pretty good job with some larger company in your line of study, just to get the practical experience and money for further training at some university over here. In the mean-time you can teach your brother a few things he has missed. What I mean to say is: go right ahead with any good study and some practical training if you can get it.

I am very tired right now. So good night and God bless you,

Your Helmut

Letter 82   *Los Altos, August 4, '51*

Hi, folks,

You don't know just how happy you have made me with your so very nice birthday letters, with the pictures and that package, which arrived only about a week ago. My birthday was spent in a rather quiet way in the busiest season of the year, as usual. Dave was here and so was Norm, of course; and Johann and Molly (2 additions from Austria) [who were working on the farm]. We had a nice little picnic on the Sunday after the birthday with fried chicken, cream puffs, and choco-late nut cake (all made by Molly).

From Mrs. Kern I got a nice leather case for personal articles (something about 4 times as large as your shaving set case) with nothing in it though; so your little set with the nice shaving articles was really very welcome; thanks, a million. You know, when I saw that cigaret case from those Egyptian cigarets I almost fell over backwards, but when I realized that the content consisted of pure chocolate, I was extremely happy; you see, I had given up smoking about 6 weeks ago. Really thanks a lot for everything.

You know, as Mr. Kern left us we were approached by a Lutheran organization whether we could not take in an elderly Austrian couple, who had been brought over by the organization, but didn't get along so well with the people that had signed for them; that was because that Austrian couple spoke only German and Yugoslav. Since Mr. Kern's bedroom was unoccupied Mrs. Kern accepted them; in other words, as soon as our family decreased by one it increased by two.

Well Johann and Molly finally caught on to our farming operations, so that they were able to feed the chickens and collect the eggs—and even feed the cows. Johann, a round little man of about 60 years, who is a typesetter by trade, is very handy with small tools, but so exact that his work usually takes much too long. Well, he and I together rebuilt a large section of chickenhouse fence, cleaned chicken houses and yards, built in a number of dark nestrooms.

I even went on a trip to Yosemite with Norman, of which I am going to enclose a few snapshots. During the apricot harvest Molly was really coming in very handy, because she cut all those apricots that fell on the ground and under usual circumstances would have spoilt. Now we finally found a real job for Johann in Palo Alto at a small printing place. Molly is still with us and will stay here until OK comes back, which may be only in October. You see, Mr. Kern seems to be really pretty bad off. He was told, that if he wanted to get cured entirely, he would have to stay at Hirsau for about 10 weeks; so I doubt that he will come by Berlin before later on in September

About yourself, now, Mart. You see, I had authorized Mr. Kern to give you D. Marks [deutschmarks] from Mrs. Kern's conto [bank account] over there, and in this way repay me partly for my services over here. If you will let me know how much one year of studying at, shall we say, the Technical High School [college] in Berlin-Charlottenburg should cost you, including all your food and other expenses, maybe I could talk it over with Mrs. Kern over here.

Of course, I would certainly not like to tell you what you should do with your future over there, and I surely don't know a thing about university conditions, and openings, and possibilities of study in Germany; but it seems to me that you might jump at the chance of studying for a few years, or at least until I can get you over here myself. And since the Kerns have enough marks in Germany, that may be spent over there only, I will probably get a better deal if I accept payment for my work over here in the past in marks and invest it in a

*good education for you, right then and there. In other words here is
what I would like to know:*

*1) Would you consider a university education, even only for a year or
two at my expense, partly; or would you prefer to start work for AEG
next year, for which I certainly could not blame you.*

*2) Please write me about your chances of getting started at Technical
High School next fall or at any other university of your choice.*

*3) Write me, whatever supplementary amount of money you think you
two will need monthly in addition to mother's pension, salary, and
whatever money there should be on hand; all sources and expenses
figured in.*

4) What do you think of the whole thing?

*If this war scare continues and I should be drafted, I hope they will
consider my knowledge of German and English and send me to Europe.
Well, I am not in yet and don't expect to hear from the draftboard until
Mr. Kern is back.*

Be well and God bless you both.
Your Helmut

8

Rescued by the Marines: *From Korea With Love*

By September 1951 the draft had finally caught up with Helmut. Chapter 8 begins with his first letter written in the U. S. Marine Corps and follows his basic training in California and first few months of service in Korea. By this time Helmut was writing virtually all of his letters in English. It was during this period that Helmut began saving the letters from Martin and his mother, which now give us the view from Germany.

From Korea, Helmut (now 21) sets in motion the process for personally sponsoring his mother's immigration. O. K. Kern, however, still has not come through with a firm commitment to sponsor Martin. Maria thinks of coming to America by herself, ahead of him, but as West Berlin is increasingly cut off by the Russians, she becomes hesitant to leave her younger son there alone.

Why, one wonders, did Helmut not give up on the Kerns at this point and seriously approach other persons as possible sponsors? No doubt it was very uncomfortable to ask people whom his family had never met, or had not seen in many years, to undertake such a serious commitment.

In Korea, Helmut wisely takes advantage of an opportunity to transfer out of Reconnaissance with its dangerous activities behind enemy lines. This decision is soon validated when his best friend is severely wounded after volunteering for the front. Subsequently Helmut is shifted back and forth from one mundane job after another during the remainder of his overseas tour.

Meanwhile, in Germany, Martin is working as a student-trainee with AEG and applying for admission to the prestigious Berlin

Technical University. There is a perverse irony in the contrast between
Martin's stimulating educational, social, and cultural opportunities in
beleaguered West Berlin and Helmut's drab existence as an American
draftee just across the river from communist North Korea.

⌘

Letter 83   *San Diego, Nov. 11, 51*
                                               United States Marine Corps

[Letter written on Marine Corps Stationery]

Dear Mom, dear Martin,
      Although I had a very good reason for not letting you know sooner
where I was, I felt very bad all the time, because I know you two are the
only ones really concerned with my future. Well it all went like this: In
September of 1950 we all had to register for the draft; that did not
mean anything. Well in February 1951 I was "asked" to appear for
Armed Forces Physical Examination, which I passed ok. Then OK was
afraid to go to Germany because he did not know when I would be
called into the services, so that Mrs. Kern was alone on the ranch while
he was overseas. But then he got sick and had to go anyway. He left
New York on June 1st. I received my first draft notice on May 29. You
see of course that we could not have called OK back for [on account of]
his health. Any news like that would have been poison for him.
      So Mrs. Kern tried her best to get me deferred and she succeeded. I
did not have to move into the services until August '51; so harvest went
over, Molly and Johann came to help us out, and in September I got my
second draft notice. This time there was no chance for another defer-
ment. Well, since OK was due in Berlin in the near future—and only
out of consideration for him—did I not let you know about my well
being in the US Marine Corps before this. I hope that he has passed
through Berlin and everything is well; otherwise don't let him know
that I was drafted, unless he should know it already. Well, I hope
everything is still alright with you. Now let me tell you exactly what
happened to me since September 26, '51.
      We were taken to San Francisco (from San Jose) and examined
once more physically. Then after one day of waiting we were given a
choice of Army or Marines, not Navy or Airforce. I chose the Marines

because Marines are a highly specialized offensive fighting unit, even more famous and distinguished then the Prussian army. Now don't think that the Marines have anything to do with the sea; they are part of the Navy, but are actually a land fighting force. Well, now you all know that I am not a very great fighting man, but I am getting along about average.

The first 4 weeks we spent at S. D. [San Diego] *in the Recruit Barracks of the Marine Corps. No liberty at any time before our 9th week is over (another 3 weeks to go). Mostly marching and classes on how to be a good soldier. Two weeks ago we were loaded into busses and shipped to Camp Matthews, shooting the M1 (Service Rifle); I think I am going to do exceptionally good.*

Around Dec. 1st we are going to be released from boot camp (which is the training and camp which all Marines have to go through). Then we will get about 10 days leave which I will spend in San Diego and Los Altos and after that we will have to report for duty at our new station which I have hopes of being San Francisco (Electronics and Radio school). I passed most of the tests in the top 5% of our plattoon (75 men). So I think I am doing alright. We have very good instructors, but very little time for ourselves. More some other time—

1000 kisses and all good wishes, your Helmut

Letter 84   San Diego, Nov. 25, 51

Dear Mother, dear Martin!

I was very happy to receive your nice letter recently and want to tell you quickly that everything is going well with me. Today I was released from a rather difficult week of kitchen duty. Last week at a shooting match I came out in about 4th place. The highest result (never yet reached) would have been 250 points. The highest performance in our unit (78 men) was 230, then came 2 x 229, and a couple of 226's, of which I shot one. The average was about 205. On earlier tests I also stood quite high, over 10% or better. Next Monday we will probably be released (Dec. 3, '51). I'll write more in the meantime.

I heard from Mrs. Kern that OK didn't receive his return ticket so he can't come back before February. She assured me that OK would visit you without fail. So goodnight then and all the best from now on, with 1000 kisses,

Your Helmut

Letter 85   *San Diego, Dec. 13, '51*

Dear Mom,
        *Another January is on its way to round the corner and with it
comes Christmas and — most important of all —your birthday . My
thoughts will be with you during the holidays. I expect to be stationed
at Oceanside, Calif, which is in the northernmost section of San Diego
County.*
        *Well, on Dec. 3, '51, I was released from bootcamp, promoted to
Private first class (Pfc), which would equal approximately a Gefreiter,
and sent on a 10 day bootleave (urlaub). I spent about one week in Los
Altos, seeing all my friends and helping out a bit on the farm; you know
Mrs. Kern is quite busy now with only Molly to help her keeping the
place going; OK is not expected to leave Germany before the end of
January which leaves Mrs. Kern sort of out on a limb.*
        *I guess that he will pass by Berlin sometime in January. Well,
anyway, then I came back down here to San Diego to spend a couple of
days with my friends down here, saw TG [Tante Guschen] in El Cajon
yesterday, who is still as she always was. Also I saw the Roberts and
heard that Maria Rosales and two of her sisters are again spending a
year or so in El Salvador*
        *Tomorrow I will have to report back from leave and continue my
training. As soon as I will know just what part of the Marine Corps I
will get into, I will let you know. But I have great hopes to get into the
intelligence corps on account of my German. May be I will come to see
you soon. Now, wishing you both a very happy holiday season, and
you, mom, a new year with quietness and peace.*

                                        Your loving son, Helmut

Letter 86   *Oceanside, Jan. 20, '52*

Dear Mom, dear Mart old boy,
        *Many thanks for your so nice Christmas letter which reached me
the other day; and—come to think of it—I don't believe that I had
thanked you for your wonderful Christmas package; well, as you can
imagine it was an immense joy to open such a lovely gift box.
Tremendous thanks for the wonderful candy, chocolates, and confec-
tions, the cookies and naturally the wonderful writing material and
books. I haven't had a chance to read them yet, but the stationary was*

an excellent idea and thanks a million again. The same mail I got your package I also got one from Mrs. Kern, who sent a large amount of wonderful cookies. All the fellows in my tent (four of them) certainly agreed that they had never tasted anything so good as your marzipan and Mrs. Kern's cookies. They were overwhelmed.

During the time that I have been here in Camp Pendleton I made friends with a wonderful guy named Ralph Eastlick from Platteville, Wisconsin. He is married and used to be a farmer, is 21 years old and really exceptionally nice...Also I have stayed pretty close to another buddy from bootcamp by the name of Bill Finlon from Chicago. He is of Irish descent with some German in him and also very temperamental but nice. Then naturally I am still closely befriended with Del Rio from San Francisco who with me is the only other intelligence man I know of.

I will probably be given a chance to take the Corporal's test together with the other fellows pretty soon. That would mean an extra $8 in pay per month and every bit helps. Two days ago we were removed from mess duty and formed into another Combat Training Co. But this Company (Love Co.) is still in training and untill they graduate those guys in training now around February 8 or so, we will only be doing odd jobs untill roughly February 15 when we will start training as the new Love Company. Any more I don't know.

Would like to wish you, Mart, a happy year of 19 [Martin's birthday was January 12] *and may all things turn out to your desire and liking. I know you are having pleasure at your job, so just keep up the good work.*

Well now, take it easy you two lovely creatures and take good care of yourselves.

Your loving Helmut

Letter 87 *Oceanside, Cal., Feb. 17, '52*

Dear Mom, dear Mart,

Just for a change, I decided to come into town, today. Ralph and I are having a pretty good time together. I sure hope we won't get seperated, because we really do get along swell. Yesterday Ralph and I had our pictures taken here in Oceanside; hope to get them back by Thursday or so. One large colored one in a folder is ordered for you, then one small colored one each for the Kerns and Norm, and a few black and white ones for Klinkerts, Rolls, Ralph, and Del Rio.

Next Friday is George Washington's birthday, which is something of a national holiday. I believe that we will get Friday, Saturday, and Sunday off, so that I hope to be able to go to S. F. during those 3 days. I still don't know, whether to stay with the Wades or the Kerns, hope that OK will be back by then, so that we could talk about Germany. Wonder whether he came to see you. If he didn't he had better have a pretty good reason or else I will be pretty mad. Will investigate about your immigration as soon as possible and relate it to you.

Well, goodbye for the time being and lots of good luck, your gong-ho Marine,

Helmut

Letter 88   *Oceanside, April 6, '52*

Dear Mom, dear Mart,

I guess it has been quite a long time again since I last wrote to you, dear people. Well, actually a lot happened since then, and then again not much at all. Two weeks ago we finished our infantry training. We were moved from tent-camp to the main area over here, where the 20th draft to Korea is being concentrated. On or about April 14 we'll be boarding ship for the Far East. Most of our time now is taken up by administrative details and besides that we have quite a bit of time to ourselves.

Ralph and I are going out together quite often, about 2–3 times a week. Last weekend we spent in Los Angeles. We went to a dance—Ralph loves to dance—walked around in Hollywood, took in all the big x [big-time] sights (there was no broadcasting going on at that time); and on Sunday afternoon we went to see the Neubergers. Now, offhand you may not recall who the Neubergers are. But you probably remem-ber Mrs. Arnstein who had invited me to spend a week's vacation at her apartment in San Francisco, when I first came to the Kerns. Mrs. Arnstein went to school with Mrs. Kern in Stuttgart.

Well, being Jews they were chased out of Germany in '38. During the war Mr. Arnstein died and with a son in the American army and daughter still going to school she slaved on a sewing machine for years and years. During that time it was that I spent the week with her. Well both her children are married, now, and so is she. She is living a very comfortable life now in Hollywood with a distant cousin of hers; Mr. Neuburger is a very placid old gentleman—a Swiss Jew—of 77, who is really a wonderful guy. The Neuburgers were out at the Kerns' ranch about 2 years ago, at which time he gave me a visiting card of his which I kept in my wallet all this time; he gave it to me with an invitation to come to see them anytime I was close by. Well, I called them up Sunday morning and got an invitation for Sunday dinner with Ralph. We had a wonderful time with Sauerbraten and Spatzele and Bockbier.

Well, next weekend, which will be the last one on US soil for a while, Ralph and I intend to rent a car and take in some of southern California's beautiful countryside. It ought to be fun. We don't have to much money, but we think we'll get by. Our plans would be nullified if they should decide to ship us out Easter Sunday or so; but what the devil, it wouldn't make that much difference.

Last week I went to the Regimental legal officer and asked him how much help I would get from the Marine Corps in case I should bring you over here. Well this is what he said: I and the Marine Corps would be able to do very little to get you, Mart, over here, but Mutty would be able to come quite easily. The government of course would be able to guarantee my job for at least another year and a half and that would be pretty good towards an affidavit. Naturally, as soon as you would reach USA, you would get, as my dependent, an allotment from the government which would come partly out of my pay. And that is that. Well, I'll enclose one picture and close my letter by wishing you both a very, very happy Easter.

> *As always with all my love,*
> *Your Helmut*

Letter 89 Berlin, April 18, '52

My dear Helmut!

I have been meaning to write you for a long time. On the one hand we were expecting the promised mail before Easter; on the other hand we were busily occupied so we wanted to write you during the Easter holidays. Then on Easter Saturday your letter came with its challenging contents, which was not so easy for us and our good friends to digest [*to fully absorb the English*]. Then too we had been invited several times to visit Aunt Anni's grave, so the days went by without writing letters. Also, we had such wonderful summer-like weather here that everyone wanted to take in as much sunshine as possible out of doors. Just two weeks ago we had ice and snow and now many trees are green already.

I'm writing this letter at the AEG on Blumenstrasse [*where Martin was working as a student-trainee*], the Train Factory/Testing Department (switching mechanisms for trains, electric cars, subway, elevated, and street cars, German Railway, and electric busses). At the moment there is almost nothing to do here. All day long we've tidied up the workshop, sorted screws and pins, labeled boxes, and so on. In other departments, on the other hand, there is usually too much work.

At home I wouldn't get to writing again today because I want to go to the discussion of a group which is connected with the YMCA. I've been there three times so far, and heard, for instance, a lecture by an American administrator about the presidential election of 1952 and by an expedition leader about the animal kingdom of South Africa. We only speak English there. A fellow student of Christa [*Christa Starkowski, the brothers' second cousin*], whom I met at a Shrovetide costume party at Starkowskis, invited me to come. [*Shrovetide is the three days before Ash Wednesday, traditionally a time of fasting just before Lent.*] About 25 men and women (old and young) who want to improve their English always get together there.

Now to you! Mother wants to inquire about some details at the consulate next week. The best would be if she went ahead and I started the first semester here before I follow her. I will be admitted to study so I hope to be able to pay the expenses by working as a trainee during the semester vacation, in case I don't receive a scholarship. Hopefully this year there are fewer applicants and more openings for students at the TU [*Berlin Technical University*]. In any case I have to prepare gradually for the exam.

After a certain period of time will you receive a furlough? Does your mail have a shorter route from East Asia to Europe via Asia than via America? In any event I wish you luck with whatever letters you may write. Have you stayed together with Ralph? Well, you're learning about Asia, and maybe you'll also get to Australia. Dad always wanted to get to Japan or India some day. Surely you'll start out in Japan, or will you only be taking care of convoys? We don't hear much about battles, but also not about an armistice. After two years it will really be time soon. Hopefully you had good weather crossing the Pacific.

On Good Friday we went rowing for the first time. Soon people will be able to bathe outside again. With my new touring bike I'm hoping to be able to get acquainted with the beauties of Berlin's surroundings. I have already undertaken a big bicycle tour of the inner half of the West Sector with friends, but soon there will be no more unknown places to be found in West Berlin.

A few weeks ago, under the leadership of a teacher, a club of former Richthofen—and Engels—students was formed, for the time being not registered but just thought of as an informal circle of friends. [*The original name of Helmut and Martin's school was Manfred von Richthofen Schule but after the war it was changed to Friederich Engels Schule*]. Even the older people are responding to a newspaper ad and are coming together in this way.

Do you remember Tsermanger and Lothar Furch? These two are also with AEG as trainees; I met them here briefly. They asked about you. Klaus Wenzel was confirmed two weeks ago (together with Karl-Heinz Belling and Bodo Dume); we were invited to a lovely celebration. Everything is changing fast around here; for example, Wolfgang Warzner is proving himself very grown up and responsible in his role as a Boy Scout leader. Your age group is already thinking seriously about marriage; so Rolf Lamprecht got engaged a short time ago, and no doubt many others that we don't know about.

For Dad's grave we want to provide a stone border now to hold the mound together. The old lady who takes care of the graves writes faithfully from time to time. Also, we hope to receive good news from you again very soon. Till next time,

Affectionate greetings and kisses, Your Martin

Letter 89 (continuation)

[*The following letter by Helmut's mother was written on the second sheet of Martin's letter. Rosemary Plettig was a neighbor from the same apartment building who had married an American serviceman, Robert Neuman.*]

My Dear Child,

Where might our greetings reach you and when? Our thoughts and prayers go with you into the wide world, which hopefully can turn around soon and be peaceful again. If possible, let us know what kind of jobs you are doing. Also we would very much like to know when your return to San Francisco might be, or maybe to Oceanside or wherever. Thank you very much for your nice little picture and of course the long letter with all the news. How was your last contact with the Kerns; he must have been back in Los Altos since the middle of March...Well, we don't want to be angry with anyone; one can never see into the heart. I would rather assume that there was some kind of good reason for his leaving out the projected Berlin trip. When did you last see and speak to them?

Dear boy, do you have any personal wish from us—how gladly we would fulfill it! Tell us what you think personally about our coming to California, especially about the time. Wouldn't it be wonderful if we (or maybe I alone first) were over there when you come back from your tour of duty? Of course, you will have to send for me from there; only then can we proceed further here. Then I will get Martin soon afterwards, as the consulate wrote. Of course it would be much better if we could both make the trip together. In no way do I want to burden you with this; instead I would like to hear your own opinion on this regarding the costs of the trip. I will inquire as soon as it's quieter again at the school. We're registering new students again now.

Well, a little more brief news from Reinickendorf. Rosemarie Neuman (Plettig) is expecting a baby—next year the whole little family is going back to Chicago. He [*Robert Neuman*] had committed himself for two terms of three years. He is only 21 and has already been here for two years. Are you together with Ralph, and what about Hugo Klinkert? When did you last see Tante Guschen in San Diego? All the dear friends send sincere greetings.

Well, stay healthy and in good spirits and receive a big hug with all best wishes and hopes from your Mutti.

Letter 90   *Kobe, May 2, '52*

Dear Mommi, hi Mart,

All is well and I am in Japan. We had a pretty wild impression of the harbor last night; but Ralph and I resisted all earthly pleasures, except 1/2 bottle of beer—which we didn't finish for reasons of taste (awfully bitter)—and spent all our Japanese money on souvenirs.

Well, first of all our trip was very uneventful with about 3 days of rough sea along the coasts of California and Japan. I was seasick off California. All in all it took us only 2 weeks and as soon as we got here we got a chance to go ashore. They paid us 15$ in occupation money [the American occupation government had issued a special currency after World War II for the use of American military personnel in Japan] *and 10$ worth of yens (360 yen = 1$). Because I had to pay back $10 to a friend I didn't have too much to spend around, but we, Ralph and I, did spend almost $30 on souvenirs.*

I bought you, Mom, a silk shawl [scarf], *hand painted, and Mart, you got a silk necktie with Japanese raised embroidery. For Mrs. Klinkert I bought a little ashtray; Ralph bought his wife a silken sports-jacket, his sister a slipper-pyjama-kimono set, his brother a tie like Mart's, his parents and in-laws each an ashtray. I still want to buy Mrs. Kern and Norm some small souvenir.*

Well you should have seen how happy I was to have some mail among the first letters that were called out as soon as we hit Kobe yesterday. There was one from you nice people, one from Mrs. Kern, and one from Ralph's wife, whereas Ralph, who usually hogs all the mail, only got one from his wife.

Mrs. Kern wrote that she was very sorry that OK came back towards the end of March without seeing you people before he sailed. She said that...he could work, but by far not as hard as he used to, and believe me that was a lot. You know, for a while I was inclined to break off all relations with OK, but I guess that if he didn't go to see you he must have had a pretty good reason. Yesterday I also heard that Ralph and I will be seperated as soon as we get to Korea (next week). He will go to the 5th regiment, 1st Marine Division, and I will go to Division headquarters, don't know what I'll be doing yet.

Hello and all good wishes from your Helmut

Letter 91 *Korea, May 14, '52*

Dear Mom, Dear Mart,
After the first week over here I think it is about time for you to hear a little something about the going-ons about me. Let me say that I am well and in a good outfit. My associates are good people, my leaders of finest caliber, the weather excellent, the war quiet, and the food good.

When I got to headquarters' battalion I spent one night at division headquarters. Then I was assigned to Recon Co. [Reconnaissance Company] *together with about 20 other fellows. They were mostly foreigners or speak at least one foreign language. When we got here—they drove us clear out to the frontlines, where Recon Co. is in position now—we found more foreigners, Marines from all over the world.*

You see, that happened like this. Since the Marine Corps began to draft people—they used to only rely on volunteers until a year ago—quite a few immigrants and people with foreign backgrounds were inducted into the Marine Corps and they were mostly given an MOS [Military Occupation Speciality] *of 0200 and thereby put into intel-ligence. You see, the mission of the Marine Corps originally was to land, seize, hold, and establish advance Naval bases. In those cases they used Recon Co. to go ashore a few days ahead of the invasion in order to gather information as to beach conditions, weather, correct-ness of maps, and enemy installations; for this purpose they needed people who knew the country to be invaded, consequently all the foreigners in Recon Co.*

Because the Marine Corps is fighting strictly a ground war over here in Korea, we in Recon have no real job to do; so they put us on the frontlines to guard a strip of river with Chinese on the other side. The Imjin River is very wide at this point, about 2 km, but consists of mostly madflats during low tide, due to its closeness to the ocean. Geograph-ically we are located at the junction of the Han and Imjin Rivers, facing west, 20 miles from Seoul. Our company with only 50 men watching the River at night is responsible for almost 4 miles of front line. Our posi-tion is definitely secure though, because of the wideness of the river, we are out of range of small arms fire, and have not drawn any incoming artillery for the past 3 weeks. There is nothing to worry about until the Chinks decide to come across some night and there seems to be no indication that they would. The last casualties Recon Co. suffered were in December of last year, when they were making ambush patrols along the Eastern front.

Transportation is no trouble for us, because this outfit actually has one jeep for every 4 men.

Chow, i. e. food, is good, except that they might be feeding us a little more fruit instead of dehydrated potatoes. Medical care is very good and so is the weather. We are all running around like little niggers.

Because of the presence of 4 or 5 German speaking people and their common interest in music and harmony, I would like to have you get me a little book or two on German Folksongs and Stimmungslieder. (Trinklieder, Marsche [drinking songs, marches] *and all you can get.) At the same time I'll have Mrs. Roll and Mrs. Kern send me some of my music.*

Hoping that you don't worry too much, I am with love,
Your Helmut

Letter 92   Reinickendorf, May 20, 1952

My Beloved Big Helmut-*Boy*!

Heartfelt thanks for the nice letter of May 2, which we've read over and over again; it brought us the first news from Asia. Just stay well—we all get *seasick*—-and in good spirits. God's ways are inscrutable, he protects everyone who depends on him, and that is what we want.

Last Sunday "The World on Sunday" brought us a picture of Panmun in Korea. Hopefully a good conclusion to the negotiations is no longer far off. Otherwise there is nothing much new here. Rosemary Neuman (Plettig) now has her little son "Peter."

Everyone takes an interest in you and greets you with many kind wishes for your well being. What is the time there in relation to California? Your news about the Kerns naturally interested us very much. We don't want to be angry at anyone [*because of Mr. Kern's failure to visit them in Berlin*] and only presume good.

Your beautiful big picture is hanging next to my bed and I greet you morning and evening before and after my daily work. What are your activities, or are you just getting further training? One would like to know so much that hasn't been written about at all. You musn't be surprised, especially since we've stayed connected only by letters for almost six years already. Yes, when and where will we see each other again? Although maybe the Kerns would sponsor Martin at the same time [*as she would come over*]. Otherwise he would just have to follow as soon as possible. You needn't be afraid that I would be a financial burden. Do you have any idea how much my assistance from the government would come to?

We can't delay emigration much longer, because when Martin is 21 (Jan. '54), then he will no longer be my "minor son" whom I can send for. We want to inquire thoroughly here at the consulate. And what do you know about this *Fall* ? Let us know more. Maybe—in case you aren't back in the USA yet—I could stay in New York, until Martin follows at least, and then we could travel on together.

Tomorrow is Ascension Day. Martin is going bicycling with friends. By the way, his practicum with AEG comes to an end on Aug. 9. Do you have any idea what the Klinkerts, etc. are doing? Where is Hugo? Tell me, are you expecting a furlough, or a transfer here or to West Germany—Europe? If the occasion presents itself perhaps you can inquire about it (maybe in San Francisco). Of course one musn't anger anyone in the process. What do you think of this?

Both of us send warm greetings for Pentecost [*a legal holiday in Germany*]. Martin has just come from work; he's now cleaning his bike for tomorrow. Tell me, should Martin bring his bicycle with him, or will that cost tax over there? Next June the Neuman-Plettig family will be going to Chicago and can transport a lot of furniture without cost. That might be an opportunity. Now I want to take care of some necessary things for tomorrow, and I kiss you 1000 times.

Mutti

Dear Helmut in the Far Distance!

Where might this note reach you? Certainly not in Kobe. We found the place on the map (of 1908) near Osaka, very small. It seems to have been enlarged only recently! At the moment I'm in the turbine unit of the large machine factory, very interesting!! Soon the application for the TU will be urgent, I am going to take a break to prepare for the [*university entrance*] exam.

Many greetings and kisses, from Martin

Letter 93   Berlin, June 20, 1952

Dear Helmut!

How is it going with you in the distant Far East? We hope good. We both have today free, mother has a school sports celebration. I've taken 12 days vacation in order to take care of my application matters in peace. Besides, today was Aunt Anni's birthday so we combined two things: the consulate and the cemetery. We had the consulate behind us in 5 minutes: as long as there is no sponsorship or an approved application from Washington, we are powerless here; otherwise mother could leave immediately. And she wants to, preferably with me of course, but it's not certain if she will be able to send for me right away.

Please do file the application to the Immigration and Naturalization Service —Form I-133 (Petition for Issuance of Immigration Visa) with the district director or the nearest branch office of the Immigration and Naturalization Service (attention of the legal officer). I don't mind staying here alone for a few months if I know that I can follow soon. Should the Kerns, for example, work things out to become my sponsors (and they were prepared to do that years ago), then everything would be all right. But as you said, we don't want to count on that anymore.

Time is marching on: I'll soon be 21 (Jan. '54) so I'm no longer mother's minor son but a regular applicant. Why should mother still be waiting? At age 60 she has to retire from the school. If she is in the United States over 5 years, she will lose her German pension anyway. The passage money matters are unrelated to the consulate; only the travel bureaus are responsible for that, so surely we could pay in deutschmarks. We thought that mother could leave in September–October 1952, and I at the beginning of '53, but maybe later when the Neuman family goes and can take baggage for us in case we want to take more than is allowed (they could take 72 hundredweight with them).

Have we already acknowledged your letter of May 14? In any case, a thousand thanks. What do you mean by *MOS of 0200*? Also we didn't understand: *"Chow, i.e. food is good." We sent you a book with German songs, did you receive it?* I just wrote this sentence in English without intending to; already the language almost seems to be flowing in my veins. We look forward eagerly to your souvenirs from Japan and especially the next mail. We and all our friends hope your service isn't too hard and that you will have some recreation. In Germany the law with regard to military participation and conscription will soon be ratified. But not yet in Berlin!

To be on the safe side I am also applying for admission to West German THs [*technical high schools, which are institutions closer to a college level*], just in case it doesn't work out with the Berlin TU.

Many loving wishes and kisses from your Martin.

Dear Helmut, good young man!

How are you? That is our number one question, and the subject of our constant prayer for you is that you will be able to perform your duty without coming to harm. So you have my most affectionate greetings with many good wishes. As Martin has already written, we are depending on your filing a claim with Washington even if I can't take Martin with me, or if the Kerns or someone else can't become sponsors for him so soon, so that I can go ahead and build a bridge that will reunite the three of us.

What do you think; should we stay with the Kerns at first, or establish ourselves somewhere else? No one needs to fear our expectations. Maybe the Feuerherdts would sponsor Martin as a formality, or Mrs. Lehner? If it could be arranged quickly, then perhaps we could go over together. Just write soon so that we know how you are and what you are doing. Receive my kisses with the hope of seeing each other soon.

From your Mutti

Letter 94   Berlin, July 5, 1952

My dear Helmut!

How are you? We had no mail directly from Korea for a long time. The mail that came today from San Diego (from Mrs. Klinkert) made up for it. What wonderful things you've sent us! A thousand thanks for the gorgeous necktie with the legendary Scylla and Charybdis on it. [*Scylla and Charybdis were a dangerous rock and whirlpool person-ified as female monsters in Greek mythology*]. You can certainly buy printed ties here with tacky pictures on them but not such beautifully embroidered silk ties. Do they have as many beautiful hand-made things in Korea as in China and Japan? Mr. Niessingh from AEG is familiar with Japan; sometime next week I'm going to ask him some things about East Asia. If only the continuing destruction of people and values would stop. The armistice negotiations [*between North and South Korea*] have been going on forever, when will they be closed?

Here in Berlin we're still hemmed in. The Russians are building encircling canals and roads to avoid going through Berlin. West Berlin-ers are no longer allowed in the Zone [*the East Zone of Germany, i. e. East Germany, which surrounded Berlin*], soon also the reverse. So big bicycle trips that were planned have gone by the board. Also, we can no longer go to Grandma [*in Wittenberg*] or to Potsdam without a very important reason.

So we have to spend our free time in the few beautiful suburbs of the Berlin area. Bathing spots are always overrun. Temporary little blockades and skirmishes on the supply roads are reported daily. Occa-sional reprisals bring about an easing of the tense situation. Hopefully we can both leave soon. There is hardly anything still holding us. My training at AEG will be finished in five weeks. Then I'll look for a job, until I can hopefully study somewhere, and if not now, then later. Malesch! [*Arabic word meaning something like "Oh, well!"*]

I just read Knittel's "El Hakim," magnificently written! Why hasn't Uncle Shawkat written in over a year? Don't you have time to write to him sometime? Now as to your birthday on the 18th, you have affectionate greetings and kisses from me. I can only wish that you will come home soon in good health. Everything else will automatically fall into place. We also send you best wishes from Grandma. Grandpa also writes now and then. Write to us again soon. With many thanks and greetings,

from Martin

Reinickendorf, July 6, '52

My dear child, little Helmut!

Our thoughts and dreams revolve only around you, you good boy. Hopefully you have received all the mail from us, e. g. guitar song book, letters, etc. Martin's vacation is over; he used it to make formal application to the Technical University, also to West Germany. In no case does he want to lose time now; he can stop at any time if the sponsorship (maybe other than the Kerns) comes about.

The wonderful silk scarf from Japan is my whole joy, a gift from your dear hand. Hopefully God will soon lead us together and watch over you and all good people here and there. So thank you so much, dear, big boy and may you have a special hug on your 22nd birthday, a wonderful age; If your brother were only with you and you could complement each other.

Rudiger Fritz is attending the Spandauer Police School for four months in order to advance. What will happen with Berlin? The noose becomes ever tighter and the constriction sharper. This throttling is terrible. Where will the politics lead? Lucky is the person who will still get out of here in good health. It's a hard test for the heart and nerves. Enclosed are a few little pictures and two copies of the last two letters from the consulate for your information. It would most certainly work out now if you would apply (on Form I-133) via Washington and at the same time Dr. Kern would apply for me and Martin to come over on one sponsorship.

It would be wonderful if the two of us could travel together. If the sponsorship were in hand here, things could move ahead very fast. And it's really important that we not let this opportunity slip out of our hands before it's too late.

Martin just came down from Tegelort, where he spent Sunday with Hansi Koppen. We're already looking forward to the next mail from you. Has Dr. Kern written you? What is Hugo doing? Did you have an opportunity to make contact with the Muhlkes before you left? God be with you, good Helmut, and many loving birthday greetings and kisses from,

Your islander-mother

*[Because of the isolation of Berlin at this time, Berliners often
compared themselves to islanders!]*

*[The following letter from Hans Georg Pohl, one of Helmut's friends in
Berlin, brings him up to date on the activities of his former classmates,
most of whom are now university students or graduates.]*

Letter 95   Berlin, July 7, 1952

Dear Helmut!

You will be surprised to receive a few lines from me for once. You
know that I accidentally learned from your mother what you have done
in the course of the year in America, and where you have now landed.

I think you yourself didn't imagine it when you left Germany in
1946. In any case, I would like to hope that you, as it seems to me, can
combine what is unpleasant there with what is useful, I mean with
regard to an occupation. We hope everything—both with you in the Far
East and with us in Germany, or rather Europe—will be resolved
peacefully. As for us in Berlin, we're leading, as far as we can, a very
peaceful and carefree life, even though the East is always trying to
torment us.

As you may have heard, I'm a student at the Free University here
in Berlin. The Free University is a West Berlin university which was
founded on the initiative of many students with American help in 1948.
I've been studying there since the summer of 1949, and am majoring in
mathematics and minoring in physics. At this time I am in the seventh
semester, and hope to be able to take the exam for my diploma in
summer of 1953.

I would like to work as a mathematician in some West Berlin or
West German industrial enterprise. Maybe I'll have luck with AEG,
where I've worked during several summer vacations as a work-student
with good extra money. It is extra profit because I have been receiving
a stipend of more than 80 westmarks a month for two semesters. Also I
didn't have to pay any university fees till now, so I have succeeded to
some extent in managing with my money.

Besides myself, a lot of other former classmates are also studying.
George Pisarek took the exam for his diploma in business adminis-
tration two weeks ago, at Berlin East University. He's going to Israel
for three months at the end of this month. Klaus Gerigh is studying

veterinary science at our university. Dieter Scherbius, Juna, and Rolf
Liege are studying the science of management, Wolfgang Klopstock,
athletics. Rolf Gelewski has become a ballet dancer. Ralph Herberg is a
salesman—an employee of Siemens in West Germany. I will be
visiting him during this year's six-week bicycle trip, which will take
me through West Germany.

So, I would like to close for today. I'll let you hear from me again
sometime. Maybe you'll also write me a few lines sometime.

Sincere greetings,
Hans-George Pohl

Letter 96 *Korea, July 10, '52*

Dear Mom, Mart,

*By now you two are probably pretty well straightened out on
Mart's future schooling and education. I sure hope he'll get to go to
one of the TUs. A little over a week ago I went to our Division legal
officer and told him all about our situation. He made a written request
to the American consulate at Pusan for the forms mentioned in your
last letter, and is expecting an answer within another week. Will let you
know as soon as I'll get any further word from him.*

*Well, now, this might come as something of a surprise, but you see,
I'm back on another 30 days of mess duty, right back here at the
division Command Post. My location now is about 15 miles to the East
of our last positions along the dikes. I'm not a messman actually,
though, because I don't handle food nor do I clean up the mess hall or
the galley. All I do is see that the cooks in the galley are supplied with
all the heat they want anytime they want it. In other words I'm keeping
the stoves in operation, fueling, lighting, and fixing them, whenever
necessary. I am the stove-boy.*

*You see, Recon. Co. moved last week Thursday and left the dikes to
some guys from 1st Amtrack Bn. We moved behind our combat regi-
ments (about 5 miles behind Ralph), where Recon. Co. is going to go
through some rugged training. A couple of days later everybody was
approached with the question: "Do you want a transfer," [because of
the exceptional risks of reconnaissance work] and about 10 guys said
yes. I was one of them.*

*As you may know, or may have been able to guess, those Recon
patrols are going to be sent in front of our lines and even behind enemy*

*lines. Now I figured this. I am a draftee, I do anything and everything I
am ordered to do (if they tell me to go out there, I'll do my best out
there and try to accomplish my mission) regardless of my own skin, but
if I'm given a chance to get out of it, I'll certainly take it.*

*So, to the surprise of many, I asked for a transfer. But as I hear
now, there are quite a few more that want to get out. Maybe they'll get
another chance and maybe they're in for good; anyway, I'm out and
I'm darned glad of it. They are looking for volunteers all over the
division to replace us in Recon Co. It takes a damned good man for
that kind of work and I'm certainly not good enough for it.*

*Well, all in all, I think that so far everything turned out to be very
good for me. Hoping for a reunion when I get back to the States.*

Your Helmut

Letter 97   *Korea, July 30, '52*

Hi, Dear people,

*It's been a long time since I last let you know how I was. Well, my
birthday passed by very quietly; but to my greatest surprise I received 2
packages just the day before, one from Mrs. Kern with cookies and
candy, and your little Zupfgeigen Hansl* '[a German song book]. *Thanks
a lot, I sat right down and went through it singing all the songs I knew
and trying those I had heard of. Thanks again.*

*Since about 10 days ago it has been raining almost steadily. It is
mostly just a drizzle with a few showers now and then. I am glad that I
am working indoors right now. Once your clothes get wet, it's pretty
hard to get them dry again. There is so much moisture in the air, you
know, that one has to watch his health. With this rain coming down I
don't care to sit in our movy* [movie?] *and get wet; so I'm spending my
evenings writing letters. What a great relief it is to be able to get some
of one's correspondence taken care of. Was sure glad to have had a
letter from Hans Pohl. And I have answered it already, too.*

*So far I haven't heard from the legal oficer concerning the
application for issuance of an affidavit of support for you, which he
had sent for in Pusan. But I should get word pretty soon, because I
notified him of my change of address.*

*Something different now. Last week I had to work nights on time,
getting the next day off. Well, I decided to take a little trip. After getting
permission from our messergeant, I took off about 8 in the morning,*

getting rides from passing trucks or jeeps. After visiting an old friend from tentcamp at Service Bn., I went to see Ralph at the lst Mar. Reg. Ralph is—like I—still on mess duty up there. We spent a wonderful afternoon together.

I left my films up at Recon. Co. with a buddy who was going to send them home to his wife [for development] *together with his own. They should be back pretty soon and when I'll get them I'll be sure to send you some first chance I have. Till then let me say goodbye for now and wish both of you good luck over there. With best wishes, Helmut*

Letter 98 Reinickendorf, August 9, '52

My dear, good Helmut!

You don't know how happy we were with your lovely letter of July 10. We were really comforted by it. Where are you located now, where else again? Meanwhile has your application been settled by Washington? We are very interested in knowing how our situation may be turning out.

Today Martin completed his practicum; at the same time the Brunnenstrasse Department of AEG is having a gathering in Schoneberg with coffee and cake, conversation and dinner—till midnight. So I don't expect him back before 1:00 a m. The summer vacation is coming to an end, school starts on August 12. Actually, it's something of a relief as the school wasn't kept open continuously for office hours. Instead there was only someone there once a week (in turns). By the way, Martin is scheduled to take the admission exam for the Technical University here on August 18. From August 15 until the beginning of the semester (Oct. 15) he has been accepted by the AEG Huttenstrasse plant (turbine factory) in N. W. Berlin.

Braunschweig [*technical school in Braunschweig, West Germany*] already sent him an admission notification. So you see how disciplined our little fellow is in everything; he's allowing himself only 4 days rest (8/11–14). If the political outlook were more peaceful I would not be so concerned about a temporary separation from him. But everywhere people are provoking each other to the point that it could still come to a war and we islanders will be sitting here isolated. God grant that everything will turn out for the good. You good young man, if it were true that we would see each other again <u>soon</u>, it would be a great joy worth all the pain—my whole longing.

I received a short letter from Mrs. Kern, according to which Dr. Kern is again in Germany (till October), and probably will take an aunt back over there. Whether I should come alone at first or with Martin will probably develop soon. Mrs. Kern probably wrote to you herself, about which way. She doesn't need to worry about us, as none of us can foresee the future. I don't expect a palace, just temporary accommodations as I've described, maybe in the neighborhood. Or are you for San Francisco? By the way, have you written to Mrs. Lehner? I certainly wouldn't want to end up standing on the street. Was your room very damp in the winter? Tell me, would Martin be drafted at age 21, or after a two-year stay in the country? There must naturally be rules about that.

What do you think of Farouk [*former king of Egypt*]? Where might he be living now? How different he turned out to be since we lived in Cairo, not far from the Abdin Palace, in 1935–39. In any case, I really found it cruel that he took away the daughter of his beloved first wife.

Time has more than gone by. For that reason we only want to take care of our family life; such a long separation was never foreseen. Already in the summer of 1948 the three of us were ready for the trip over, four years ago! Just stay well, young one.

Hans Weiss is bouncing around here with his auto. He will be getting married in spring and go back to Philadelphia. Also Rosemarie Plettig-Neuman will go to Chicago then. If worse comes to worst, I'll stay in New York to begin with if necessary. Just don't worry; everything has always worked out.

Heartfelt greetings and kisses with best wishes from Mutti

Letter 99   Berlin, August 10, '52

Dear "Stove Boy" Helmut!

I'm finally getting around to answering your last nice letter. Until yesterday I was in practical training, and now I'm waiting for the next step. The entrance exam at the Technical University will probably determine it. I already received a card from Brauschweig informing me of my admission there. So do you advise studying in [*West Germany*]? Globetrotter that you are, you would probably make a quicker decision to change your place of residence. But as long as Mother is still in our Berlin home, it would be harder for us old residents of Reinickendorf to leave Berlin; it would be different if I were alone. Also I can study here first and study over there [*in the U. S.*] later. Living would certainly be more expensive in West Germany, especially because of scarce housing.

Yesterday evening, at the AEG summer party (with a variety program, dance, and lavish entertainment) I wore the beautiful tie. Many people really admired it. Among the AEG people was Lathar Furch, you must still remember him. He worked as a trainee for two terms and in November will go to the Beuth School of Engineering. Also one of the Amler brothers is going there and Ralph Nagel already has it behind him and is an engineer at the Hohenzollern dam. Who knows when I'll get finished. So what are you planning for your future? Will you stay in the service, go back to the farm, or what do you think is best? If only we could discuss things personally and not just through letters! Maybe we'll experience that soon—inshallah! [*Arabic: God willing*]. The main thing is that we never lose sight of each other. I wish you always "Mabruk!"

Greetings and kisses from Martin

Letter 100 [typewritten]   *Korea, August 14, '52*

Hi, you two lovely creatures,

You don't know how happy you made me with that little song collection I had in the mail yesterday evening. I've been going through the book last night and to-day and keep finding so many old songs I still remember having sung in good old Germany.

You may be surprised to see me writing this letter on a typewriter, but that's just what I'm in charge of now. You see, when I was transferred off mess duty three days ago, I was assigned to the company First Sergeant's office, where I hope to be spending the rest of my time overseas. I was made company mail orderly and office clerk and as such I will naturally have to learn how to type.

I think that I'm doing alright, considering that I am writing almost entirely without looking at the keys anymore. It's still pretty slow for the time being, but I guess that speed will come with time and experience. And writing a couple of letters every evening on my own time gives me all the experience I'll need with a chance to afford to make a few mistakes now and then. Once writing will become a habit with me I'll have it made. The First Sergeant who seemed like an awfully rough guy before I went to work for him, turned out to be one of the nicest fellows I've ever met.

*Yesterday I was able to get my affidavit for you Mother straight-
ened out. The Division legal officer has sent an awfully nice letter with
the affidavit and a statement from my "employer" to the American
Consulate in Berlin Dahlem. I also asked Mrs. Kern to send you a
statement as to my former employment, since it just might be good to
have it should they want it..*

*About 10 days ago I had a small accident. While refilling a hot
stove at the messhall, the gas can I was holding caught on fire, and
dropping it I spilled some of the blazing gas on my right trouser leg.
Although I was able to extinguish the fire within a matter of seconds I
still suffered 2nd degree burns between the foot and the knee of my
right leg. The skin came off just like that time in Cairo when I scalded
both my legs with boiling water. Due to the advances in medicine new
skin has already formed over almost the entire area, I had been getting
penicillin injections daily. Since I have been working all the time,
though litely, you can imagine that it could hardly have been very bad.
So please don't worry about me or my leg.*

*Let me sign off for now, wishing you lots of good luck on your next
trip to the consulate.*

Love, Helmut

Letter 101   *Korea, 17 Aug. 52*

*Heard from Bill Finlon yesterday, who is switchboard operator at
A Company 1st Med. Bn.* [Medical Battalion] *that purely by chance he
happened to see Ralph's name on the casualty list of Aug. 13. Ralph
had been there only for a couple of hours that day and then was
evacuated to the hospital ship. I still have to find out which one he is
on, so that I can write to him. The fool was in regimental headquarters
Co. for 3 months and had to ask for a transfer to a line co. After he got
transferred he got hit right the 2nd week during the struggle for Bunker
Hill. I don't know how badly he got hurt, but I sure hope that it won't
be anything permanent because he didn't deserve it.*

Till later,
Helmut

Letter 102   Berlin, August 19, '52

My dear Helmut!

   I just have a free half hour at work as my supervisors are away and I don't have anything to do. However, I'm thinking about you and have taken up paper and a copying pencil in order to write you again. At the moment I'm a work-student till October 18 at the Moabit turbine factory (AEG) for 1.05 marks student wages. They always keep me busy there wherever I'm needed. I'm substituting (as far as is possible) now for a man in the termin bureau [*possibly payroll office*] who has gone on vacation. In two weeks I'll be located at the milling machine or at the drawing board. As you see, an experience rich in variety, in which you keep learning something.

   Yesterday morning I took the entrance exam at the T. U. In my estimation I did very well. For about 10 minutes I was interrogated on a stream of technical, mathematical, physical, and historical subjects and then was allowed to go. In the middle of October I'll find out whether I've been accepted. I finished my practicum on August 9.

   This factory here is very interesting with its gigantic halls and machines. Mr. Skowronek, Manfred's father, who is the foreman here, has already been able to show me so much, and through the work in the office I am also learning more about the piece work system (with pre-calculation and accounting), parts-storage, etc. I will always be able to work in a similar way during semester vacation.

   We enjoyed reading your letter in which you told about your birthday. We're already looking forward to the promised pictures. I hope you've survived the period of cold weather. May everything continue to go well for you.

                                    Many greetings from Martin

My dear, good Helmut!

   Loving greetings and all the best wishes to you in whatever you may be doing: success, patience, and above all health! Everyone greets you with faithful thoughts and in the hope of a happy reunion. Meanwhile I wonder if you have received an answer that gives some foreshadowing of the future. Perhaps we will soon hear further details from you, my darling.

   Recently I have had such a peaceful feeling, as if everything is coming onto good paths and will one day prevail over the endless wait.

A silent prayer also helps for peace and clear thinking. Even Grandpa wrote with special greetings for you, that God alone directs everything rightly. It's important that you're taking care of your health and is reassuring to us. What can we do for you that would make you happy? We've already consulted with the Plettig-Neuman family, and perhaps a small connection for later [*when the Neumans would be in the United States*] is not to be sneezed at.

Yes, Martin is temporarily a work-student with AEG. Each person brings something new into his life; it is in no way time lost. He is a fine, efficient worker, for some probably too solid, which for him and for the pocketbook is only to his advantage. Don't worry too much, everything will turn out the way it should. Hans Pohl received your letter the same day as we did. More another time; for today stay well and just write as soon as you can—at least a sign of life! What would a small room for me cost there (in San Francisco) in case the Kerns back out (the aunt, etc.). We'll see what he is going to do.

Hearty kisses from Mutti

Letter 103   *Korea, 25 Aug. '52*

Hi Mom, Hi Mart,

Long time no see. Got your big letter yesterday and thought it best to answer it right away. At the same time I have received those long overdue pictures from Recon and so I am able to enclose a few for you people.

Now that your vacations are over I imagine that you are both in deep work again, Mom you in your ancient element of stenographer and you Mart probably in a brand new one, or at least one similar to the one you left a little over a year ago. I think you should have been able to take care of the entrance exam without any difficulty and from then on it could hardly be anything but the routine of hard learning that could keep you on top; and I know you'll be there.

Good luck on this new venture of yours and good wishes from me, who I wish I were in your shoes. You don't know how much a real German education means in USA. Maybe not so much in credit—they give damned little—than in actual knowledge, which with a finished education means everything over here.

Do you know as yet which field you will try to branch off into later on? There is refrigeration, electronics, and some others besides just

plain electrical engineer and it might pay to specialize in something,
but then, I'll leave that all up to you. I know that I would like to get into
electronics (radio, telephone, and television) when I get out of the
service but that all depends on a few things to come.

My leg is in excellent condition, skin all over the second degree
area and certainly beginning on the third degree area. My boss is
being very nice about everything. I think I told you about Ralph's
getting hurt on Bunker Hill. As I found out, now, he got it in the right
arm, shoulder, and leg, and can't be in any too good a condition. The
fool, I warned him so much not to ask for a transfer to the front lines; I
can't mention it anymore now.

Be good now and so long with all kisses and good luck. Your old
(22) Helmut

Letter 105   Berlin, Sept, 6, '52

Dear Writer Helmut!

We were very glad to receive another letter from you with the nice
pictures. Now we can get an idea of the Korean landscape and you
guys. There don't seem to be any forests there, only shrubbery and
street trees. The shape of the houses is also peculiar! Everywhere in the
world one finds beauties and unique characteristics; it's just a shame
that the times aren't peaceful.

We read about your injury with dismay, but it's good that
everything is healing well. Hopefully there will be no lasting damage.
Also we were very sorry to hear about Ralph. But who knows what he
might have been saved from through it. I can imagine, for example, that
captivity is very unpleasant. Is it certain that service on the front lines
lasts nine months? And how long will you probably stay there altogether? If you should still be in the clerical position, then we would be
professional colleagues for the moment. At the moment, in Warehouse
II, I have to make long inventory lists, and rummage in dusty card files,
but soon the demands will be heavy again.

Now we're anxiously waiting for the next mail from the consulate,
since so much depends on the decisions of the consul. As long as
nothing is yet decided we're still enjoying the Berlin atmosphere, as far
as it's worth experiencing. Sometimes we go to a movie, hear an
operetta or an opera, take evening steamer trips on the beautiful West
Berlin lakes, or visit friends, of whom we surely have more than
enough. I'm too tired in the evenings to undertake a lot more, so I read

good books (e.g. by Tolstoy, Hesse, Wiechert), or sometimes play the accordion. School hasn't begun yet and I'm enjoying my freedom.

With greetings and kisses, Your Martin

Letter 106   Reinickendorf, Sept. 7, 1952

My dear big Helmut son!

You have no idea how interested we were in your little pictures and how happy they made us. You have our sincere thanks and our heartfelt greetings and wishes for your painful injury to improve well. Well, I really know that you are in good care and, with God's help, step by step, will overcome everything. Continue to be patient; after all, you were in the hospital and maybe now you can use the typewriter for your future activity in the service.

In any case, the time of our reunion is drawing ever closer, isn't that wonderful? What do you think? Should we stay in New York to begin with in case the passage money for two should be tight? Mrs. Kern wrote me that if she can house me, she would take Martin in if necessary.

Well, God knows where I will find a modest little room; that isn't important. I don't want to force myself on anyone. So was your little room so damp that it would be out of the question for me in the winter? But then one can collect warm things. Where there's a will, there's a way. My darling, the thought of being at both of your sides again in a small home with advice and help [*for them*] makes me happy and will overcome everything. When do you think you will actually return?

Greetings from all the dear friends, e.g. Hn. Heimbach (who thinks you should always just duck if something comes flying!) and many more. I'm sending you a little package from Berlin, which you may enjoy. For today greetings and kisses from,

Mutti

9

Berlin Island: *Life in a Beleaguered City*

Most of the letters in this chapter were written by Maria and Martin from Berlin, especially during a three-month month lapse on Helmut's part when his taxing work as a baker on mess duty seems to have left him too exhausted to write much of anything at all.

In contrast to Helmut's matter-of-fact reports about everyday life as a GI, the letters of his mother and brother reveal a more global perspective, reflecting solemnly on the dismal world situation. Martin's letters describe in detail his life as a student at Berlin Technical University and the letters of both mother and son convey the extreme tension of life in incendiary West Berlin as the city becomes more and more insecure and isolated.

Meanwhile, back home in the United States (but apparently without the expected funds), O. K. Kern again raises their hopes, and again fails to follow through. He invites Maria to live on the farm while his wife now goes to Germany, and again offers to sponsor Martin, but then appears to leave the matter completely up in the air.

Also, communication between Helmut and his family about their immigration seems somewhat out of sync. Maria and Martin apparently consider their departure to be imminent, while Helmut sees it as taking considerably longer to effect, especially for Martin.

The situation is further complicated by the ambiguity of Helmut's own future back in the United States. He has not really made up his mind about what he wants to do after the Marine Corps, or indeed whether he wants to settle in California at all—even as his mother and Martin look to him for advice about their own future residence!

Letter 107   *Korea, Sept. 19, '52*

Hi Mom, Martin,

It's really a shame to let you wait for a little letter like this for such a long time. Several things have changed with me in the meantime. Our personnel officer transferred the main (and only) typist out of the First Sergeant's Office and refused to replace him unless one of us 3 non-typers would get transferred also. So the Top got a new typist and I was transferred back to Guard Section.

After standing post for a few days I was put on Division outpost with 5 other good fellows, our purpose up here being to keep constant watch over the limits of the Division Command Post (Headquarters area), to see that no civilians enter the area except through the main gate and to stay on the lookout for enemy troops that might have infiltrated, concentrating for an eventual attack on the C. P. [command post] We stand various watches day and night getting plenty of rest and 12 hours every 3rd day to do what we want.

From where our OP [outpost] is located up here on one of the ridges surrounding Div. Hq. we can see quite a lot of Korea. During the day we can make out the dust clouds raised by exploding shells on the front lines about 10 miles away and at night we can see the flashes from Bunker Hill and other areas of conflict.

About the affidavit of support and the employment statement which I had asked Mrs. K. to issue, I have never heard again. She does write a nice letter, now and then, telling me about the goings-on about the ranch. I am also in constant correspondence with Mrs. Klinkert, Mrs. Kempf, Norm, and Ralph and Ruby Eastlick. After spending two weeks in a naval hospital near San Francisco [Ralph] has, finally, been transferred to Great Lakes Naval Hospital near Chicago, only 5 hrs drive for his wife from his hometown of Platteville, Wisconsin.

The writing of this letter had been interrupted for a few days, because I had to move once more. I was taken off Outpost and put back on mess duty, where I am now working as helper in the bake shop. My address should remain as guard section, though, because I am receiving my mail promptly and that will be the outfit I'll return to after this stretch of mess duty is over.

I have a request to make for a buddy of mine, who is on the OP I was on. He will be going home sometime before Christmas and would like me to find out whether it would be possible for you to purchase and send to the States to his mother a Schwarzwalder Kukuksuhr [Black Forest cuckoo clock] and Dirnd'lkleid [dirndl dress] for his wife. He

*thought of spending something like $40 on both together, and would
rather have something good and lasting than some cheap imitation.
Could you find out whether you could get these items in Berlin, how
much they are and whether it will be possible to send them at all and
how much that would cost, and how you would want him to send the
money (check, money order, cash). Let me wish you well now in all
your ventures and*

Bye from your Helmut

Letter 108 Berlin, Oct. 19, '52

Dear, good Helmut!

Unfortunately I haven't been able to write without being interrupted lately, which you will please forgive. About the requested gifts for your buddy, I dashed through Berlin and made a survey. It's best to have both, but I must ask you briefly again how much to allow for the clock and how much for the dirndl dress. Forty dollars, which he would best send by check, making allowance for postage and duty, comes to 150 marks, to be divided! How much of that should I spend on the mother and how much on the young wife?

There are Black Forest clocks for 30–150 marks (with cuckoo, musical clock, etc.) In dresses there are of course authentic costumes in all colors, all attractive, some more simple, for daily use, but also elegant ones made of silk; perhaps with a jacket, etc. The measurements can't be matched very exactly; the width of the waist is larger in all the dresses. Of course that can be made appropriate by taking it in or using elastic there. That's not important. If the money arrives we'll be glad to take care of the desired measurements.

We're anxiously waiting for further news from you and from the consulate, to which we're not supposed to go without being called. Have you not yet received the sponsorship, or are you waiting for a sponsorship for Martin too? Perhaps many applications are being processed. About when will you return to the U. S. and to where? As soon as you hear about it, let us know. And never make careless trips close to the front. You must not tempt fate from here on out.

The situation in Berlin remains uncertain for young people especially, which is why I would like Martin to be away from here too, only we can't pay for two households. The sinister East is too close to us, the encirclement very uncomfortable!

The world is a powder keg; too many ideas are opposing each other. If everything were resolved bloodlessly, then mankind would be happier again. We need reconstruction everywhere, and can scarcely endure more destruction. My dear child, you are constantly in our thoughts and hopefully we will see each other again in good health and confident of facing a new future; the three of us should be joyful about that and pray for it.

For today a warm hug and many good wishes from your Mutti. We'll write more soon.

Letter 109   Berlin. 10-27-52

Dear Helmut in Distant Korea!

Although a vacation may sometimes seem so pleasant, I haven't been very satisfied in these two free weeks between work and study. It wasn't only the uncertainty about the immediate future (incidentally, my admission to Berlin TU arrived today), but especially a kind of guilty conscience in the face of all of you, who actively in battle or passively in prison camps, have been affected by present-day politics. When someone, like me right now, has time to listen to the daily news or read the papers, and to hear personal accounts, he begins to brood—don't be surprised at that!

The person is fortunate who is so absorbed in his work or his passion that he can shut the world out. There are already too many like that, and how easily one falls into this passivity, but if you consider how many, for example in the East Zone like Uncle Paul, are waiting for a change and have to go along helplessly, then it's sad to see the self-satisfaction in the countries (especially West Germany), which has gripped a large part of the population. Again and again there are wars, in which people lose their head or limbs, or at least valuable years, and all that never to the benefit of mankind. How gladly would any one of us help you carry the burden, and on the other hand how glad we are that for the time being there is "only" a cold war here.

So we can only wish that you come back soon safe and sound. Then we three will certainly see each other again. Neither the Kerns nor the consulate have reported anything so far, so we will have to inquire again. Tomorrow I'll get registered and then begin the first of two pre-semesters in the humanities. For this semester I will thankfully decline the Aachen and Braunschweig TU's. I'm enclosing one of the passport photos which I need for my student ID card. This past week, at my leisure, I looked over our photos and leafed through atlasses and diaries. In this way I re-experienced what Dad was moved to write down in Italy, Spain, England, the Canary Islands, and Egypt, as well as at home and in the U. S. Unfortunately, the diaries from Ireland and Egypt are missing.

(Incidentally, in case you've kept our letters that would make us happy because we aren't keeping any diaries and that way we could record some interesting things for later. Your letters are collected in a letter file. Memories are something wonderful and the mind loses them too fast. Well, neither of us is old yet, but, as they say, time flies until one becomes old).

The dissolution of our "household" certainly won't be difficult for us! Let us hear from you again soon! Stay well and cheerful!

Many greetings and hugs from your Martin

Letter 110 Reinickendorf, 10-30-52

My dear, good Helmut-*boy!*

We are already yearning for a new letter from you; you had already spoiled us with mail before. But we hope to God that things are going tolerably for you and are tremendously happy about the ever closer reunion, isn't that so? Then everything else will soon work itself out, in a way that is good for us. Easier immigration is being discussed here again; hopefully things will soon come together for our Martin. Otherwise I will come alone first and we will send for him as soon as possible. The main thing is that nothing serious will intervene for us islanders. Then one would end up reproaching oneself in the end.

Incidentally, Martin (despite starting with the T. U. here) will obviously start with practical work over there (most likely in an electrical trade, we thought something with Westinghouse). But he must first accustom himself to the language. All in good time. What do you think about the Kerns, are they backing out? Well, it will continue this way despite all the promises that were given. A change (without resentment) is sometimes intended by Fate for the good.

Don't you have any wish? We would so gladly fulfill it for you; this can be done without our suffering hardship. So go on with God, my dear Helmut, whatever your situation. Don't fret about anything or anyone, and trust your Lord God, he will make everything go well.

Kisses and greetings, Your Mutti

Letter 111   Reinickendorf, Nov. 17, 1952

Dear, distant Helmut-*boy!*

Hopefully things are going all right for you; maybe we'll get mail from you soon, which we wait for with longing. I just wrote to Dr. Kern about his letter of Nov. 3, in which he invited us to come there. He wants to send us an affidavit for Martin now. His wife will travel to the homeland next year, as soon as we are over there; she will stay here at least half a year. O.K. wants to pay for Martin's transportation from New York to San Francisco.

Well, you'll be happy that our travel plan will really start moving soon. Martin is still diligently attending the first semester (humanities) at the TU. He has a full schedule; in addition he's attending lectures on higher mathematics, English, music history, etc.

Yesterday we were at a family gathering at Dr. Eva Starkowski's [*Maria Dost's cousin*]. Christa [*her daughter*] is in the 8th semester of medical school. Evelyn [*another daughter*] is studying to be a medical technician. Both girls are so lovely. Everyone sends you greetings The poor people (including Uncle Ernst Krummery as school principal) are suffering greatly emotionally under the Eastern system, as well as from hunger. It can't go on that way for long. Ilse Steffe [*Maria's god-daughter*] has been imprisoned in Potsdam since March 1951. As a technical draftsperson she made an engineering design that they designated "espionage-sabotage." Grief everywhere! May God help all good people to carry on in this chaotic world. Well, we are rejoicing in a happy reunion soon. With kisses and many good wishes for the future.

                                    Your Mutti and Martin

Dear Helmut! [*note from Martin on margin*]

How goes it? Are you very busy at the moment? I hope you sometimes have some free time so that you can hear the same American hits that I hear on Rias [*a radio station*]. Every week there is a "Hit of the Week." I like most of them a lot, only not when Louis Armstrong sings.

Letter 112   Berlin-Charlottenburg, Dec. 10, '52

Dear Helmut!

I finally want to write to you once again from the so-called "Green Room" of the T. U. I just had experimental physics with Prof. Ramsauer, that is the mechanics of liquid and gas-forming solids. I have some time until 2:00, then Certified Engineer Spoerel will lecture on "Introduction to Mathematics." These lectures and "exercises" are seen as a bridge between the institute and high school, and enjoy wide popularity since many people have been out of school a long time and "Mathematics I" already assumes a lot. I have also registered for Math I in order to at least try to follow it.

Five semesters of mathematics are scheduled for the engineers, besides two semesters of representational geometry with Prof. Dr. Rembs. These three subjects alone take up so much time for home work that there isn't an hour left for all the rest: Literature (Pr. Altenberg) "Great Novels of World Literature;" Philosophy (Prof. Heyde); Introduction to Dialectical History (Prof. Herrmann) "The Congress—Founding of the Reich;" Anthropology (Prof. Muckermann), a kind of Biology of Man combined with ethics, psychology, philosophy; Music History (Prof. Stuckenschmidt); English (Prof. Blacker) "Modern English Drama;" and "Creation of Public Opinion: Press, Broadcasting, Education."

Well, that's what my program of studies looks like; 34 hours a week. Often I had to come here twice a day; because of the involved trip I usually choose to stay here over the noon hour and attend to personal things. In the reading, club, and other lounges you can sit down just as you like. Incidentally, the lecture rooms are so widely scattered over the large TU campus that you usually have to hurry in the half-hour breaks in order to get an acceptable seat.

For me Monday and Thursday are fully booked from 8 a. m. to 6 p. m. You can well imagine that after 10 hours of working with concentrated material I don't have the energy to do more of the same kind of work at home. So then I have to sit behind the books (notes) on Saturdays and Sundays or meditate under the Christmas tree. You could use the semester vacation just to digest the material and solve the problems that were put forth during the semester.—Enough of that!

In spite of everything, it's still a joy to listen to such men. Often too there are important events at which I have met, for example, the English high commissioner Sir Ivone Kirkpatrick and Darwin's nephew, an author. Four days ago I was invited by the "medical students" of the Free University to a formal ball at Schoneberg where I met among others Ruth Pisarek, Evi Starkowski, and Irmtraut Saum. Besides demonstrations of ballet and ballroom dancing, there was also a fashion show to see. Very conservative clothing and deportment.

Do you have any kind of opportunity for private amusements over there? If not, what do you all do in your free time? We haven't received any mail from you since the 24th of September! Nevertheless we hope to hear from you for the coming holidays in December and January. Meanwhile have you learned the Korean language yet? Or don't you mingle with the Koreans? How is the weather over there? Here snow has fallen exceptionally early (end of November) and it's stayed on the ground till now; at the moment black ice on the roads in its worst form. The latitude of Korea is much further south than Berlin, but is it so much warmer? How is your leg, and what do you hear from Ralph? We haven't heard any more from O. K. and the consulate, but we inquired more closely at Hapag's (passage to New York $170–$180 payable in DM plus 100 DM apiece for visas). The number of places is no longer so limited.

For Christmas I wish you very peaceful days in good health and pleasant surroundings, and hope you will soon be released from your post.

Till next time affectionate greetings and kisses from Your Martin

Letter 113   [*no date*]

My beloved, big, dear Helmut!

The holiday is drawing nearer and—God willing—also the time of the reunion we've so longed for. My dear child, the last waiting period is coming to an end; then there will be a lot to tell. We have made the plans up to now only in broad outline; with the three of us and possibly with further thoughts from Dr. Kern things will move forward. Martin is diligently learning whatever he can lay hold of. You two will complement each other wonderfully with such completely varied experiences. You must surely be happy about that. However, we don't want to celebrate a lot here; the three of us will do that together over there.

Darling, will you please transfer promptly to New York (Hapag-Lloyd office) the money for my transportation to California. Dr. Kern wrote in November that he wants to assume the cost of Martin's trip to Los Angeles.

Everybody sends their best wishes. If possible send us a few lines again soon. It's our only comfort in this confused world. Our building is fortunately well heated, also the office and the university. Has Mrs.

Lehner written to you? I had solicited a possible sponsorship [*by her*].
In any case it's good to have two.

So now, *1000 kisses from your old Mutti.*

[*The following letters from Martin and Maria, sent together as Letter
114, reflect their concern about the fact that there has been no word
from Helmut in almost three months*].

Letter 114 Berlin, Dec. 21, 1952

Dear *Yankee* Helmut!

It's Sunday evening before Christmas, a mountain of mail is lying
in front of us, part finished, part not yet. You know our extensive circle
of friends, and woe betide us if we forget one of them! Why hasn't any
mail come from you even for Mother's birthday? Hete Steffe came
from Potsdam; she still hasn't heard anything from Ilse (since she was
arrested two years ago). Dieter fled to West Germany after he was
spied upon (as a "reactionary " teacher).

Today Christmas vacation started for us (till Jan. 4, 1953). I will
have to work a few hours every day for the TU. But in the long run it's
all fun! On New Years Eve we want to hear Beethoven's 9th Symphony in the Tegeler Humboldt School. We hardly have cause for great
jubilation. The only purpose for getting intoxicated would be the
stupor. You are still giving us the most concern, because we're not
hearing anything from you. Everything else is unimportant to us. So
now, write to us once! May everything go well for you in 1953!

Greetings and kisses to you,
Martin

My dear Young Man!

At the turn of the year your mother also sends you the warmest
greetings and wishes. Meanwhile, what all may you have experienced,
little Helmut? We would love to know, and can hardly wait for your
next letter. You had spoiled us a little bit [*with mail*] in July, August,
and September. Certainly you can't always write when you want, but
from time to time. Have you received the two book mailings and the

little Christmas package? If you have experienced anything terrible or difficult, just write to me about it from your heart, since we are the ones closest to you, my darling. We would rather wish for you a nice pleasant experience. That will all come at the right time. So, dear child, I commend you to God's protection, wherever you may be. To a quick reunion then, with you over there, or will you perhaps come here [*on leave*]? So, then, happiness to you in 1953 and a hearty kiss from your Mutti.

Letter 115   *Korea , Dec. 31, 52*

Dear Mom, Dear Marts,
    Hope that your holiday season was a pretty happy one. Received all your correspondence with the keenest of interest. It was wonderful to hear about Mart's schooling, especially. And your package got here about Nov. 15. Although I haven't used the chess board yet, I hope to be soon, now that I have so much more time to myself.
    Here is what happened to me. First of all, my leg is as good as normal. Then, I have spent the past 3 and 1/2 months on mess duty here at Headquarters Battalion. During all that time I was working in the bake shop here, with narry a moment's time to myself during the day, and much too tired to do anything at all in the evening. Well, in the beginning of December a friend of mine from the lst sergeant's office came around and told me that I could be promoted to corporal if I were to become a baker. With the consent of the mess sergeant and four chief bakers I was changed from "Basic Intelligence" to "Basic Food Handling" and two days later to "Baker."
    I didn't —until now—know that the Marine Corps passed out any Christmas presents. But I think I got the nicest one of them all: another stripe on my arm and a pay increase of at least $10 a month. So now I am a corporal and have two stripes on my uniform.
    The essence of the whole thing is that I am well and hoping the same of you. I won't write any more right now, but soon there will be more (all about my ideas about you two). Till then the best of luck,

                                                    Your loving Helmut

Letter 116 *Korea, Jan. 6, 1953*

Hello Mart,

Happy birthday, fellow. I immagine that it will be over for now, so sorry I am a little late, but better late than never. You don't know how I felt not having written Mother for her birthday; but at that time I was working constantly and incapable of doing anything at all after work.

Well, all that has changed now, and I have all the time in the world to write letters—also the facilities. My desk is completed but still without light. I've been using it pretty steadily every second day of late, and it really makes me feel good inside. I am working with two nice fellows and can't complain about the people in my tent either. They are really a wonderful bunch. Most of them came over from the States only a month ago. Some of them came off the lines after being wounded badly enough not to be able to withstand any more combat. They are all mess men except for myself.

In another four months I should be on my way home. Once I get back to the States I'll start looking for a good job. You see, I am going to take one of those capability or aptitude tests. They are ways of finding out what kind of work you are bestsuited for (through education, upbringing). As I see it, a man will be able to produce better and more in the field he is best in. Consequently he should be most valuable in just that field and therefore get paid more at that kind of a job than at any other—unless it should be some kind of a racket. I immagine that it'll turn out to be electronics or research as a whole for me. Then, with valuable training gained and a tidy little amount of money made—with you two over in the States—I may think of going to college.

The way I figured it out it should take roughly a year to make enough money to get mother over on my own. With her it wouldn't take too long to get her visa after her affidavit has been furnished; and I still doubt that I'll get anybody to do that. So I guess it would be best to rely on myself for that.

Now then, if Mrs. Kern issues your affidavit, I immagine that it will take you at least a couple of years to get your quota and visa to enter the States. In the meantime you would be continuing your education—with a little help from me (monetarily) if necessary—and that would of course decrease the risks the Kerns are taking. I mean with those extra years of learning and experience you ought to have no trouble at all finding a good job once you get to the States. If you people have any wishes as far as merchandise or money is concerned, please don't hesitate to ask

Let me say it again: Happy birthday and many more of them. All the good luck with your studies too With a fond Hello and a hug for Mother I am as always

Your loving Brother Helmut

Letter 118   *Korea, Jan. 24, '53*

Hi Mom, Mart,

Just want to let you know that I'm alive and well, same as ever. My job is the same, the winterizing of our tent has been completed. About a month ago I had to move into our baker's tent, and fix it up same as I did the one I used to live in. But as I said, that's all done with now.

I got your letter yesterday. It took 10 days to get here, which is no longer than your letters usually do. I also got your package with the candies and marzipan. Thank you very much

They have some USO (United Services Organization) and Army shows traveling the frontlines here, and occasionally they come back here too. So we were able to see Carolina Cotton, Dick Contino, Mickey Rooney, and many others over here at the improvised stage in our messhall. Some shows are better than others, but as a whole they are pretty good entertainment.

My friend Ralph Eastlick is over his 30 day reconvalescence leave, and probably back at his new duty station somewhere around Chicago. We are corresponding regularly. He did a lot of work during his leave, and says that his leg is just as good as normal. I'm glad for him and his wife because they are such wonderful people. He is going to try to get some leave when I get back to the States in three or four months so that we can spend at least a few days together.

As I wrote you before, I am going to live where I'm going to find the best job. So chances are pretty good that I'll move to the Middle-west, that is around Chicago somewhere. There I'll be around all my friends from the Marine Corps.

Well, let me wish you good luck and close with a fond hug for the two of you.

Love, Helmut

Letter 120   Berlin, Feb. 5, 1953

My dear Helmut!

Four letters from you in four weeks, we really aren't used to that, especially after a silence of more than a quarter of a year. A thousand thanks for this mail, you're making us happy with every line! In the last letter, which came today, we found more pictures again, which we immediately examined closely. Tell me, does the man in the helicopter want to jump off, or can't he wait for the landing? I must tell you that your pictures are always nice, everyone that sees them finds them sensational (since they come directly from that hot spot, Korea).

After you get home will you be discharged immediately from the service, or will you still have to complete two years? I would like to hear you prattle in English sometime! Can you competently bawl out the bakers who are under you? Or isn't that customary in the Marines? Also, I'm interested in how you heat your tent.

On January 21 the humanities department, to which I still belong for the present, had a ball with a little theatrical production and midnight cabaret called "Humanistic Magic." A first-rate band ("Franz Bucherl") played for the dance. The audience was very international, so at my table a Persian woman sat next to Ramsi, and a Chinese man sat at a nearby table. Soon you should have a picture of my "festive matriculation," which we experienced recently. That was the reception of those newly matriculated into the student body. The chancellor, vice-chancellor, and deans of the eight faculties appeared in festive regalia. Prof. Muckermann delivered the speech of the day.

Now there are only four more weeks till the end of the semester; the time went fast, because I was scarcely conscious of it. I will surely attain the goals which I have to reach; in the first of the two math classes I got 12 out of 16 points, that is "good." Until the beginning of the new semester I will whip up the geometrical drawings. I've applied for a job as a work-student with AEG during the five-week vacation. Hopefully there will be something (prospects are bad).

First we'll celebrate Shrovetide here in Berlin. On the 17th (Shrove Tuesday) my electrical engineers are organizing a masked ball, which I would like to attend; however, I still don't have a costume. I want to be sure and participate in the "electro-alcoholic" experimental field if I have to miss the "Off-Center Escapades '53," the famous and very expensive event of the high school for visual arts. On the 11th I'm supposed to act as a table partner for a young woman at a silver wedding celebration.

By the way, I'm happy to hear that they're giving you opportunities for diversion occasionally. Recently we were at the "Nuremberg Trichter," a modern cabaret with wonderful performers. Lore Haase from Werder visited us one Sunday. They say that the Zone [*East German*] residents will soon no longer be allowed to come to Berlin. I'll close for today and work on Lesson 11 for Higher Math. So I'll just say in Berlinese: Mach's gut!

Greetings and kisses from Martin

My dear Big Boy Helmutlein!

Your happy mother wants to thank you just as sincerely for all the nice mail that has reached us already in the New Year. Your photograph is wonderfully clear; and who is sitting in the airplane? With three magnifying glasses I haven't been able to recognize you. Did you take the picture? So from now on, "Mabruck." Recently we received a nice letter from Aunt Anna Schram [*their old friend*] in the Bronx. She will be 83 years old and hopes for more mail from us soon, and news about when we will be coming to New York. I was very happy about it (as she was with our New Year's greetings). I wrote her that Mrs. Lehner might be willing to take over Martin's sponsorship.

Our Grandma is somewhat heavy-hearted; yes, she feels strongly the separation caused by the actions of the East—insurmountable. How can that leave old people any kind of hopes for the future? Grandpa and Grandma are going on 79 and 77 years old now. We can't go there through the blockade against people from the West. Who can do anything about it? Everybody asks about you and sends greetings.

By the way, you musn't change anything by mistake: Martin and I still go by the old quota numbers; but we must bring a sponsorship; for me yours is sufficient as long as you're a soldier. Recently changes have probably begun: I've read in the paper that separated families will be reunited. This year Martin is still a minor; who knows what will happen after that?! It doesn't matter to us who takes over the sponsorship; the sooner the better. Martin wouldn't like to remain here alone, as he recently expressed emphatically.

[unsigned]

Letter 123   Reinickendorf, February 25, 1953

My dear Golden Boy, *big-baby!*

How happy we always are when we receive mail from you, possibly even with photos. We always put them under the magnifying glass and thus establish that your dear little face looks serious, of course, but just as good and fine as before. After all your experiences in the country and overseas that means so much to us that you can't even imagine it. So, Helmutlein, receive a kiss by letter until hopefully you get one in person soon, mouth to mouth.

Enclosed are some photos from Martin—little brother's experiences during the recent weeks; a little diversion from his busy life as a student. Now whatever may come in relation to our early move over, we will deal with everything together, even if it should turn out somewhat harder and entirely different than up to now.

At the beginning of May Rosemarie Neuman will emigrate to Chicago with big Robby and little Peter. Anneliese Wenzel has lost her mother; a dear soul went to sleep. We were at the cremation. Otherwise everything is as it was in the past, until the politics of Berlin comes to a crisis point, about which we prefer not to brood too much. We can only ask God not to abandon us to a sudden attack by the East. They are dangerous and we are islanders.

1000 kisses and good luck everywhere, good big fellow.

In love, Mutti and Martin

Letter 124   *Korea, March 5, '53*

Hi, you two lucky people,

This is Korea calling. Your big boy, or baby as Mom calls me, is writing you another letter with a teeny-weeny witzy picture in it, which he took himself.

I just heard about a bit of news broadcast over the radio. There is supposed to be some talk about extending draftees for about 6 to 12 months. According to that I guess I won't get out of the MC before October '54. Well, it doesn't matter much. I'll be able to save a little more money that way.

By the time I'll get back to the states I'll have about 450 dollars in the bank (Norm deposited them for me) and close to 700 dollars in Security bonds. Those bonds I get at the rate of one $37.50 bond a

month since Dec. of '51. They mature after 10 years into $50 bonds
and can be cashed anytime along the line. If discharged in September
of this year I'll get another $500, 200 for leavetime due, but not taken,
and 300 customarily paid upon discharge for buying new clothes. That
will leave me close to $1000.00 in the bank by the end of this year—if
discharged on Sept. 28—and $850 in bonds. The money in bonds I'll
never touch till you guys are coming over then it'll be ready cash . Also
I'll leave the $500.00 on the bank in case I'll ever need it in an
emergency. That way it'll be pretty secure.

Here's goodnight now. Till the next time, best wishes and good
luck.

Love and kissse, Helmut

Letter 125   Berlin, March 23, '53

My dear Helmut!

In recent months it's probably the first time that you've been
writing more letters than we. We're happy about that, but you'll be mad
at us!?

Your last letter with the *teeny-weeny-witzy picture* took only 6 days
(usually about 10). It takes about that long for a letter from Bergfelde
bei Frohnan (East) to Reinickendorf. You must know that we haven't
been allowed in the East Zone for a long time. For some time the
separation of the U-[*subway*] and S-[*surface*] railway systems has been
pushed by the East. "Border stations" will be transfer stations (for
better possibilities of controlling passports); residents of the East with
Western tickets have to pay 5 marks fine, there is no more transferring
between sectors [*of Berlin*], etc.

You can see that Berlin Island is becoming ever smaller. In the
summer the Hafel [*River*] is the only bathing beach. Children, with
their parents and grandparents, relax (not always to everyone's delight)
on every piece of existing grass. We poor city dwellers can no longer
go to the Muggelsee [*a lake*] in the neighborhood of Potsdam, or to the
Wandlitzsee [*another lake*], like before. On the way to the T. U. I am,
thank God, independent of the public conveyances that travel through
the eastern sector. In summer I will always go there on my bicycle (25
minutes). At the moment I'm already training for it (for eight days I've
been a work student with master craftsman Timm of the large machine
unit in the Brunnenstrasse division). Well the time for me at this rough

work will not be long. After work I occupy myself at the drawing board and try to keep the week ends free.

3/24/53

Yesterday evening I interrupted this letter because I had a movie ticket for "Don Camillo and Peppone," a French-Italian Association film of Julien Duvivier. This film was strongly recommended to me and I can only advise you to see it if you have the opportunity! Until 10 minutes ago two school friends were here who sometimes like to play something on the piano. Music lovers are certainly welcome here, so we're happy if someone comes and plays.

Now you've heard something about my—maybe very boring—"experiences." For Easter you and your bakers will surely be very busy!? But even so we wish you a couple of nice, quiet holidays [*in Germany both Easter Sunday and the following Monday are celebrated as holidays*]. In recent days we heard only of battles on the middle western front. Are you still in that area? Have you had much to suffer from guerrillas? It would be nice (for everyone) if you would be released and not have to give up still another year.

So then happy Easter 1953! and good luck until you go home.

An affectionate greeting and a kiss from your Martin

Letter 126 Reinickendorf, March 22, 1953

Dear, good Helmut-*Boy!*

We hug you for all your nice mail, the latest from March 5. Thank you for everything you shared; it relieved us and made us happy. Today the newspapers set forth some hope; may everything proceed towards the rapprochement of the people, for the benefit of all suffering human beings. Please let us know your future plans, or your field of service and location. All the friends here are asking whether you could serve the rest of your military time here, even in Berlin. That would be so lovely; however, it ought not to divert from your and our plans for the future.

Easter is just around the corner; we are always together in hearts and thoughts. I've already thought about whether we might send you the accordion ahead of time via Rosemarie Plettig.

What kind of agreement have the Kerns made with you about the future and Mrs. Kern's planned trip to Stuttgart? We have heard nothing from them since November 3, 1952. Although Dr. Kern invited me by letter to come over there, maybe to help out...he wanted to undertake the sponsorship for Martin as soon as possible and to send the documents here. My dear boy, have you sent the documents for my entry to the consulate? The endless uncertainty of everything is hard for us, but hopefully now we will soon arrive at our goal, my brave child. May God arrange everything the way that is best for us.

Martin is seeing a good "happy" film today, which a person can use as a break from work. Meanwhile I will go to the Plettig-Neuman family (apartment 109) for a little while to see how their travel plans are going. The alarm is sounding again already, who knows why; hopefully not the sector turmoil again. Everyone sends you greetings. Now look at everything calmly; you don't need to do anything hastily. We recently received a very nice letter from Mrs. Bertha Dodge with good news and interest in you. She would like very much to see you again, etc. More about that soon. For now many kisses and best wishes. To a happy reunion!

Your Mutti in Berlin—still

Letter 127   *Korea, March 17, 1953*

Hi Mom,

Just want to let you know that I am well. My job is fine, I have more time to myself on the off-days and get a lot of time to work on my Elementary Algebra course—correspondence—which I hadn't been working on for 4 or 5 months. I'm merely refreshing that long-forgotten Algebra I had 7 years ago. I'm doing alright at it too, turning in two 8-hour lessons every second day for corrections. I have begun sending packages with my gear back to the States to Norm, like camera and equipment. Soon I'll send my personal gear and then I'll be all set for rotation.

The way it looks now I am scheduled to leave this country around the middle of next month. With an invitation by the Wades to spend my leave with my friend Norm I should be able to get mail there from May 5 to May 10. But this has yet to be confirmed. As soon as I hear that I'll be leaving a certain date, I'll let you know immediately. There is not much news otherwise. Sure hope Mart will find some time to let me know about his progress at school. I am sincerely interested in his studies, you know. Let me close now. I'll write more, soon.

As always, your loving son Helmut

Letter 128   Reinickendorf, April 1, 1953

My dear, good Helmut-boy!

Easter is right at our doorstep; hopefully the holiday will bring us all closer to the longed-for peace—it looks like it. In any case we wish you above all a good closing-up and a happy trip back. We're tremendously happy that this period, with God's help, will soon be over for our brave, upstanding big fellow. If only we could receive you over there [*in the United States*]! We will do so in spirit and with our whole heart!

Sometimes I wonder if you might be able to come to our area in the course of your service—if not to Berlin, maybe to Europe? Well, soon you'll be in beautiful, familiar California, at least closer to us. Tell us your news and maybe your plans; we wouldn't want to make any mistakes. Till now our emigration hardly had a purpose, but now our interminable separation is slowly ending; on the other hand, to have broken off here too soon would have been thoughtless. Our home is always yours, and finally the other way around, *n'est ce pas?* [*French = isn't that right?*] If only the constant threat of war [*in Europe*] would fade, or best of all, of course, end completely. All the nice mail from you and the photos are our whole joy; our three lives now belong together.

Yes, Mrs. Dodge wrote such a nice letter; she would like to see you again. Anne [*the Dodges' older daughter*] is a medical doctor and a year ago married *"a classmate," she and her husband are serving their intern year in Seattle, Washington, on the Pacific Coast but far north of California. Perhaps her husband will have to serve next year in the Army or Navy Medical Corps. Mary, of nineteen,* [their younger daughter] *is in her second year at the University. She is chiefly interested in music and plays the viola quite well. Do you remember still your first meeting in 1946? Lastly, Mrs. Dodge wrote, "May this year of 1953 prove a fortunate one for your family, and may fortune arrange for us to meet again. With best regards from the Dodge family,...Bertha Dodge..."*

She also mentioned your prospects after release from the Marine Corps. *You are also eligible for government aid in continuing your education, it will include tuition, board and room, books and some monthly allowance for one more year than the man spent in service.* You are probably also informed about this, or will be.

You know, it's very touching how loyal this family remains to us after 23 years of acquaintance through our trip from Guatemala to New

York—in spite of Dad's death. It must be our destiny. Perhaps they
would provide the sponsorship for Martin if nothing works out elsewhere. Write to them when you have time. We must be thankful for this
Christian love. Easter greetings and all good wishes for your future
from your mother who hugs you!

By the way, George Pisarek has now visited us, but we didn't give
him your address; he will probably send a note with us. Caution is
advised because he may be unsafe politically.

Mutti

[*George Pisarek, a friend of Helmut and Martin, had apparently had
communist leanings, even having attended a university in East
Germany. Thus neither Maria nor Martin are sure that he can be fully
trusted and caution Helmut about discussing political matters with
him*].

Letter 129   Berlin, April 3, 1953

Dear Ex-Front Fighter!

Hearty congratulations on your completed service on the front in
distant East Asia! Everyone who hears about you is breathing more
freely now that you're returning to the States. Your remaining service
at home will surely no longer be very dangerous!?

I'm really unqualified to answer your questions about photos;
therefore I've asked George Pisarek to handle them. Incidentally, his
political views continue to be unclear, although he doesn't give a hoot
about his studies at the Linden University (East) anymore (political
economist) and might want to begin afresh at the TU. Better not to go
into politics if he should write; just small talk or general chat. Last
summer he was in Palestine with his sister (about 100 students, an
international group) and worked in a communistic settlement (commu-
nal land).

In three weeks my second semester begins. New subjects coming
with it: Chemistry (inorganic), Introduction to Machine Building
(mechanical drawing, normschrift [*probably some type of writing or
lettering*], etc.), Mechanics, Technical Work Materials, Dictated
Sketches (freehand). In the second semester I can step into mathematics
in peace, after I have gone through the second exam. Hans Pohl will be

finished in summer. As a mathematician he doesn't want to teach, but to work in industry.

Greetings and kisses to you, Martin

Letter 130 *Korea, April 18, 1953*

Liebe Mutti, lieber Martin! [Dear Mother, dear Martin]
Just to show you I can still write German, I thought I'ld start out in German. But actually I've only written two or three letters in German since I've been over here. Many, many thanks for that big letter I got the other day. It held so much wonderful information that I don't believe I could match it by any means.

If the Neumans want to bring the accordion with them, that suits me fine. But don't you think Martin would rather play the accordion than I, since I haven't had an accordion in my hands in eight years. So if Martin ever plans to use it, then just keep it. But if the Neumans do bring it, it would, if possible, be best for them to take it to Chicago, because Ralph Eastlick could easily pick it up there and keep it until I come to visit him next summer.

When I get back to the States and calmed down a little, I'll write a letter to the Dodges. Yes, I think that that was awfully nice of them to write you, but I am sorry to say that I don't quite remember what the daughters looked like. What she says about my subsistences is not quite correct. The government used to pay about $65 for a single veteran while he was going to college (for food and rent) plus paying for all books and equipment (needed for studying) and tuition. The way they handle it now, they grant you education (1 and1/2 days of education for every day spent on active duty) and pay you 110 dollars monthly if you are single, out of which you have to pay for all your schooling and board and room. Loans are available for veterans, also financial help during on-the-job training. But since you can only apply for one of these assistances, I think I'll forget all about the deal until I start college. And I have 9 years after I get out of service to complete my education.

Just address the mail to me c/o Norman Wade. I'll probably be there from May 22 till June 1. After that I'll inform you of my new address as soon as I know it. Good night for now. Best wishes as always from your

Helmut

Letter 131   *On Board USNS "General Walker," May 5, '53*

Hello, you two,

Since we left Inchon, Korea yesterday morning, we are expecting a few hours of liberty this noon sometime. We are headed for Japan and expect to get there around 11 o'clock this morning.

I am working in the bakery 4-6 hours a day; got to go to work at 10:30 and might miss all chances for liberty this way. They have me baking bread.

The ship is a comparatively comfortable troopship—much nicer than the "Pope," the ship we came over on. Meals are excellent and swaying is a minimum as yet. Just a few guys are seasick. We expect to get to the States between the 15th and 20th of this month. I guess the Wades are waiting for me. Maybe I'll take a short trip to Wisconsin and Illinois to see Ralph. I would really be a lot happier if I saw him soon.

The two of us have grown to be very good friends, even though we haven't seen each other over a period of 10 months. He is a very fine man, even without much education, and very smart. At the age of 13 he managed a 160-acre farm with the help of his 12 year old brother, doing all the work themselves. He and his wife have been writing me constantly. Ruby Eastlick has really been wonderful at sending me packages, too. For Easter she sent a telegram, wishing me well. If I can possibly swing it I'd like to go to see them. Even a few days will do very well.

I think I'll hitch-hike, that means stand by the roadside and have someone pick me up who is going to Chicago or that general direction. If I wear my uniform I shouldn't have any trouble getting rides that way. Ralph and I always used to travel that way when we went on liberty from Pendleton to San Diego, or Los Angeles, or Hollywood. Once, when I had a 3-day liberty I hitch-hiked all the way up to Los Altos, which is about 600 miles. Now I think I can do it all the way from the west coast to the Middle West. It should be fun and very inexpensive. With my camera along I ought to be able to take a lot of fine pictures. Well, enough of that now. I just feel that I have deserved a little fun to my liking and am going to get it if at all possible.

If George was not able to get the Praktica camera, just let me know what the specifications are and the prices and taxes for different models. I'll let you know whether to buy it or not later. It is really a fine camera, but maybe I better think of buying a car rather than an expensive camera.

I'll close for now, hoping that this mail will leave the boat in Japan alright. Till next time let me wish you well and send you my best regards. I assure you I am as happy as you are about going home.

With love, Your Helmut

10

Back in California: *Helmut Re-enlists!*

With Helmut back from Korea and the issue of Martin's sponsorship still unsettled, Maria begs Helmut to use his 30 days of accrued leave to visit them in Berlin. But this possibility seems to have been thwarted—in ways that are not entirely clear—by Helmut's unexpected decision to re-enlist in the Marine Corps.

At this point Helmut sees this as his best opportunity to study electronics and eventually enter guided missile training. A conflict now appears to emerge for Helmut between finally getting on with his own education and helping his family resettle in the United States. His schooling with the Navy will involve several changes in location, and he also feels financially unprepared to give them the kind of start he believes they ought to have.

In Germany Martin continues his university studies while the situation in Berlin becomes critical. There has been a major uprising in East Germany and Russian tanks are surrounding West Berlin. Maria, now 59, is preparing to retire from her job at the school and would like to come the United States before she is 60.

Back at El Toro Marine Base, Helmut is looking forward to seven months of study in Memphis, Tennessee in the field of aviation electronics—only to learn that his application has been rejected. Instead, in January 1954, he starts out at the ground electronics school on Treasure Island in San Francisco Bay.

Totally frustrated by more than seven years of separation from her son, Maria hopes to visit him in California the following spring. But meanwhile, as one of the highest scoring students at Treasure Island, Helmut has been selected for a special six-month Naval program in advanced electronics in Pomona, near Los Angeles, beginning in May, 1953.

Once again, Helmut—ever practical—puts his mother off, arguing that he would not be able to see enough of her to make her trip worthwhile. The chapter ends with a letter sent at the beginning of Helmut's studies in Pomona, which will be followed by an assignment at the highly restricted Naval Ordnance Testing Station at China Lake out in California's Mohave Desert.

⌘

Letter 133 Berlin, May 16, 1953

Dear "Big Brother"!

If I were to keep a diary, I would draw in three stars and inscribe: "Helmut has left Korea" (according to his letter of May 5th)! That got us all excited.

I want to acknowledge the picture in which you're sitting at your workplace. It's nice; thank you! From the previous letter something is unclear: do you still need 9 years after time in the service until you're finished? Do you mean 9 semesters, or how will such a long time come together? Summer has come very early here, so that I'm going to the TU in short pants. On Pentecost we'll surely be able to go bathing.

If only I had more time for recreation! I'm way behind in my continuous work because suddenly recognition of participation in mechanical drawing was required of the basic practicum (26 weeks) and I had to repeat the delivery of detailed reports for this purpose. After Pentecost I have to produce drawings for representational geometry (from the first semester), and then I will soon have to take a course in DIN A2—Normschriftbogen [*a form of lettering used to label technical drawings, etc.*], all time-consuming work to do after hours [*at home*]. Of course I shouldn't neglect math and mechanics (physical-mathematical), otherwise it won't work out well in the exams. So at the moment it's a race against time, because everything is important; you just ask yourself what's the most urgent.

Today I took your accordion to the bellows repairman (one small hole). It will be ready on the 18th; then it will soon swim in the direction of Chicago. In the workshop of the little accordion factory I learned that our accordion is not, as we assumed, an Italian one

("Tonelli"), but comes from Klingental (today in the East Zone), a post-war, mass-produced one, not as good as present-day West German handmade instruments. However, since it cost only about half as much, it's certainly not as bad as people make it out to be (probably to defend their own brand). For all that, you're sure to be happy with it, and if you want, maybe we could buy another one and bring it with us.

In your letter you compare a camera to a car, which you may prefer to buy. (Mother is already happy that you will pick her up in a little car). But, tell me, are these two things really comparable? Here only in a ratio of one to ten. If autos are so cheap, then I can understand. And gasoline must also be dirt cheap! ? Here only prominent people and businessmen have money for cars, and also hitchhiking here is some-times connected with payment.

On your leave I wish you fine weather, good recreation, and very nice experiences, no matter where you are! Let us know your address soon.

Kisses from Martin

Mr. Kern has written that his wife will be leaving as soon as I arrive and that a sponsorship for Martin will follow as soon as possible! (?) He surely waited for that; a sponsorship must be used in two-three months. Everything will probably work out now. Dear big boy, my good Helmut! How happy we are that you have Korea behind you, and now how long still and where? Greet all the dear friends who took care of you in our stead and who now stand at your side. Now God be with you and we hope for a happy reunion there or here. We can hardly wait.

A hug from Mutti

Letter 134   *Menlo Park, May 27, '53*

Hello you two sweet people,

How are you getting along? I am just fine, myself. Thanks for your letter with the picture in it. As far as the catalogues and descriptive literature of cameras is concerned I never received any yet. When I said that I thought it better to keep my money and invest it in an auto-mobile a little later I meant just that. A five or six year old car, like a Chevrolet or Ford, with about 50,000 miles on its speedometer costs around 700 dollars, wheras a good camera costs anywhere from $100

*to $400 and more. But new autos cost from about $2000 for a Chevy or
Ford to $4500 for a Cadillac and Lincoln.*

*If you want to know anything about my voyage I can only say that
it was uneventful and stormy. I was seasick (a little), but didn't have to
heave. We got to S. F. on the 17th and started our leave on the 22nd.
Although I'll have 30 days of leave if I want them, I'll be going down to
El Toro (Santa Ana, Calif.) to report for duty tomorrow. The Wades are
awfully nice to me.*

Till later, love, Helmut

Letter 135 Reinickendorf, May 27, 1953

My dear big Helmut-*boy!*

By now we hope that you are in your new home, with good friends
who have received you and surrounded you with love, as far as this is
possible. An important period has been reached in your and our family
life. It will now be decided where and how long you will spend your
last segment of military service. How was your trip back? We're
already looking forward to your next mail. Did you see more of Japan
this time? I have always imagined it to be storybook-like despite the
bustling life of a huge port city. Well, you will hardly have become
more acquainted with it on your short visit.

Then came your reception in the USA. That must surely have been
a wonderful experience, which we would love to have shared with you.
Now, for the moment, we must take comfort in the hopefully no more
distant future, in which we will experience almost everything together.
Isn't that right, my Golden Boy? Sometimes when the doorbell rings, I
wonder whether you could be standing in front of our door! Incidentally, in such a case be advised not to go through the East Sector (that is,
the city center) under any circumstances. Instead, transfer once more
inside the West Sector. Couldn't you apply for a leave with your
mother after some seven years of separation if you can't obtain a sponsorship for both of us in any way? Just recover first from your year in
Korea, which involved a mental strain for all of us. Martin has now
registered for mechanics as a new subject, very new and interesting for
him. Nevertheless he would interrupt everything on the spot if we could
only see you again and make plans together.

Helmut, if things don't work out for us to get over there, then by all
means come home to visit us—without obligations—after your release
from the service; we have so endlessly much to share and have to get
reacquainted again. Also, here you might be able to go to the TU with

Martin as a guest-student. I also think that near the Zehlendorf railroad station there are some American university divisions; I read something like that once. Incidentally, there in the direction of Argentinian Street, whole rows of newly constructed American buildings, lodgings for Americans, have gone up. They've shot up from the earth like mushrooms.

There is a lot of grief everywhere; the worst is probably Aunt Dr. Eva Starkowski's loss, both of whose daughters have gone to the TB hospital in Heckeshorn near the Wannsee. More than anything we want to be able to maintain our health. Bodies that are too thin have no reserves to fall back upon in an emergency. By the way, when Mrs. Lotte Lehner last wrote me on April 9, she said she wants to continue trying to obtain a sponsorship for Martin, if possible. Tell me, wouldn't your friend Ralph do it, or someone in his family? Or have you asked Norm Wade; after all, it's only a formality.

Now, one other matter: Martin may be eligible for the draft here now that we're finally a federal republic. Wouldn't it be better in any case for him to serve the time over there? In this regard the two of you above all belong on the same side.

Pentecost Saturday the two of us went with the Muller family on an excursion to the Heiligensee [*one of several lakes in Berlin*], where I went to a ferry restaurant on the bank of the Havel. On the other side you were always aware of a Russian base, with loud radio music, singing, startling shots at individual swimmers, etc. If only they would go back East. We feel their presence everywhere, especially the poor sector [*east Berlin*] and East Zone inhabitants. But on our side heavenly peace!

[*The last paragraph of this letter began with references to a woman who had been trying to promote a relationship between her daughter and Martin*]....Martin has pulled back a little, since she was making a great effort to draw him in. He still has no time for a serious relationship, that would only hinder him from his work. That will all come soon enough, when the right one comes along. And you won't remain a single "crab" either—you must really be laughing at that. [*Helmut's mother is referring to the crab as a sign of the zodiac, Cancer, which was Helmut's astrological sign*]. Of course I don't know where this letter will reach you. In any event may it bring you many affectionate greetings and all the best wishes for your future from both of us in BALIN. [*This is no doubt a play on words, comparing insular Berlin with the island of Bali*].

In love, your Mutti

Letter 136 *El Toro, June 2, 1953*

Hi Mom, Hi Mart,

Here I am at the base now. I spent a whole week end in casual section before I was assigned to my current outfit. It is Marine Air Maintenance Squadron 10, Marine Training Group 10, Marine Air Corps Station. From there they put me in the station Bakery, where I'll probably go to work in a few days. I was offered a term at Naval Electronics School either in San Francisco or Chicago. In return I'ld have to extend my enlistment for two years.

Well, tomorrow I'll probably be taken before the major. If the subject of reenlistment should come up, then I'll put my terms in front of him squarely. If I get all possible assistance through the Marine Corps or otherwise to get you, Mother, over here—if possible during my two-year term—and if I'll get to go to Electronics School and change my Spec Number [occupational specialty number] *from baking to electronics when I get out, and if the outfit is willing to release me for further training in guided missiles—if I should qualify for it, then I am going to agree to extend for two years.*

The only reason why I would want to get out of the MC, now, would be to get enough money together to be able to get you over. Wades are going to take care of Mart when the time comes. If I can do all that, and go to school and get training in electronics staying in the Corps, I'll do that and extend for a couple of years, but only then. Well, I'll keep you posted promptly.

Till later, your Helmut

Letter 137 *El Toro, June 5, '53*

Hi, you two,

Well, your little Helmut is going to be a soldier boy for another 3 years. He will get out of the Marine Corps on the 9th of June 1956. In the meantime he will get good training and experience for civilian life in electronics (ultra high frequency radio and radar) with a 30 week course in Aviation Electronics at a Naval School in Memphis, Tennessee in the near future. Pretty soon I'll apply for another affidavit for you Mother (they couldn't do any more than reject it again due to insufficient funds) and if they should accept it, you should be on your way over here before long.

The Wades will give an affidavit for Martin when the time comes. I would like to try to keep the Kerns out of this entirely. By the way, the Kerns held a chicken picnic in my honor during my leave, during which OK presented me with a "C Soprono Blockflote" he had brought back from Germany especially for me. Also he gave me an expensive German photo-electric "Sixtomat" lightmeter after I admired one he had. All these were counted as belated Christmas presents. Mother when you loose your job in December I'll try to get you as a dependent. That way you will get some money from me <u>and</u> from the government, which you can use towards Mart's education. It will save me from paying a lot of taxes.

I am already working in the electronics shop, first day today. They had me washing coffee cups and bringing in water for coffee. I should start school late in summer. Till next time lots of love

Your Helmut

Letter 138   *El Toro, June 12, '53*

Hi people,

I feel the urge to write you again. Actually I can't recall having thanked you for the two letters I got while I was with the Wades. And now Norm writes that there is another one and a couple of books in German. Well, you guys are really outdoing yourselves.

Yesterday I got my first mail here at the base. One letter from Norm and one from Ralph. Norm and his Dad didn't think I should have re-enlisted on two accounts. First because they thought that it was doubtful that I would get into electronics, they thought those were only promises. But, you see, I am in already and going to go to school next month probably. The other reason was that they thought that I could get you over sooner if I were a civilian. Well, I don't know about that either. I am going to try to make out another affidavit around Christmas. Maybe the Consulate will accept it as sufficient, then.

As for myself: I'll try to give you my reasons for re-enlisting. When I would have gotten out in September I would have gone to work either as an apprentice machinist or in the electrical-electronics field. Shall we say that after 1 or 2 years I would have been called back into the Corps (my status would have been "reserve" for 6 more years) then I would have had to go back into the bakeshop. My training would have been interrupted invariably.

This way I'll get 7 months of intensive schooling, then 2 and 1/2 years of experience, maintaining and repairing radio transmitter and receiver sets. When I get out in June of '56 I'll be able to step right into the aviation electronics field, making pretty good money; and later on I can always yet go to school, when I'll have started a home for you people, I mean our position will be stable. I don't think I made a mistake by re-enlisting.

Well, on my way to Tennessee I may get a week of leave or so, which I would like to spend with Ralph in or near Chicago. Maybe I can look up the Neumans then if I knew where they live. God bless you two. Till next time,

Your Helmut

Letter 139 [*Undated*]

Dear Helmut!

I read your plans for the next three years with interest and would like to ask whether the period of technical training can be counted wholly or in part towards later study. The practical training you're receiving is certainly good, hopefully not too specialized. Hopefully too always in peaceful surroundings.

What if we were to meet again at Tempelhof [*airport in Berlin*]? At the moment one reads a lot about the political tension in East Germany. Maybe we can visit Grandma sometime soon. We last saw her three years ago.

Tell me, is Memphis located in the area of the southern states, where the black people predominate? Two years ago I read "*Blow for a Landing*" by Ben Lucian Burman, about Mississippi. When you have time, read this novel! Some weeks ago I saw the color film "*An American in Paris*" (with Gerschwin's music) starring Gene Kelly. I thought the film was great and would like to recommend it in case you're not familiar with it already. In Berlin we're having a film festival week now; the German film industry is and remains lame compared with Italy, for instance.

Greetings and kisses from Martin

Letter 140   Reinickendorf 6/21/53

Dear, good Helmut!

A crazy week lies behind us in Berlin, although we two weren't directly affected personally by the ungodly tumult. But it's hard on the nerves for everyone who takes the incidents seriously. We're sending you something from our newspapers as printed matter. Of course you will also be informed about the happenings there. Yesterday Martin went with Bergitte Muller to see an Egyptian film (film festival) in the Gloria-Palast on Kurfurstendamm. All of poor East Germany is in high agitation over their cruel situation. But hopefully everything will enter a more peaceful course and no second Korea will develop here.

Thank you for your nice letter from June 12; you will already have taken the right actions. We wish you good success in all your endeavors and are standing with you in our thoughts as long as we cannot yet be with you in person. But the sooner the better—with the increasingly isolated situation. We don't expect a big house, only a modest place to stay not far from you. This week I had an unpleasant dental treatment, six teeth pulled; not very comfortable. But hopefully it will work out well. Then I'll have a clean slate and won't need to cause any problems or expenses over there. No, one doesn't get any younger.

Hungary, etc. are rising against the severe East Regime; what a shame that it's costing so many victims; only great desperation brings people to the point where they will risk everything! The young man who was shot to death here (in a Russian court martial) is from Reinickendorf West, has a wife and two children. It could just as well have been somebody else (as a horrifying example).

6/22 Early: I'm going to the school in an hour, have two hours telephone duty while the school has an outing day. Then I'll be back and Martin too, with his homework; I'm sitting on the balcony and chatting with you, my boy, from a distance. Everything is still in an uproar; fortunately we're not located at a sector border point. All of West Berlin is hemmed in by Russian tanks, etc. together with the East German police; one dares not dwell on it. We didn't let ourselves dream that the situation would become catastrophic so suddenly. May God soon grant a marked change for the good—we want to ask him for that. The despair was so great, you know, it had to come to an explosion. Tomorrow Adenauer [*president of West Germany*] is coming here for obsequies. Dear child, be embraced, and may all go well for you.

                                                                    Mutti

Have you received an actual refusal from the State Dept. or have you received no answer to your application to bring mother? Robby Neuman rightly asked what area we would move to, since it probably belongs to a sponsorship to provide accommodation for the immigrants. What do you want then, should we go to Los Altos or start out in the Middle West? If there are problems with mother's affidavit she can surely go over temporarily as a visitor; thus she would retain the right to a pension from Germany. Wouldn't the state subsidy you mentioned apply to mother as a visitor? Does a visitor have to leave the country again after a certain time?

Greetings and kisses from Martin

Letter 141 *El Toro, July 4, '53*

Hi, you two good people over there, I realize that you are due for a letter from me for quite a while now. I got two of them from you and one through the Wades two weeks ago. Also those camera catalogs. Thanks for everything. I guess it'ld be best if you forgot about the cameras until some later time, when I'll probably ask you to buy me some little 35 mm camera. But till then I won't need one.

By the time they will have my occupational specialty number changed from baker to aviation electronics and assigned me to that school in Memphis the summer will be over, thank goodness; as I understand it, temperatures down there are around 100 degrees F. day and night. Here in Cal. we have a consistent drop in temperatures at night, at least along the coastal valleys. This coming week I'll take my final examination on that course in Elementary Algebra which I started and finished in Korea. Right now I am attending 3 hours a night, 3 nights a week for 6 weeks a class on Television at one of the close-by colleges. I am more or less only sitting in on the lectures, without getting any grades at the end of the course (I do not have the necessary prerequisites required for this course) but I am sure learning, if not all everybody is learning. The course is free except for the books and I am using someone else's.

Today is Hugo Klinkert's birthday. You know; he is married, has a son about 1 and 1/4 years old and lives in Long Beach, about 30 miles from here. So far I spent two Sundays with him on the beach. Tomorrow I'll probably go to San Diego. Since he's down there for the week end, I might be able to get a ride home with him. So long and God be with you.

Your little Helmut

Letter 142   Reinickendorf, July 4, 1953

Dear Good Helmut, Boy!

The 18th of July is approaching again, your 23rd birthday. At the moment we don't know your latest address but I would still like to start a little letter to you. Where might you be right now? It's Sat. night, I'm sitting alone on the balcony, but the gnats are too lively, so I'll probably have to go back in soon. Martin went to the Mullers for a little chat with Brigitte. We're having hot days, so I am glad to be alone once and talk to you, my darling. You will probably also have a nice girl sometime for company and I'm sure you will have good taste.

We're anxious to know if you will see the Dodge family in St. Louis soon. In any case they are touchingly faithful in their letters, and that is sometimes the most important thing in life, to know someone on whom one can depend. I will never forget how Mr. Dodge formerly wrote us that if something happened to old Aunt Augusta he would stand behind you. That reassured us so much; I would ask you to take an appropriate attitude, as you feel led—natural and friendly, without shyness—towards true friends, for up to now they have always treated us kindly and felt for us, and perhaps that can be meaningful for one's whole life.

Yesterday Mrs. Fritz and Mrs. Froscher came for coffee with us. Rudiger [*Fritz*], as a policeman on the sector borders, sees and is aware of many things. Building manager Pirecki from the school is worried; his son hasn't returned home from the East Sector since June 17. Unfortunately many West Berliners are detained there, are harassed, etc., viewed as agitators—such nonsense. The uprising—without any weapons—arose from desperation and has grown spontaneously. Unfortunately one can't tell how many victims it took with it.

Dear boy, I've already written you that Uncle Richard (age 79) and also Greta Neustadt (from Merseburg), about 54, were released from their suffering (cancer). If only the Starkowski girls don't come to a catastrophe; I'm going to inquire again from their mother, Aunt Eva. I suppose you're now beginning your new term of service. Please tell us about it in your next letter. Well, we can hardly meet this time on your 18th of July. We will spend the whole day with you in spirit, my dear, big boy, and for the present send you many heartfelt greetings, best wishes, and loving kisses.

                                        Mutti

Saida Helmut Effendi! [*Arabic: Hello Mr. Helmut*]

Esaiak enta, ya habibi? [*How are you, dear fellow?*] That's about
as far as I can go [*in Arabic*]. Malesch! [*Too bad!*] Congratulations in
everything for the future! I want to wish you, ya uallet [*boy*], plenty of
filus [*money*], good health, and happiness, privatim wie generatim
[*Latin: personally as well as generally*]. A letter that might reach you
in Memphis must properly be in Arabic; so don't be surprised if I speak
to you in Arabic. [*Martin is referring to the fact that the original
Memphis was in Egypt, where Arabic is spoken*]. I am always annoyed
with myself for retaining so little.

For over a week it's been at or above 30 degrees C; the water was
so warm that bathing in Tegel Lake hardly cooled you off. I don't want
to take my "vacation" till September, when the worst heat is over. The
holidays begin July 20, the winter semester begins around Nov. 1; I
want to work 6 weeks; the rest of the time I have to have for myself, or
rather for the T. U. There will hardly be any time left to prepare for the
intermediate examination in Humanities; there is so much to calculate,
draw, and prepare. At the moment I'm preparing for the second math
exam of the semester, which is on the 14th (on partial diversions,
higher order functions, and complex functions). I passed the first one,
inshalla!! [*Arabic: Thank God*] with "satisfactory" (3.0). About 3/4 of
all the people were supposed to have <u>failed</u>. (A lesson from Vector
Analyses).

Incidentally, we have a few female students among the machine
builders and electrical technicians; we call them "Intelligent Beasts"
(mostly ugly).

Until next time a thousand greetings and kisses,

Martin

Letter 143 [from Helmut's mother]   Rdf. July 13, 1953

Hallo, boy—good dear Helmut!

*These lines may bring you our heartiest greetings and best wishes
for your birthday, that means health, success, and luck on the whole
line—and good camerads and true friends. We add* [a letter] *and foto of
Rudiger for your 23rd birthday. The boy had last weeks also hard
service here at the Wedding-Sector-frontiere.* [The sector border in a
neighborhood called Wedding]. *Never mind, he is nearly three years in*

police service, and this profession in this time of insecurity is somewhat harder than in normal circumstances.

But now, more in German; with it the letter will end well. Well, we've just gotten the accordion started on its trip. The things will be picked up at Apt. 109 tomorrow morning. Rosemarie will fly to Chicago with little Peter on July 16, via Frankfurt; her husband, and his mother, are very happy about their coming. The baggage, of course, is going by ship. Her address is: Rosemary Neuman, 6940 S.E. Marshfield, Chicago, Ill. So ask first by letter when it's appropriate to visit—after the baggage has arrived. In any case we're happy that you'll be able to "play" again, but also keep it for your pleasure. It brings faithful greetings from little brother and mother through a childhood friend from Reinickendorf.

Of course, we would prefer to fly right with her! But our day to travel will also come. Incidentally, Robby's brother Alfred has been in Lichterfelde [*a section of Berlin*] for two weeks for the termination of his service (he was also in combat in Korea). How life turns out sometimes—Well, stay well and be embraced by us two Islanders. As Mrs. Schmidt wrote today, Mrs. Kern wanted to be with us in June—now she can scarcely be expected to come here to the "Berlin Situation!" We will certainly find out.

[*unsigned*]

[*The following letter, enclosed in Maria's, is from family friend Rudiger Fritz, who was serving with the West Berlin border police*].

Letter 144

Dear Helmut!

You will be surprised to get a letter from me. I really always wanted to write you, but it just never happened. Whenever I saw pictures of you at your mother's place, I resolved to write. Now I really have a good reason because your birthday is right around the corner. Hopefully my birthday wishes will still arrive on time. They really should have gone off much earlier but I've hardly been at home since June 17. Even now it's still not peaceful in the East. I don't think it will ever be peaceful again as long as the Russians are in the country.

So now we're right on the subject that people here are most preoccupied. with. I don't dare enter the East Sector [*of Berlin*] at all anymore, much less the East Zone [*East Germany*]. Maybe you will be surprised at the difference between the "Zone" and "East Berlin." You can only enter the Zone if you have a permit from the East German government. It may be harder to get this pass than to go to America. Only it's the opposite from the Zone to Berlin. The whole city border here is barricaded with boards or barbed wire. Only within the city limits there are still no barricades between the east and west sectors.

If anyone from the East ventures beyond the border it can very easily happen that he will be wounded because the border is watched very closely from the East by the Volkspolizei [*East German police*] and also the Russians; tanks are even brought in from the East in some places. The Volkspolizei are no longer distinguishable from the Russians, since the uniforms and the weapons are the same. We from the West do our patrols only with rifles.

No, I didn't think that I would end up with the police. It happened exactly like with you when you went to Korea. I doubt that I will stay with the police my whole life, because it isn't ideal. It was and remains an expedient; however, it's just very hard to get anything different and better and after all one is dependent on money to a certain degree.

Surely you must know that Rolf [*Gelewski*] is married. Horst Lazile is studying law. I'm with him often. Georg [*Pisarek*] has recently been wanting to study in the West. He's fed up with the East too. Darselle wants to emigrate to Portland (USA). So this is all, as the sheet of paper is filled up. I hope you've been happy and now, most importantly, best wishes for your birthday.

Many greetings from Germany, Rudiger

Letter 145 *El Toro, July 19, '53*

Hi Folks,

I guess when a fellow reaches my age he stops having birthdays. I received your nice letters—and Rudigers—last week, and let me thank you very much for all the information and interest. Outside of those letters there was a package with a fruitcake to remind me of my birthday. The cake was from Mrs. Kempf, who had saved it for me from last Christmas. It never occurred to me that yesterday was my birthday until I happened to spot a cake around noon.

My work is certainly very interesting now. I am learning how to repair and check and install radio receivers and transmitters. I guess I'll be sent to school around the beginning of September. As I heard it costs the Marine Corps around $10,000 to send one man to this Electr. School at Memphis. I can only say that there is a fine bunch of men in this outfit. All of them certainly of much higher intelligence than the ones I was overseas with.

Although I will look in at the Dodges when I'll be in Memphis, I have learned to get along without favors from friends, entirely. I am depending on myself only from now on.

Your Helmut

Letter 147

Rdf. 7-24-53

Dear Son, good Helmut!

Again you made us happy with such a nice letter; it reached us enormously fast: in just three days—heartfelt thanks. Everything is so interesting to the two of us here, as you can imagine. Enclosed are pictures of Rosemarie and little Peter's departure for Chicago from Templehof on July 16, 1953. Her first letter to Mother Plettig arrived today. The flight lasted 40 hours and went well; her reception and first impressions were as she had wished. We are happy for them; for the three of us, with God's help, there will also be a reunion, about which we will certainly be no less happy.

Martin achieved a 2 again in his math exam; otherwise, too, the second semester ended happily, about which we're glad. Monday he begins to work again as a trainee in the turbine factory of AEG. It helps now, although he could certainly use long vacations for all of his university work. In September he needs to relax after 9/5.

Dear boy, it's wise of you to free yourself from the good will of "strangers;" in so doing you will not bring pain to anyone who has honorable intentions; on the other hand the faithfulness of true friends is a joy that many people hardly know. It would make me sad if you had bad experiences. Pour out your heart; it gives relief. I have experienced a lot and understand almost all situations.

Greetings and kisses from
Mutti and Martin

Letter 148 Berlin, Aug. 11, '53

My dear Helmut!

We are glad that you like El Toro and that you're enjoying the work. If the training in Memphis is so expensive, then you will surely get a lot out of it; hopefully your application will be supported. I imagine that you are momentarily in a precision workshop, is that right? Or are you repairing the sets on the spot? In any case, this is a kind of basic practice that every technician needs.

For the past two weeks I've been a work student again with AEG, namely for six weeks in the Moabit turbine factory. The director, a certified engineer, kept me busy in his office the first three days. I had to interpret charts. Then I was assigned to my real destination: to build the standing parts of generators and to set up an experimental generator in the test bay (a new kind of cooling with hydrogen instead of with air). For four days I was used "upstairs" where I had to draw curves of the energy paths of an inductor and after various trifles I am taking extracts from a technical journal on "Smooth Cylindrical Surfaces."

As you see, this time I'm earning my money in very pleasant and instructive employment.

Last Saturday the factory party was held at the Tegel Lake pavilion. The company gave the employees a plate of pork roast, coffee and cake, four beers, and four brandies; also a guest could come free. I invited Brigitte Muller. It was very nice, even if not as elegant as any of the dances at the TU.

Now I would like to make a request: Please get me a course catalog from some American technical college for the direction of my studies (electrical technology, power current technology, engineering). I would like to compare it to the local ones, in order to determine how much of what I'm learning here I can use in a continuation of my studies in the USA.

It's a question of an overview of the whole curriculum; which subjects are to be covered in which semesters, how many lectures and practicum hours there are, and when one is tested in individual subjects. Maybe you can inquire about whether and how far a partial German education is recognized. As far as I know, even completed studies aren't always recognized (for example medicine). Many of our friends are advising me urgently to finish my studies here; others to go over there immediately. What do you think about it? Do consider all of the circumstances.

A short time ago Mrs. Braunsdorf [*a friend from East Germany*] was in Berlin to pick up the food packages donated to her and Grandma. She was with us two days and two nights and told us a lot about Wittenberg and Grandma. Everyone always sends you greetings.

Your faithful Martin

[*Note added by Helmut's mother*]:

My darling: *Good evening and many thanks for all fine post. Today I like to inform you that Mr. Neuman had to go to Sacramento—California; Rosemarie will follow him with Peter. I will inform you if I know more, I mean about the accordion…they will dwell in the houses of the military families.—Do you know anywhat about Sacramento, isn't it near Los Altos?*

Letter 149   *El Toro, 16 Aug. '53*

Hi Folks,

Just a few lines to let you know how I am. Everything here is fine, including myself. Currently I am getting ready to fire our rifle for requalification—this ordinarily is done about once a year. You don't realize just how hard it is to get in and out of some of these firing positions. They have us fire everyway except on our heads. But it's a lot of fun; and marksmanship has always been my hobby. You might be interested to know that I finished that TV course at OCC with a "C" (satisfactory). Although I wouldn't be satisfied with a grade like that ordinarily, considering the fact that this was an advanced course and I just a novice, I am satisfied. Also I know a little about TV.

It is entirely possible that I'll make sergeant in October. That will mean a handsome increase in pay. Also—unless it'll be changed—I'll leave for 20 weeks of school at Treasure Island (San Francisco Bay) around the middle of October, to be continued by another 3 months of school at San Diego or so. You see my application to enter the Aviation Electronics field has been rejected. Instead I was assigned—or rather will be at the time of transfer—to Ground Electronics. Although my Electronics Officer and Sergeant and the squadron commander are going to try to keep me in Av. Electr., when something comes from

*Washington not much can be changed. Although I would have
preferred Av. Electr., it doesn't matter much one way or another.
Maybe I can get into "guided missiles" (V-2) in this way.*

Good luck and much luck, Your Helmut

Letter 150   *El Toro, Sept. 21, '53*

Hello Mom, Hi Mart,
     *I just received your letter of September 17. Another one of those
that only took 4 days to get here.*
     *There was quite a lot of news in it. I think it's just wonderful that
you, Mother, want to come to Calif. next spring; but in a way I think
that a voyage of this kind takes a lot more than sentiment and enthu-
siasm. I tell you what: Let me think this thing over all the way. Give me
a week and I'll write you the details. Maybe we can arrange for you to
stay here permanently even before you come. That would be alright
wouldn't it; but it's rushing me quite a bit.*
     *So far I don't even have a place for you to stay. And to buy one
would be foolish as long as I'll be in the Service, because if you'll come
over here, we'll want to stay together. As soon as you come over
here—maybe not as a visitor though—you'll be eligible for some $110
or so plus $90 for me. I'm sure that we could get along on that and still
save some for the future. As you probably already know life over here
is awfully expensive. Why, do you know that I spend an average of $40-
50 a month, most of it for clothes, cleaning, and soap and such stuffs. I
have a beer now and then and permit myself to go to a movie once or
twice a week. To own and operate a car would come to something like
$50 a month, although that figure could be reduced considerably. I'm
sure that we could make a go of it.*
     *Now to something a little more immediate. On the 10th of next mo.
I'll report at Treasure Island for 20 weeks of Electronics Technician
School. I'll be only 45 or 50 miles from Menlo Park and 120 miles from
Sacramento. Treasure Island, or TI as I'll call it in the future, is a man-
made island in the middle of San Francisco Bay. It was made for a
World Exposition held at S.F. some years back. A Naval institution is
there now, part of which is this ET school. Next year March I'll get
through with that, then follow either 20 weeks of school at Olathe,
Kansas, or 12-20 weeks of school at San Diego. Although I wanted to
get into Aviation Electronics, I was denied that wish. Ground Elec-*

*tronics is the next best thing though. Schools are supposed to be as
good if not better.*

*I heard from Ralph, where his wife is going to have a baby. That'll
mean that I'll become God-Father. I requested it. There was a time
when he thought he never would make it, but now he turns out to be the
happiest man alive.*

Well, be good. Many thousand kisses,

your Helmut

Letter 151   Berlin, Oct. 16, '53

Dear Helmut!

We have thought about you a lot lately, since you are probably on
the move from El Toro to San Francisco. In that case you will have had
no time to write. In any event we are still waiting for the letter you
mentioned with your decisions or intentions. Still, we don't want to
leave you without mail, even if we don't yet know your new address!

Do you have to take courses to become a sergeant, or is one
automatically promoted? Your education on Treasure Island is no doubt
purely technical. You've probably made a connection with Rosemarie
P. and maybe even received the accordion from her. Her latest
acquisition is a 1940 Buick (for $150) which drives like the Devil!

Meanwhile Maxe Genz (75) has died here (heart). Two weeks ago
he still visited us with his wife and made all kinds of jokes; he would
gladly have lived till 90. He still had no grey hair. I went to his funeral
on Tuesday, since mother had school. Do you remember how he took
pictures of us all at your departure?

On the 19th the new semester begins for me. Right at the beginning
I have to take the "Intermediate Humanities" exam. The new subjects
coming up are Machine Elements, Physical [*hands-on*] Practicum, and
Introduction to Electrical Engineering (with Prof. Mohr/AEG).

I'll close for today, since I still want to go to the movies: *"Hocus
Pocus,"* a film whose plot I'm already familiar with from a nice radio
drama.

Greetings and kisses, Your Martinus

Letter 152 *[undated]*

My dear, good Helmut-boy!

Dear big boy, how are you, have you already become a god-father?—a lovely role. Fortunately you have more normal conditions than prevail here. My goddaughter Ilse Steffe in Potsdam was arrested in March 1951, since then there has been no trace of her (she is 30 years old now). Cruel!

I wonder if Mrs. Kern is back in Los Altos. She wanted to go back at the end of September. Martin will start his third semester on Oct. 19. He wants to learn and work as much as possible. But his big hope is still to resettle as soon as possible in your America, for you probably won't come here as easily—or at least with the military. Just come at Easter towards the eastern part of the USA if at all possible, if you have a choice. Although Mrs. Plettig thinks I could live with her at Rosemarie's, which would be nice. But the main thing is still that I move close to you, even if we can't be together. Tell me, don't you have a lot of vacation leave coming, or has that been used for something else? Now let us just stay well, then everything will be all right; as it says so beautifully in the song, "Only a Little Courage."

By the way, warm thanks for your last nice letter from the end of September; but just don't buy a car—there is time for that—till everything is clear. First a modest place to stay and then your departure, isn't that right? We don't need to rush. If need be, there may be one to borrow; besides, we still travel everywhere by train and bus.

Thousand kisses, my boy, from your mother.

Letter 154 *Treasure Island, 11-30. '53*

Hi Mom, Mart,

Your last letter came on the day I was leaving El Toro. Since I finished checking in here today, I have a little time to drop you a few lines. I am one of a dozen Cpls and Sgts who are going to school here at TI and who are at the same time reigning over 300 overfresh Marines just out of Bootcamp who are also going to school here.

My duties will consist mainly of going to school, but since I am making more money than most guys here and also since I am supposed to have more experience than most guys here, I am also required to show some rare qualities of leadership. Well, I don't know how I'll be doing but I'll try.

When I reported in last Friday night I was given my liberty card and permission to remain on liberty till Monday morning. Altogether I spent five full days at the Wades. I intend to spend the Christmas holidays at the Wades' too. Norm and I are going to take a short trip to Sacramento, then, to see the Neumans.

Say, Mom, I really wish that you could hold up your visit till a later time. I am just getting a small bank account built up, and I am not going to count on any outside help. Also this school I am getting ready to go to is going to take me till well into May, if not June. After that there will be more school probably till the end of the year. When you go to school like this you can't get leave unless you happen to be granted some between schools.

Another point I'm considering is that, even though you want to pay for the trip yourself, the money will be almost wasted but for the few times you'll be able to see me. If you are going to spend the money to come over here—for a visit—you might as well stay; but as it is: I am not only not yet ready for you, but don't see how I could get ready with me moving from school to school.

Now, Mom, I know how you feel about wanting to see me, but your coming now would only gum up the works. Sure, I want to have both of you over here, as soon as possible, but that "possible" means in another year or best of all, when I'm out of the service. You have no idea, how I'm trying to save money. At the present time I have about $1000 in Security Bonds (in safekeeping at Washington) and a savings account of $850 in Palo Alto Mutual Savings and Loan Association drawing 3% interest, compounded semi-annually. An allottment of $80 a month out of my pay—which is about $120 now—constitutes about all the money I can afford to save every month. At the time of discharge I hope to have close to $5000 saved and a moderate car paid for. Then, with a pretty good Technician's job (steady income) and the savings and transportation we could easily start a home.

If you should come before then, I will have to stop my savings allottment and even if we won't have to touch the savings account or the Bonds it won't be easy living on what we make at the present time. That of course excludes all chances for a car and a start of a home. In other words we will be at a standstill until I get out and make a little more money. Since I was thinking of studying (going to college) a few years after my discharge, you can see that this would have to be postponed for two to four years until we will be financially stable.

Well, Mom, I sure hope you are going to be able to see this my way. If you only could—that would save me about three years of my life.

At the same time I've been thinking of another angle. I'm going to try to catch a hop to Frankfurt and Berlin as soon as these school months are over. With a thirty-day leave that'll give me enough time in Berlin with you to make up for all the years we haven't seen each other. Wouldn't that be nice? And I think it's possible.

Well, I'm going to include a picture or two. And please don't think of buying me something to wear. In the first place I have plenty of clothes and in the second place I can buy all the things I need and in the third place you need the money yourself. After Christmas I'm going to send Mart some money for a suit; please consider that my Christmas present. As always,

Your Helmut

Letter 155   *Treasure Island, Dec. 18, '53*

Hi Mom, dear Mart,

Today is your birthday, Mother, and I would like to wish you the best of luck and lots of good health. Naturally, with Christmas coming around, Christmas greetings are also on the order. The Wades invited me for Christmas to spend all of my 16 days leave with them. Right after New Year Norm and I will drive up to Sacramento and visit the Neumans.

It looks as though I won't be starting school until the beginning of January. People here are very nice and of high intellectual standard, an entirely different class of people than you usually find in the service, especially in the Marine Corps. This also is the best school the Navy has to offer for enlisted men. There is one man in my dorm who was an assocate professor for English Literature at the University of Bonn. He speaks very good German and is very educated; four years at Harvard U. and one in Rome. At the present time he is reading the novel "Der Tunnel" by Kellermause, which you sent me last year.

The Wades have opened their home to me completely and I am spending all my weekends with them and leave, too. Every Sunday we go to church and Norm and I go out to a dance, now and then. They are the finest people you can imagine and I wish you would write to them once. I am sure they would be delighted to hear from you.

As I wrote you before, if you ever need any money, don't hesitate to ask for it. I have more than enough in the bank to help you out when-ever you need it. I don't see why you should have a tough time getting along, if I am saving, here.

I'll close for now. Lots of good wishes and a very merry Christmas and luck for the New Year...

Your good old Helmut

Letter 156   *Treasure Island, Jan. 26, '54*

Dear Mom, Mart,

Like many other weekends I spent the latest one with the Wades in Menlo Park. When I got there I found your letter with the correspon-dence from the American Consulate and your wonderful answer. The Wades were as ready as ever to give Martin's affidavit of support and if mine for you, Mom, should not be sufficient they are willing to furnish any additional affidavit necessary. Also, I can always count on the Wades for sound advice and solid guidance.

As you know, my bank account has increased to something like $2000 which would be enough to make a downpayment on a house, a car if necessary, some furniture and clothes; but then there would be nothing in case of emergency; and to expect anyone else to foot our bills would be entirely out of the question. One other thing I'ld like to mention is that I'll be moving around for the next 2 and 1/2 years during which my company would be most valuable if not necessary to you. Besides of course the fact that we all would like to stay together once you got here. Unless absolutely necessary—according to further word from the consulate—I would like to ask you to be patient until I'm out of the service.

Now, for general information, I'ld like to ask you to answer a few questions and give some instructions in case of a negative answer from the consulate. Can you pay for your way over here and will it be possible to pay for the trip to S. F. over there; how much weight may you take with you in the line of household goods when you come. Will any pension or insurance be paid to you when you leave Germany, or while you are over here. Would you be willing and able to take on some household work.

Now to the visit to Sacramento. Norm is engaged to a young lady by the name of Bert Nye. Bert has a sister Alma who is engaged to a sailor. Since she would have sat at home doing nothing, we asked her whether she would like to join our little party, which she graciously did. She is a very nice kid, 16, a music lover—she plays the bass fiddle in the Peninsula Symphonie Orchestra—and the kind of girl I'ld like to get married to some day.

By the way, due to no fault of the Neumans the accordion was stolen before I ever saw it, together with all of Bob's civilian clothes—suits he had made in Germany. Although this is very regrettable, it was not due to neglect or any such thing except the delinquency of some nice fellow citizens.

Since I still have a lot of homework to take care of let me close for now.

As ever, Your Helmut boy

Letter 157 *Pomona, 10 May, '54*

Hi Mom, Hi Mart,

Sorry, long time since you people heard from me. I was very busy—at school. As you probably know, I re-enlisted in the Marine Corps to get as much schooling and special training as possible. Well, every 20 weeks or so five privileged Marines get to go through a specialized electronics course. They have to be of high class standing during their first 20 weeks of basic course, and a full two years to go in the service will help greatly. So, when the Lieutenant got a call for five men, he told me that I had to finish the last four weeks of the course in two, in order to be able to be one of the five men for this special course. I finished the 17 weeks that I went to school up at TI with a 97.35% average; out of 450 test questions I failed to answer 12, which made me one of the best students to ever get out of that school. Last Saturday I checked in here.

All in all this course is going to take approximately 24 weeks. My next duty station is probably going to be Inyokern in the Mohave Desert, about 100 miles east of Bakersfield and 200 miles north of L.A. Right now I am located about 30 miles east of L.A. The weather here is nice, but promises to be very warm later on in the summer. I might buy a car a little later in the year, so that I can get around a bit better on the weekends. Since I'll need one anyway when you come, I may as well get it early.

Figuring on me getting out of here about the middle of November, it would be nice if we could set the date for your arrival around

Christmas of this year, or thereabouts. Mom, you can either live in the desert where I'll be stationed or else near San Francisco. Mart, you can do what you think you'll want to do.

Let me know what you think of this plan, then I can go ahead and sponsor you, Mom, and Mart will be sponsored by the Wades. Hope to be hearing from you soon. My present address is on the envelope.

Best wishes and cheerio, Helmut.

11

Homestretch: *Countdown to Reunion*

With the Wades' sponsorship of Martin's immigration, the long-awaited reunion is at last clearly in sight. As Helmut immerses himself in his studies at Pomona and the subsequent guided missile training at China Lake, Martin is completing his final year at Berlin Technical University.

Although Helmut mentions receiving many letters from Maria and Martin, there is a lengthy gap in the correspondence from Germany—probably lost or not saved—between October 1953 and February 1955.

The focus now—from June 1954 to October 1955—on both sides of the Atlantic is on preparations for the big move. Helmut applies for a military allotment to help support his mother; Martin and Maria receive their American visas. Letters discuss what should be brought along and how it should be shipped. Martin asks for information about universities in California; Helmut expresses concern about his brother's draft status as a new immigrant.

There is mounting excitement in Reinickendorf as Martin and Maria dissolve their household of so many years and decisions are made about how they might best cross the United States.

The letters end with Helmut's final plans to drive across country to New York City and for the meeting at the dock on October 15, 1955, when the new arrivals will disembark from the *"Berlin."* Even though final decisions have not yet been made about the best place for Martin and Maria to live while Helmut completes his last year in the Marine Corps, this is of small concern compared to the joyful prospect of being together at last!

Letter 158   *Pomona, June 26, '54*

Hi Folks,

Just a short thank you for the pictures and nice letters. Also I want to say that I'm going to Menlo Park next weekend to talk things over with Mr. Wade.

I was at the Immigration Service here in Los Angeles last Friday and found out that I can petition your preferred quota; but to do it I'll have to have Martin's birth certificate, Mother's marriage license (or a certified copy). Also they want to know the number under which you were deported and complete dates of previous entry into the states.

Friday 10 days ago I bought a 1946 Dodge. The car is in very good condition. I paid $400 plus about $100 for one year of insurance. Well, I'll write more real soon.

Love, Helmut

Letter 159   *Pomona, Aug. 28, '54*

Hi, you two,

According to the date it has been eight years since we saw each other; time is running shorter though, because I can hear those wheels clicking every now and then that say that you people's transfer has begun and official channels are working.

Yesterday I got word from LA that neither my birth certificate nor Martin's baptismal certificate had any mention of our parents' names. Actually they said that they couldn't keep working on the case till that new set of documents came in. Do you think you may be able to incorporate that information in another set of baptismal certificates. That is the only way in which we can keep those official wheels in motion. Sorry to be of so much trouble, but American bureaucracy is as bad as the German—at times.

I am standing my watch right now. Actually it is somebody else's; but since he wanted to see the football game in LA, I consented to stand by for him. Now I'm waiting for him to get back so he can stand the rest of his watch; because tomorrow morning I'm going to take a trip down to San Diego.

Love as ever, Helmut

Letter 160 *Pomona, August 22, 54*

Hi folks,

Many thanks for all your many letters I received recently; also for all the books, pictures, the birthday candy, and the things you sent through Mrs. Plettig—who sent them to me about a month ago. I'll try to cramp much news into little space. First of all here are some pictures (color taken at T. I. and the black and white down here).

That fellow who is in two of the pictures is Richard Votoupol. I met him in San Francisco. He was in my dorm there, going to school in my class. We used to go ice skating now and then, we went to see some musical shows and had lots of fun in general. I had him down at the Wades once. He is from Granite City (East St. Louis}, comes from a pretty poor family, has had a pretty rough life, has a fine character, and much ambition to learn to become a Catholic priest. He is very serious about it.

For 8 weeks I had been going to evening classes at Santa Ana JC [junior college] (about 30 miles from here). I was attending classes on analytic geometry (plane) 2 hours for three nights a week. I finished that course last week with a straight "A." About four weeks ago I applied for your advance quotas. I haven't heard anything since then. All the papers were to be returned (to me, I guess). All that remains to be done is for me to make out the affidavit. For this I still have to get the Marine Corps' statement of employment and a bank statement. Then with the Wades' affidavit as a foundation, there should not be much to keep you from getting here by Christmas.

Have you studied talking, at all? It is going to be pretty difficult for you at first, but you'll get used to it soon. Unless I tell people about my background, they never know it. Most of them think that my English is better than the average American's; but, then, that is very easy, because the Americans are mostly sloppy in their speech and spelling. But you'll make out, alright.

As far as you, Mom; I don't know what we'll think of as far as location is concerned but we'll find something good. Maybe San Francisco, San Diego, or Los Angeles. I'ld kind of like to keep you out of the desert; there is absolutely nothing but heat and sand out there and living facilities are very few. We'll arrange something though.

Best wishes, and many kisses,
Your "old" boy, Helmut

Letter 161   *Pomona, Oct. 10, '54*

Hello folks,

I've actually forgotten how to write a good letter or perhaps I never knew how, in the first place. I'll sure be glad when you two finally get here. We'll have to get acquainted all over again. I know that I have changed and I am expecting Martin to have changed too. Maybe I won't even know how to address the intellectual, but we'll soon find things to adjust to each other.

Well, last week I got word from the office of Immigration and Naturalization in Los Angeles—when they returned all the papers they had been evaluating—that the application for advance visa for you two had been approved and sent on to the State Department, from where notification would be sent to the American Consulate in Berlin. They also made it clear that it would be useless to act until we heard from them.

I have a statement of employment from the Marine Corps and am expecting similar statements from the bank for which I have asked. By the way; I have one account at "Palo Alto Mutual Building and Loan Association" in my name, which is being fed by $80 each month coming directly out of my pay. I also have a joint account at the association's Menlo Park branch (jointly with Norm). The Palo Alto account...contains approximately $500, now. The Menlo Park ...account contains approximately $1000. It is jointly with Norm only so that he can get me some money out of the account in case I should ever need any. The money is all mine. I am writing about my financial standing so that you may know what I have in case of emergency. Also, in the event of my death you will receive 6 months pay from the government and $10,000. My pay right now comes to about $129.00 [per month].

My school here will be over in less than two weeks. We are graduating on the 22nd of October, at which date we will proceed to Inyokern for an apparent year and a half of duty. You'll hear from me as soon as I get up there.

I am not the proud owner of a car anymore. I had to sell it for junk after a friend of mine rolled it (sideways) from a speed of about 50 miles an hour. Three people [including Helmut] were in the car at the time (two asleep) and not one got hurt. No other car was involved. The driver insists on paying me back for the damage he caused, but since I think it really wasn't his fault and because I should have had the car insured against damage to the car itself, I feel that I should be strictly

*responsible for the loss in terms of money. It was miraculous that no
one suffered personal injuries. The guardian angel was certainly close.*

*I have no plans of buying another car until I'll need one. It is a lot
better to be saving money without a car and buying a pretty good one
when the time comes and you need one than buying an old one now
with little money, spending money on it and with it and never being
able to improve your assets without great expense.*

*You have been asking about my recreation. Well, I usually don't go
to the movies but once or twice a month. I don't drink and haven't
smoked since the end of May—thanks to Rich. I don't dance—primarily
because I don't know how. I went to church (almost) every Sunday as
long as I had the car. My reading is rather slow, but I do some of it,
mostly technical or scientific or philosophical. Rich is home right now,
in St. Louis, on leave, before reporting in at Camp Lejeune in North
Carolina (on the East Coast). He is quiet, serious, solid, has good
traits, and an eager philosopher. He is a good Catholic and avid
athlete. I guess mostly he is a substitute for a Brother. A few weeks ago
I became interested in ping pong; and now I spend about an hour or
two a day practicing. Well, you'll hear from me as soon as I'll get up
there to Inyokern. Till then I am yours as ever*

Your loving Helmut

[The following letter is Helmut's first from the Naval Ordnance Testing
Station at China Lake, California].

Letter 162   *China Lake, Nov. 21, '54*

Hello, Mom, Mart,

*How are you two holding out over there? As soon as I got here I
went to see the Legal Office. There a nice lady, the Secretary, took the
case into her hands. Within one week or so, the affidavit should be
finished. Then I'll send you your copies and one to the Wades, so that
they know of my intentions and have an idea as to how to make out
their own affidavit.*

*The weather here is out of this world right now. It is warm and
drops to almost freezing every night. The base (Naval Ordnance Test
Station) is located right in a huge basin surrounded by mountains*

about 3000 or 4000 feet higher. Less than 100 miles away—you can see it in the distance—is Mount Whitney 14500 feet high. That is the highest mountain in the USA. It is in the southernmost part of the Sierra Nevada crest. To the East of here about 100 miles away is Death Valley, a part of which is the lowest point of the USA, about 250 feet below sea level. The whole territory is just a desert.

Within five miles of the base are two little towns; one is Ridgecrest and the other Inyokern. The base itself is swarming with scientists and other civilians. There is a regular shopping center on the base here with a bank, post office, library, commissary food store, post exchange (Warenhaus für Militar) [department store for military people]*, theater, and high school with gymnasium, and a restaurant and a community center (club house). The Commissioned Officers Club offers odd jobs for $1.00 an hour. I've just started to work there, about four or five hours for four nights a week.*

The GM Bn is housed in one of five Navy Barracks. Marine Barracks is a separate building housing guard company. My work is very interesting but I can't write about it. All I can say is it consists of maintaining electronic equipment. The people I'm working with are the best.

For recreation I used to go to the movies a lot. But now I am working most of the time. I'm reading books on clear thinking and handling problems of all sorts. Also I am quite interested in the local church. Every Sunday and most holidays several of the boys and I attend the services at the Lutheran Church in Ridgecrest. Tonight they are having a sacred concert and we'll be sure to go.

My friend Richard Votoupal is now stationed at Camp Lejeune, North Carolina. Norman Wade is now attending the University of California at Berkeley, on the East Shore of San Francisco Bay. He may be getting married pretty soon.

Myself, I am going to stay single unless I should find just the right kind of girl. I've been out of circulation too long to be common. I am different in most of my habits and that requires a different kind of a girl. I don't go and care much for the girls around here. And the nice ones I know are married—to my friends. They are the kind I am looking for.

It'll sure be great when you'll finally come. I haven't given the housing or dwelling problem much thought yet. There are things you'll have to learn that are peculiar to the life in these United States. Things like hairdo and haircuts and clothes will come naturally. It would help if you could get yourselves a couple of suits if you can afford them.

Don't load yourselves down with shirts and underwear and socks,
though. Those things are rather cheap here and must be considered as
part of your average living expenses

If you can't afford them, write me and I'll send you the money.
Because as I said I've saved for your coming and I'ld rather see you
get something good over there with it than buy something expensive
over here. I said this before, so please don't mind me saying it again:
be sure to get your teeth and eyes fixed completely just before getting
here. Again, if necessary I'll send you the money. Consider it yours,
after all, it is.

When you get to New York I'll have some money there for you
someplace and tickets for LA or San Francisco. Please don't think me
hard if I'll ask you to not stay there over a couple of days at the most,
because life in New York is expensive and we won't be able to afford
much. I'll probably meet you at the plane, [in Los Angeles] but it is
possible that I'll meet you at New York; just possible. Well, I've gabbed
enough.

With much love as ever, Helmut

Letter 164   *China Lake, 1 Jan. '55*

Hi, you two Berliners,

Have you had a nice Holiday Season? I got your Christmas-written
letter and loved it as much as the gift parcel which got here last
Thursday. Thanks an awful lot. That Marcipan is always delicious and
the cookies never make it in anything but crumbs. I can certainly use
that leather pen case, and the harmonica enchanted one of my friends
so much that I gave it to him to use till he got one of his own. He'd
been looking for a Hohner for some five years and never was able to
get one. As far as I am concerned, he can keep it, because if it makes
him that happy to play, I am happy too. I am glad you liked the
watches. Martin's watch is selfwinding

The little yellow silk ribbon is a bow-tie with adjustments for
various neck sizes, or were you just joking when you called it a tape
measure? Rich, Norm, and I all have one just like it. That sort of makes
the four of us a club of friends. Please give the Kerns' address as your
future or expected living area; although we will probably never move
there, they always have room, just in case someone wants to investigate
from over there. I spent Christmas with the Wades in Menlo Park.
Congratulations for your retirement, Mother. You won't have to worry

much about duty for one complete photographic outfit. You can always call it your hobby, like the violin I brought with me. Hope we'll see you soon.

Helmut

Letter 165   Berlin, Feb. 25, 1955

My Dear Helmut-*boy!*

How are you in the distant West? We haven't heard anything from you since January 1; we hope to get mail from you soon. Today we finally went to the consulate in Dahlem. We could only hand over our passports and a couple of documents. We would not have been admitted in person without an appointment, but we received some very good information. Actually, in the wake of the mass operation of the postwar period there has been a yawning gap in the waiting rooms and corridors.

Who still goes to America if things are going well for them here—mainly just visitors. Over there, compulsory military service; here not (yet)—no one is suffering from hunger here anymore. But, that's nothing against the USA; who knows how long it will stay this way here? For our family in any case the situation is different from that of most other people. A lot of people can't understand why we don't want to stay here—but mostly people who only know and value their own four walls!

Now, after this digression, to the point. As your family we are entitled to a preferential visa; so they don't have us registered at all on the normal quota waiting lists, but are waiting for us to say when we want to go. The 60-day waiting period was only set because they wanted to know whether we seriously intend to emigrate. So this question seems to be resolved; we will get our visa when we want to have it. But for that we still lack the sponsorship (we've taken care of everything else).

Since mother would already be added to my application, one sponsorship would probably be sufficient at the mention of both our names. On the basis of your occupation (and maybe savings) you could provide this for us alone. They are no longer so strict about the fat bank account, etc., no doubt not at all, with my fitness and willingness to work. This formality (notarized certifications) is thus the only obstacle which still blocks our way, and which surely could be overcome. If Mr. Wade causes difficulties, then we'll try it without him. I hardly believe that the consul will change his mind. Only we will not undertake if at all if this sponsorship isn't here.

Our preferred leaving time would be August since my preliminary examination takes place in July. The consulate is no longer concerned with the trip itself; for years that has been a private matter to be handled with the steamship lines. I think this plan will be feasible for all parties. Please keep it in mind. When you have everything together, it's best to send it to our address.

I'm supposed to greet you for Hans Pohl. He was sick (overwork) and is now taking his diploma exam. For a long time already he's been working as a physicist in the AEG laboratory for current and voltage transformers.

I have now reached the end of 5 semesters and have completed all the training necessary for examination, as well as I could. What comes now are my preparations for the exams; lectures would only be attended for a later possible High Diploma examination. Lately I have hardly had any rest, so I am happy about the coming "vacation."

For today affectionate greetings and kisses from your Martin

Letter 166 *China Lake, 13 March, 1955*

Hi Folks,

There is so much to be said and yet not much time to say it. I am still working at the Club about three nights a week. Also I am spending at least two nights a week at church. I've found wonderful friends there and lots of interest in our Christian religion. It is "Our Savior's" Lutheran Church in Ridgecrest. I may even become a minister.

I think that the Wades have made out an affidavit for you; but if you'll want to come around August, then I'll start making out another one in May or so. That way the dates will be within three months of your departure. Also let me know the complete income about April, that I can declare mother a dependent. Even if a couple of checks will be going to Germany, we may be able to get furniture and so on moved to Calif. (at least from New York) at Government expense, especially if I should make Staff-Sergeant.

Martin, before you come, it is necessary for you to get the following information, in order to continue your education here, sooner or later, and also in order to be able to apply for a job according to the education you've had.

Get the number of hours you spent on each subject per week per semester. For instance: you took an hour of math for five days a week, and perhaps a sixth day with a test on that subject for that semester. You should be able to compile between 20 and 25 hours or more per semester. The University of Cal. at Berkeley gives a "bachelors degree" in Electrical Engineering for about 130 points. Did you get some sort of a certificate for your year with the AEG? If not be sure to do so.

Since the middle of January I again have owned a car. This time it's a '49 Dodge, black and in very good condition. My friend [*the one who caused the accident*] paid for it. The letter writing is going twice as easily because I am listening to some wonderful record music of Mendelssohn and Schubert.

Greetings from Helmut

Letter 167   Berlin, March 27, 1955

Hi, Helm! Dear Big Brother!

One has to gradually practice speaking colloquially as people usually seem to over there. We received your aerogramme of March 13 after a 10-week pause, and were happy with the gratifying contents—the same with a letter from Mr. Wade. As a result, the sponsorship should rest with the consulate now, which we surely will receive confirmed from there soon. Your fears that we could now come too early will probably be hardly necessary, because the affidavit is valid for three months, and the visa another four months. It's going to work out now.

We're glad that besides the Service you have enough time left that you can work for the Officers' Club and the church. However, you would also do a Christian work if you would spend an hour every two weeks to send your mother a sign of life, which means more to her than any medicine. Otherwise we might have the prospect of receiving just two more letters before we leave, which couldn't tell us everything we need to know.

The question of where we would live, for instance, is still not clarified. The Wades seem happy to have us with them; we haven't heard anything from the Kerns, or is it better to live in Los Angeles (Pasadena—CIT)? [*Martin is referring to the proximity of Los Angeles to Pasadena, location of the California Institute of Technology, a school he is considering*]. People will ask us about this. Is the university in Berkeley also a technical university like Pasadena? So Norm is there; what line of engineering is he in then? My studies are all outlined in the so-called text book and will be completed through examinations. Thus my eagerness to make it for the finals. Thank you for the tip about the certificates and testimonials regarding study and work. I'm having everything verified that's still lacking. We congratulate you on your new Dodge and rejoice with you about the compensated loss. Much luck from here on—

Greetings and kisses from Martin

Letter 168   Reinickendorf, 3/28/55

Dear Big Sonny!

After the social Sunday of the 50-Year Jubilee school celebration in the "Lichtburg" [*no doubt a large conference and social center*], I greet you affectionately, as do the faculty members. Perhaps pictures will follow as an awful lot of them were taken on Saturday (a ceremony in the school, to which I also had an honorary invitation) as well as on Sunday. Four photographers wandered round about us.

Yesterday I sat at the Old Teachers Table and ended up with Headmaster Utpott on my left. Next to it stood a long table with the young faculty members between 25 and 45. Mr. Simon directed the order of festivities, dance, etc. There was much to tell about, but where should one begin? Shakespeare's *"As You Like It"* was the excellent, amusing student performance. Later I'll tell you about it personally.

But now, most importantly, after receiving your nice letter of March 13, 1955, we were very happy about its contents, and then came Mr. Wade's very friendly letter to Martin. After that he gave his sponsorship documents to the consulate in Dahlem. Next week we will present our police certificates of conduct, with which the proceedings for the visa can begin. How does it stand now with your application for me [*for an allotment from Helmut's pay*]? In case it hasn't happened yet, it should be started as well. My income is still unchanged since January. Except that the employees and widows pension is now 54,10 DM instead of 51,10 DM. My old age pension is just now being decided on; no decision has been presented as yet. I would have it sent later. I'll close now with affectionate greetings and kisses

from Mutti

Letter 169   Reinickendorf, 4/23/55

Dear Helmut-Boy,

Today briefly a couple of lines for your information. Mr. Wade's sponsorship is in the hands of the consulate and from there we received a letter to Martin written April 7, with the note: "As soon as there is a quota number available you will receive an invitation to a personal conference."

We have come very close to our goal. In the next few days we want to check with Hapag-Lloyd's about the reservation or deposit for our places on the ship; otherwise it could happen that the visa is issued but the tickets are jeopardized.

I am still waiting for my pension decision, that is the payments from January. Of course, we had to dip into our savings, unfortunately. We aren't wasting anything, and by the way, we are allowed to bring plenty of money with us, which is comforting to be sure.

From tomorrow until May 5 Martin has exam days; then further studies till July, when the last preliminary exams will follow. Then the departure could follow in or after August, according to human reckoning, if Fate means well for us this time.

In case we don't make it from Bremerhaven on the *"Berlin"* on August 9, the *"America"* (U. S. Lines) on August 30 would be a possibility. Have you taken the current military allotment for me in a lump sum? Where is your Service location likely to be in the future? According to today's paper, the world appears somewhat less war-hungry; that would be desirable. How do you like your Dodge? We congratulate you! Yes, we wish you much pleasure with it.

By the way, Mrs. Plettig travelled well from Sacramento to New York in a Trailway Bus for about $70.00. Maybe that would be practical for us too and cheaper than express train. The stations: San Francisco, Sacramento, Reno, Salt Lake City, Ogden, Cheyenne, Grand Island, Omaha, Des Moines, Chicago, Toledo, Cleveland, Harrisburg, New York—How would the express [*train*] go and how expensive? For today stay well and receive affectionate greetings from,

Mother and Martin

Letter 170 *China Lake, 22 May '55*

Dear Mother, Martin,
Thanks for your last letter, and of course for the wonderful Easter package. The harmonica of course stays with me. I promise I won't give it away. It is too beautiful.
Sent you a $60 "remittance order" through the "Bank of Amerika." All I got is a copy of the order and you will get the money from some bank in Berlin. Please let me know how you like the arrangement whenever and as soon as you receive your money. The bank, here, would like to know how convenient it is. I'll be sending you that much until September inclusive, then when you get here I can claim you, mother, as my dependant and demand the usual subsistance. So you think you'll get to NY about Oct. 15. Well, I'll arrange for your trip across the US from this end.
Next weekend three of the fellows and I are going to take a short trip into the Sierra; west of Lone Pine about 12 miles to Whitney Portals. I am teaching Sunday School at the church, Bible stories and religious instructions for 10 year olds, in my class. In a couple of weeks we are having a dinner as a surprise for the pastor and his wife for their twentieth anniversary. I was asked to play a couple of numbers on the Piano. Also when the pastor and his family goes on vacation, I may play during Sunday services.
The job at the club is still keeping me busy at least three nights a week, last week it was five nights. So, you see, recreation for me consists of working, writing letters, and maybe an occasional ping-pong game.
More about your coming some other time. God keep you; with lots of love,

Helmut

Letter 172 *Lakeshore, June 24, 55*

Dear Mother, Martin,
I am on leave and vacationing for a week in the beautiful High Sierra. Huntington Lake is a large artificial reservoir east of Madera. Since I have one day before moving on, and some time left, I am writing a few letters.
Listen, if you can sell all the furniture there, it would be just as well. We would not just have to consider the transportation, but also

*the storage. And transportation across the US wouldn't be cheap
either. I really think it better to buy furniture here, as we are able to
use it. Until we are settled someplace, we'll be moving every year or
two, that is until Martin and I have our steady jobs.*

*In case you should have some money left, when you leave
there—and you mentioned possibilities of going through
Lünen—perhaps you could leave some sort of a copper wreath or so
there* [on his father's grave].

*It's getting cool now. And I'll probably roll up in my bag before
long. Love,*

Helmut

Letter 173   Rdf. 6-26-55

Dear Helmut-*boy!*

Your nice vacation letter with three lovely photos arrived here to
our pleasure; we thank you very much for them. It is certainly wonderful for you to get into a cooler landscape in contrast to the military area
in the heat. (So enjoy what God has allotted you, then you will accomplish your duty faithfully). Also be careful in dangerous territory not to
run out of anything. That's how a mother, thinks, you know, in spite of
all the pleasure that she would like you to have.

Do you know that Martin and I have been called to the consulate
on July 8 and are supposed to bring money for the visa? You know, the
nearer the day comes, the more exciting it is. Martin has calculated
exam days from July 4–16. We're hoping that everything can be completed without difficulty. Perhaps not too much will be required of us.
We have to get vaccinations once more for the trip; but first we want to
wait for the visa. Just keep your fingers crossed.

Dear Helmut, just now an engagement announcement came in:
Evelyne Starkowski became engaged to a Hansjorg Meyer on her 23rd
birthday. She had many admirers, not surprising with her charm and
intelligence, etc. It's a shame that they, both sisters, have such delicate
lungs. Evelyne has taken a course of treatment twice already, but her
doctor mother seems to think she is cured for good.

Christa has been married since about Easter. She wants to take her
physician's exam in the Fall. For the time being she is practicing in the
Virchow hospital. So the next generation is moving forward. And one
day the sons [*Martin and Helmut*] will also arrive there, when the right

partners come along and the situation allows it. I never want to stand in your way when you've found your happiness and want to establish it.

The warm summer has come punctually; now the sun is shining just beautifully. Now our balconies are all getting similar lattices, etc. Then we can finally put out a few little flowers. As it is one sits too much in the limelight. But that should hardly concern us much longer. Now I want to close for today with many good wishes and sincere greetings. By July 18 you'll be back in the service again. Let me hear from you again soon, my good boy. Above all, stay well and all good things! Go with God, young man.

Mutti

Every couple of days Martin brings home some kind of successful grade. Sometimes it worries me; it could affect the nerves. For him a change all the way around is in order as soon as possible. However, we do want to make good use of the weeks till mid-September.

Letter 174 Reinickendorf, 7/10/55

Dear Helmut-*boy!*

Greetings from Berlin, where we have lived the longest. On July 8 we were at Clay-Allee [*Clay Street, named for U.S. General Lucius Clay, where the American consulate was located*] to take care of the outstanding visa questions. Our appointment was at 8:15 and it took until 5:00 to get everything settled. We received Martin's completed documents; mine will be handed over tomorrow since I still need new photos. I'll mail this letter tomorrow after getting my visa in Dahlem; then you'll be fully informed.

Then our departure can be expedited most quickly in every respect, that is—ship passage, living situation, baggage, money settlement, etc. I still lack the pension decision, etc. which hopefully will work out now without delay. Otherwise we'll make noise in the right places!

How did the rest of your leave go? Thank you for the greetings from the lake shore, especially the very lovely picture in front of the church [*sent with the letter written at the lake*], which was an excellent likeness. Yes, we have so much to share, little by little, since nine years of separation have brought a lot for you and for us. Our joy is boundless, come what will over there.

Well, my dear boy, your 25th birthday is coming soon, which hopefully you can celebrate healthy and happily. Then we will catch up quietly and enjoy being together, which isn't possible now. That's nicer for us than a big celebration. When you have the chance, please greet the Wades for both of us, who are thankful for their help. As our travel destination we gave their address. What happens then we will await patiently and leave to your plans and our joint decision. You know well that we don't expect a house and home, just our dear Helmut within reach.

By the way, we sent you two books, which hopefully will reach you safely as printed matter and will interest you. Please let us know if you receive them; especially since *"Atom"* was inspected here (open on both sides), which made me nervous. It's a good book. It's always such a business with the mailing. That will be a lot simpler in the future.

Now we wish you much luck with everything you're planning. I'm so happy that you brothers will finally be united after we were separated by Fate to such an extent for almost nine years.

Greetings and kisses from Mutti

Dear Helmut! Today just in haste a heartfelt wish for your birthday. Stay well and in good spirits as in the first 25 years! After getting through (hopefully well) the exam on July 12/13 I'll be more rested.

Your brother Martin

[*Note from Mother*]: Up till now everything has worked out, but he is quite strained and needs rest urgently after this extra stress; he must have it.

Letter 175   Berlin. 7/20/55

Dear, good Helmut!

Soon the last letter will be exchanged between Berlin and Calif. How little a person can say in a letter about everything that would be interesting to report.

When we will come now lies entirely in our own hands. We have no more to do with the consulate; our visa is good for four months from July 8, so the time of our departure from Berlin (October) has been suitably selected. A passage is already paid for, so we are securely booked for a two-person cabin on Deck B. We've already studied the map of the ship with interest.

Before departing from Bremerhaven we will probably go briefly to Lünen and Rheinhausen; the Schneiders have invited us to visit them for years. So we will give up the apartment at the end of September. The cellar is already a problem for me, besides the contents. Liquidating a household is more trouble than it's worth.

Where should we address our large baggage to? Are the Wades the right receivers? That isn't so important, but if the baggage arrives properly it will certainly save us a lot of trouble. If Norman is studying technological subjects at Berkeley, perhaps it's best if I connect with him and pursue the studies as soon as possible. Does he go from Menlo Park every day, or how does he do it?

My last exam was at <u>13</u>:00 on July <u>13</u>. [*The family seems to have considered 13 a lucky number!*] Everything worked out as expected. With that I am now a "Kandidat" (Candidate in engineering), which corresponds approximately to your bachelor's. Before I leave the university I will be certified for as much as possible. We will have our hands full of things to do in the remaining two months.

At the moment it's mid summer here. In the first bathing of the year I immediately got a sunburn that knocked me out for three days. The unaccustomed heat reduces any spirit of enterprise. Have you become accustomed to the continuous warmth? Hopefully you had a nice vacation.

What do you think of the following idea, which we can't get out of our minds? You must be familiar with the modern little upright pianos, which are about half as expensive as the old big ones. Shouldn't we bring a piece like that over with us? We would trade in our Trautwein piano, but then have a worthwhile piece which would certainly make you happy. Over there pianos must be so inhumanly expensive. The transportation of a small piano would surely be considerably cheaper than a big one. If all of the financial matters should finally work out, would that be something to consider? I'll close now for today.

Loving greetings and kisses
from your Martin

Letter 178   Berlin, 8/17/55

Dear Helmut!

How are you, old desert sailor? Good, we hope. Yesterday I read mother an article, *"Rocket Launchers on the Sound Barrier"* (from HOBBY—June issue), which deals with SNORT, the project of Drinkwater and Nelson. That naturally interested both of us. Also you aren't all that far from Las Vegas, Nevada [*associated with rocket testing*]. In any case your work seems to be very interesting. We're now anxious to know how Part II of the trip, the journey from New York to California, will take shape. Should we perhaps make a short stop in St. Louis [*to visit the Dodges*]?

I've been pasting in new and old photos all day here, in order to end the disorder; the effort has been worthwhile. Our daily work now consists of sorting, giving away, destroying, and "offering for sale." However, as you know, our household doesn't contain many valuable things. So all the more junk.

Our many friends who aren't aware of our departure will surely be displeased if we don't say goodbye in a big way. We could just celebrate our leaving for three weeks, you know, if we told them about our plans. Yes, such are our "cares." But they will soon belong to the past. What will the future bring? With this thought I greet and kiss you

Martin

Letter 179   *Aug. 22, '55*

Hello Mother; hi, Martin,

Beg your pardon for the long pause. As an explanaton I have to say that I have been very busy and when not too busy, not relaxed enough to write. You know, I have to be in the mood to write. And when you are too tired, the letters you turn out aren't worth writing.

Well, as far as the money is concerned, I sent $120 in July, for June and July; and another $60 for August was sent about a week ago. Please don't bring any furniture with you. Bring only the better clothes, Martin, don't bring any short trousers, because, as a rule, they are not worn, here. Underclothes are a regular expense, here, and not too expensive. Could you get a hold of a couple of good chromatic (with the slide) mouth harmonicas, one of them with only one row of holes *(reeds). They are for a couple of good friends who would be absolutely delighted and to whom I am obligated in a small way.*

At the moment I am planning to take leave on October 3rd and start off for New York, so that I can meet you at the dock, on or around the 15th of October. I think that's the date which you mentioned. Now, on the way back we can stop over in St. Louis if you wish. In case I should not be able to make it, I will send you enough money to make it to California, but about that I'll write next time.

If I could make it to New York, and I probably will, we would have that much longer to talk about the future. If we can keep Martin out of the military service for one year, I would be only too happy to send him through school till he gets his Master's Degree. The University of California at Berkeley where Norman is going would be the most likely place. There is absolutely no employment for you, Martin, within about 150 miles from here, because it requires "secret" clearance to work on the base, here, and there is no industry anywhere close by. As far as I am concerned, I'll be here till January or February, then we'll all (the battalion, that is) go to another base around here. It's a problem alright.

Well, the lights will be going out in a few minutes. Bye, now, and I'll be writing again, soon.

With lots of love, Helmut

Letter 180   Berlin, September 1, '55

Dear Helmut!

Thank you for your nice letter with the pictures, from which we got so much! Above all, we're happy that you want to come and meet us. Till now you haven't left California yet either [*except for Korea*]. What kind of transportation are you thinking of using? Probably not your own car? The money you sent for August arrived - *thanks a lot!* We are coming out well financially, as we now see clearly. Thus a further mailing isn't necessary. Finally, too, mother has received her pension decision; the money due for 9 months is coming in a few days.

We've already found a buyer for our radio and the pillow set. Today we bought an opera glass and an atlas. A good pair of field glasses and maybe the desired telephoto lens should also follow. I brought with me recently a 1- and a 2-row mouth harmonica. Today we located our cabin, No. 415, B-Deck. According to the map the cabin contains one double bed, 2 small closets, 1 commode, 1 wash basin; it doesn't have a view out, except right near the WC.

Will we find each other right away in New York? Will you have a uniform on or will you be in civilian clothes? In case there is still something to tell at the last minute, then write to the main post office in Bremen, general delivery. On about 9/28 we'll leave here and clear the way for the Riesack couple. Mrs. Riesack is mother's successor in the office; they have to vacate their apartment in Waidenamslust by October 1, and will be installed as our sub-lettors (if it works out).

Mother has tried to retain the right of residence temporarily for all eventualities—for various reasons. Thus, for example, our piano can still stay until we know what will happen with it. Is there any possibility for mother to live with you in the restricted area? If not, then would it perhaps be best if we two lived for the time being in or near Pasadena, which is located much closer [*to Helmut*] than Berkeley, and which also has the best technical college in the USA, after Boston, as the professor of foreign institutes told me. A permanent solution to the residence question is probably not yet possible now, as long as you are still a soldier.

Loving greetings today
from Martin

Letter 181   *China Lake, Sept. 6, '55*

Dear Mother, Dear Martin,

Got your letter of Sept. 2 today. Thanks for all the information, which was very complete. In answer to some of your questions: I'll probably be in civilian clothes; but I'll find you. And I intend to take my car. It is in pretty good condition all the way around and shouldn't give me any trouble.

Also I'll be taking enough money so that we can make the trip by commercial means if necessary. I'll send $300 to a bank in New York, where both of you and I can get hold of it without any trouble, just in case I should get sick or delayed somehow, in reaching New York. The address of that bank will follow later.

In case we should miss each other, contact the Wades by telegram, about me. I'll do likewise. In case you'll leave to make the trip across country by yourselves, make the $300 last and get your tickets and travel information through "traveler's aid" which is at the larger train terminals and at ship docks. The Wades would help you after that. Just write to me, when the ship is due to arrive in New York. Well, bye for now.

Love, Helmut

P. S. My German is a little rusty.

Letter 182   China Lake, Sept. 18, 55

Dear Mother, dear Martin,

Time is drawing to an end, now, during which we were separated, geographically, though never in spirit. Still, our separation was a lot more bearable than those involving deportation to Siberia, or captivity in Korea or Red China, or even prison. We were free all the time with minor restrictions. Most of the time—the exception was when I spent the last four years in the Marine Corps—I was free to return to you. I think you will find that the US was well worth the time which you had to spend waiting to gain entrance.

Well, my car is slowly getting conditioned for the trip. I intend to stop in Wisconsin to see Ralph. If we should happen to miss each other at the dock, go to the "traveler's aid" desk where your ship lands and ask them for a message from me. If you should be out of luck there too, then proceed to a hotel—if at night—or to the Manufacturer's Trust Company head office at 55 Broad Street, New York 15, N.Y. There you will be able to pick up $300.00

The money will be sent there this coming week; if not, they will at least have a message for you. As I explained before, I may have an accident on the way East—you never know—and this way you will still be able to make it to California without further assistance. Then you can contact either the Wades in Menlo Park, or Pastor Neipp here in Ridgecrest at "Our Savior's Lutheran Church." Both the Wades and Pastor Neipp would help you. But, God willing, I'll be able to do all the helping.

I have not sent any more money this month. Mother, with your total income at $65 at the present time, I couldn't even claim you as a dependant, now. But how much of this will you be getting after you get to this country? It is wonderful that you were able to get a good set of binoculars. They are always nice to have. And since you have a good camera be sure to get those telephoto (and possibly wide angle) lenses

to fit it. Yes, Mother may be permitteed to live right here on the
base—as my dependant.

It might interest you to know that I took off to LA last week
Thursday and Friday. There I was able to get much information. First I
saw the US Army recruiter. He said that you could join the Army for
three, four, or six years after you receive your "first papers." Now
ordinarily it is not necessary, any more, to get first papers except for a
special case like joining the service. Then you would be eligible for
American citizenship after 90 days and with your education you could
probably get a commission (become an officer) then. And if you should
decide to enlist for a minimum of three years, you would be guaranteed
any school the Army has to offer.

Then I saw the selective service commission (draft board). An
American has to register for the draft 10 days after he turns 18 years of
age. This also applies to aliens (you) except that you only have to
register within six months after you hit the States. So there is no great
hurry on this account.

Then I went to Cal Tech. in Pasadena. I talked to the graduate
school counselor. You are considered to be a graduate student if you
start school there; in other words your present education is equivalent
to at least four years of college in this country. Then I talked to the
Freshman Dean (first year advisor and troubleshooter), a Mr. Strong.
He was of the opinion that it probably would be best for you to go to
the draft board in November, volunteer for the draft with the Army and
get in this way for 24 months; only, the Army has been releasing their
draftees after 21 months, and that would be Sept. or Aug. of '57. Then
you'll be just in time for the '57-'58 school year. Otherwise you'll have
to wait till Sept. of '56 anyway. Cal Tech does not accept anyone in the
middle of the school year. But we can talk it over when we are on our
way back to the West Coast.

In case this should be our last communication by letter for a while,
let me wish you a nice journey and that God be with you throughout.
See you in New York.

Helmut

Letter 183   Berlin, 9/19/55

Dear Helmut!

From Berlin today the good news that the big baggage is out of the house. After packing only till noon today we're now free of the big burden. Each china, book, and laundry carton was picked up together with a big cabin trunk and duffle bag (with bed pillows and blankets) by a Moabite moving company. They are now going to be cleared by customs and will go, if everything is *o.k.,* direct to San Francisco (via Hamburg), so that neither of us has to worry about it at the railroad station in New York.

Because of the expensive train freight across the continent, we were urgently advised to choose the direct transport by freighter via Panama. Even though on the *"Berlin"* 250 kg goes free, this way still amounts to a savings of about $35.00. The trunks will be transferred one time less (at least!) and we won't have to bother with the baggage as soon as we arrive in California, but can get everything prepared in peace before the shipment arrives on about Nov. 10.

The payment of about $700 from Hamburg to San Francisco we'll settle in deutschmarks. We've already sent ahead to Bremen a cord suitcase with Mother's wardrobe. It will be in our cabin when we come aboard. So for the airplane we only have one more suitcase besides bags. On 9/29 at 12:15 we'll go from Tempelhof to Hannover. [*The East German government did not allow Berliners to take ground transportation to the West*]. We want to be in Bremen by the 3rd, so that we will have three days on the Rhein. We'll certainly go briefly to Lünen.

Our apartment is so bare already that every word echoes loudly. Tomorrow another piece of furniture will be picked up by an elderly refugee couple from East Prussia. Uncle Hermann Hintz will still be picking up a couple of things, so everything is being disposed of; nothing is being carelessly wasted. After the renovation of the outside front of the building, the inside rooms (they're dirty to be sure) will follow in October (without cost), so that our successors will have an even nicer apartment.

Yesterday Mother went to a concert, the *"Samson"* oratorio by Handel in the music college. I was with Inge Frase at the neighboring Tribune Theater for the happy play *"Banbury"* or *"The Importance of Being Ernest"* by Oscar Wilde. I only received one ticket for the concert. So in the end (for the last time) we still had an artistic treat. This morning the black suit was dropped into the suitcase.

Life is now somewhat Gypsy-like with the remaining inventory—but it's almost fun—in anticipation of the big trip. The enclosed photo was taken on a little outing with the paddleboat on Tegel Lake. A little fore-taste of the Atlantic? So we're slowly getting travel fever; up till now we just had no time for it.

Enough for today; greetings and kisses from

Your brother Martin

[The following letter is the last one written by Maria before she and Martin left for the United States, where Helmut met them at the ship. Helmut recollected later that not only was his mother fearful of encountering wild animals on the cross-country trip, but expressed concern about the possibility of being ambushed by Indians!]

Letter 184   *[undated]*

Dear Big Boy!

Our days here are now numbered and in spite of all the chasing around and commotion in dissolving our local connections, we are really happy, indeed blessed, in the hope of our soon-coming reunion. You probably feel the same way. But don't undertake too much with the long West-East trip. Who will be with you; is someone coming along on whom you can fully rely? On difficult stretches, do give up the car and travel such stretches only by train. For you must not overly task yourself or completely lose your way and come upon animals which could bring you danger. Also avoid getting over-tired. But you haven't been reckless up to now. God will stand by you as always in life.

Thank you again for your last nice letter and all the plans made. In any case, the *"Berlin"* is supposed to be in New York on October 15 at Pier 97, North River, Foot of West 57th Street, New York City.

By the way, a double mailing of money arrived smoothly for June/July and the August mailing after it. So, *all-right.* Thank you for all the love and provision! Don't worry too much; everything will turn out well. I am very tired; that's why I would like to close now with many loving wishes and kisses and a happy "Auf Wiedersehen!"

Your Mutti

AFTERWORD

By the time the newly united family had driven together from New York to California, Martin had apparently decided to join Norman Wade as a student at the University of California in Berkeley. There Maria and Martin rented an apartment together. Helmut enrolled at the university as a freshman on the G.I. Bill of Rights when his service with the Marine Corps ended in June of 1956. Maria remained in Berkeley until her death in 1964.

Because of the equivalency of his studies in Berlin, Martin soon had his B.S. degree in engineering and stayed on at Berkeley to obtain a master's degree. While pursuing his studies, he was employed as a research assistant. Both of the brothers were married in 1957, Martin to Rosemary Young, a secretary in the engineering department, and Helmut to Sylvia Diederich, a university librarian from New York City. Helmut continued at the university until he received his Ph. D. in physics in 1965.

Martin went on to an engineering career with I.B.M., where he was employed for the rest of his working life, and settled in the San Francisco Bay area. After receiving his doctorate Helmut obtained a position with the Center for Naval Analyses in Arlington, Virginia. There he worked as a researcher and weapons systems analyst. After the death of his first wife in 1974 he married Elizabeth Arnswald, who had been one of Sylvia's classmates at the University of Michigan. In 1979 they moved to the Seattle area where Helmut was employed by Boeing Aerospace, a division of the aircraft company which specializes in defense-related projects. Helmut never revisited Germany.

As Helmut preceded his brother in coming to America, he also preceded him in death, but only by a few months. In March, 1994 Helmut died from complications following a devastating stroke. The same year Martin was diagnosed with an aggressive brain tumor which took his life in July. The brothers were 61 and 63 years old. Helmut was survived by two sons, who now live in St. Louis, Missouri and Vancouver, Washington. Martin's widow, daughter, and two sons all reside in California.

Maria Dost continued to correspond with Bertha Dodge for a number of years after settling in the United States. The Dodges' daughters, now living in Florida and West Virginia, continue to use the old family home in Vermont during the summers.

Helmut eventually lost touch with the Neuman family, Augusta de Boer, the Klinkerts, and Mr. and Mrs. Kern. The Kern farm in Los Altos Hills has long since been replaced by an upscale residential area.

Helmut and Martin maintained a lifelong relationship with the Wades. Norman, who worked as an executive with Aramco in Saudi Arabia, is now retired. He lives with his wife aboard their yacht off the Pacific coast. His mother, Hilda Wade, now widowed, lives in the same house in Menlo Park, California, which Helmut considered his American home as a young man.

At the time of this writing, Helmut's badly wounded Marine buddy, Ralph Eastlick, is still living with his wife, Ruby, on the family dairy farm in southwestern Wisconsin.

ABOUT THE EDITOR

Elizabeth Arnswald Dost grew up in the Chicago area and later attended the University of Michigan where she earned a dgree in history and English. She taught high school English, and has ten years of experience in the field of journalism. She worked as a staff writer on *The Toledo Blade*, a daily newspaper in Toledo, Ohio; was a copy editor for the *Palm Beach [Florida] Daily News*; and edited an interdenominational Christian monthly in the Seattle area. Mrs. Dost has always had a penchant for travel and foreign languages. She loves the Pacific Northwest and makes her home in a suburb of Seattle.